# RECONCILIATION, FORGIVENESS AND VIOLENCE IN AFRICA

## Biblical, Pastoral and Ethical Perspectives

Editors
Marius J. Nel
Dion A. Forster
Christo H. Thesnaar

SUN PRESS

# DEDICATION

In memory of
H Russel Botman

*Reconciliation, Forgiveness and Violence in Africa: Biblical, Pastoral and Ethical Perspectives*

Published by African Sun Media under the SUN PReSS imprint

This publication was subjected to an independent double-blind peer evaluation by the publisher.

Stellenbosch University and the publisher have made every effort to obtain permission for and acknowledge the use of copyrighted material. Refer all enquiries to the publisher.

Views reflected in this publication are not necessarily those of the publisher.

First edition 2020

ISBN 978-1-928480-52-5
ISBN 978-1-928480-53-2 (e-book)
https://doi.org/10.18820/9781928480532

Set in Palatino Linotype Regular 10/12

Cover design, typesetting and production by African Sun Media

SUN PReSS is an imprint of African Sun Media. Scholarly, professional and reference works are published under this imprint in print and electronic formats.

This publication can be ordered from:
orders@africansunmedia.co.za
Takealot: bit.ly/2monsfl
Google Books: bit.ly/2k1Uilm
africansunmedia.store.it.si *(e-books)*
Amazon Kindle: amzn.to/2ktL.pkL

Visit africansunmedia.co.za for more information.

# TABLE OF CONTENTS

# LIST OF CONTRIBUTORS

**NEW TESTAMENT**

PROF. MARIUS J. NEL

Associate Professor of New Testament

Chair of the Department of Old and New Testament

Stellenbosch University

Stellenbosch, South Africa

https://orcid.org/0000-0001-5922-1594


DR. GODWIN ETUKUMANA

Provost ECWA Theological Seminary Aba, Nigeria.

Research Fellow Department of Old and New Testament

Stellenbosch University,

Stellenbosch, South Africa


DR. ENDALE SEBSEBE MEKONNEN

President of the Shiloh Bible College, Ethiopia

Research Fellow Department of Old and New Testament

Stellenbosch University,

Stellenbosch, South Africa


**SYSTEMATIC THEOLOGY**

PROF. DION A. FORSTER

Associate Professor of Systematic Theology and Ethics

Chair of the Department of Systematic Theology

Director of the Beyers Naudé Centre for Public Theology

Stellenbosch University

Stellenbosch, South Africa

https://orcid.org/0000-0002-7292-6203


DR. ALEASE A. BROWN

Post-Doctoral Fellow, Desmond Tutu Centre for Spirituality and Society

University of the Western Cape

Cape Town, South Africa

## REV. JACO BOTHA

Minister of the Dutch Reformed Church

PhD candidate

Stellenbosch University

Stellenbosch, South Africa

## PRACTICAL THEOLOGY

## PROF. CHRISTO H. THESNAAR

Professor of Practical Theology

Head of the Unit for Reconciliation and Justice

Beyers Naudé Centre for Public Theology

Stellenbosch University

Stellenbosch, Western Cape

https://orcid.org/0000-0001-9388-1895

## REV. BENAYA NIYUKURI

Director of the Paraclete Counselling Mission

PhD candidate

Stellenbosch University

Stellenbosch, South Africa

## DR. OHOLIABS D. TUDUKS

Minister in the Evangelical Church Winning All (ECWA)

Lecturer in the Department of Religious Studies of Gombe State University, Nigeria

PhD candidate

Stellenbosch University

Stellenbosch, South Africa

## BEYERS NAUDÉ CENTRE FOR PUBLIC THEOLOGY

## DR. WILHELM VERWOERD

Researcher, Beyers Naudé Centre for Public Theology

Stellenbosch University

Writing on some themes is seldom the prerogative of a single theological discipline, let alone of a single theologian. Some themes require reflection that comes from a variety theological disciples, each with their particular methodological, and theological, resources. In fact, some themes are simply so multifaceted, and so central to the gospel and to our faith, that they must be reflected upon by all theological disciplines. Examples of such theological themes include those in the title of this publication: reconciliation, forgiveness, violence and, to the background of these, the theme of human dignity.

Within, at the Beyers Naudé Centre for Public Theology we tend to agree with David Tracy, that all theology is intrinsically public discourse across the publics of the church, the academy and society at large. This volume contains a variety of rich and challenging essays that contribute to the wider discourse on public theology on the African continent as it relates to reconciliation, forgiveness, violence and human dignity.

We are extremely proud of it, not only because it is the first publication from the Unit for Reconciliation and Justice that is housed in the Beyers Naudé Centre for Public Theology, or because it contains contributions by colleagues from all three the disciplinary environments in our Faculty, but also as it showcases the work of some of our doctoral candidates and doctoral alumni from across the continent. May this publication also represent a first step for them in a long and fruitful scholarly journey.

**Len Hansen**
*Series Editor, Beyers Naudé Centre for Public Theology Series*
*Stellenbosch University, February 2020*

This book is the result of an inter- and trans-disciplinary engagement with three ethical themes from an African perspective by researchers from Stellenbosch University. The themes in question are reconciliation, forgiveness and violence. The contributors firstly engaged with one or more of the identified ethical themes from their specific disciplinary perspectives in their respective contributions. Thereafter, a symposium was held at the Beyers Naude Centre for Public Theology at Stellenbosch University on the 13th of April 2017. The aim of the symposium was to expose colleagues working in different disciplines in the Faculty of Theology to the contributions of those working in disciplines other than their own. This resulted in an enriched multidisciplinary perspective on these complex themes within the African context. The contributors each reflect on issues that arise from their varied African contexts. However, it needs to be acknowledged that the character of the project is informed by the theological points of view of a group of scholars linked to a particular institution – the Faculty of Theology, Stellenbosch University. It is, however, the hope of the contributors that this publication will serve as a first step towards a much more dynamic and inclusive conversion with scholars elsewhere in Africa, throughout the varied contexts of the Global South, and the wider wold.

The publication is structured in such a way that it draws upon the disciplinary experience of three theological disciplines (Biblical Studies, Practical Theology and Systematic Theology – with a particular focus on Public Theology and Ethics). The engagement of these three disciplinary perspectives facilitates a nuanced and textured understanding of the complexity of reconciliation, forgiveness, and violence in various African contexts. The aim of the engagement of these three disciplines is to enrich the understanding of notions of human dignity in relation to this conversation. The relationship between the discourses of human dignity, violence, reconciliation and forgiveness offers a wealth of material for interdisciplinary academic research. This, in turn, enriches and further develops the disciplines from which the original contributions came.

This book is premised on an understanding that human dignity is a complex concept that requires careful and rigorous consideration in order to explicate the implications for sound theology and practice. One of the challenges with human dignity discourses is that they are easily collapsed into utilitarian discussions of human rights and planetary rights. While this is a necessary outcome of responsible scholarship in the field, it cannot replace the need for a primary engagement with the multi-faceted notion of dignity that precedes the discourses around responsible rights – namely the dignity discourse.

Violence against persons and creation stems from an inadequate and jaundiced view of the other (whether it be other persons, communities, or aspects of creation). The expression, or performance, of violence is predicated upon a poorly developed understanding of the dignity and value of the other. This research project engages such beliefs and constructs with an aim to enrich the understanding and development of the descriptive and applied ethical considerations of dignity-based justice. A multifaceted understanding of the dignity, value and beauty of human persons impacts the ethical engagement with concepts of forgiveness and reconciliation.

This publication therefore brings together a variety of disciplinary, and intersectional identity, perspectives to enrich and texture the discussion. The disciplines it draws upon are Biblical Studies, Practical Theology and Systematic Theology (with a particular focus on Public Theology and Ethics).

The first three chapters focus on reconciliation, forgiveness and violence in the New Testament. **Marius J. Nel** focuses on Matthew 1:21 in order to understand how the author of the First Gospel appropriated the first century Jewish messianic hope for salvation for his particular community living within the context of the violence of the Roman Empire. Nel attempts to discern what Matthew wanted to achieve with his intertextual engagement with the Old Testament and argues that the manner in which Matthew addressed his context can provide contemporary African churches with appropriate hermeneutical guidelines for how to engage with their own analogical socio-political contexts. **Endale Sebsebe Mekonnen** studies violence from the perspective of Paul's letter to the Romans. He argues that in the context of the Roman Empire where violence was ubiquitous, Paul presents such violence as being part of the concept of evil (κακός). Paradoxically, Paul perceives violence constructively in the experience of the Messiah as a means of creating reconciliation, peace and glory. **Godwin Etukumana** focuses on reconciliation as an important topic in contemporary political, social, economic, and religious spheres, since it has the ability to redefine human relationships therein. The specific focus of his chapter is on the various ways in which the Gospel according to Luke describes the reconciliation of those who had become estranged from their communities with special reference to the case of lepers in Luke 5:11-16. Using a socio-historical hermeneutics he further investigates whether the metaphors used in Luke are similar to those used in African society's engagement with lepers.

The next three chapters approach the three themes from the perspective of Systematic Theology (with a particular focus on Public Theology and Ethics). **Dion A. Forster** engages the complexity of a politics of forgiveness in South Africa 25 years after the end of political apartheid. He draws upon a four-year qualitative empirical study of how Black and White South African Christians understand the processes and notions of forgiveness in the light of South Africa's complex economic, social and political context. **Alease A. Brown**, in turn, uses a postcolonial hermeneutic to demonstrate the ways in which a re-conceptualisation of the human renders possible a theology that uncouples humanity from political subjectivity. She draws on Sylvia Wynter's ontology of the human in order to argue for substituting the conception of Jesus as Man, for the conception of a Jesus in his kenotic, Kyriotic, and mediating human genres. Brown also argues that the incidence of violence in the life and teachings of Jesus is a warrant for apprehending aspects of the life and teachings of Jesus as constitutive of violence. Finally, she suggests that Jesus' human genres may be understood as demonstrating a necessary engagement in violence by those who would be like Jesus, and who would pursue the flourishing of creation. **Jaco Botha** investigates empire, structural violence, and the missio Dei by using the social location of Mgecineni Noki, who was killed in the conflict between Lonmin's Marikana mine management and their workforce life, as a lens to critique the Church's engagement in issues of violence which undermine the dignity of the most vulnerable peoples in the new South Africa.

The last three chapters focus on the topics from the perspective of Practical Theology. **Christo Thesnaar** investigates how the lack of implementing the recommendations from the Truth and Reconciliation Commission (TRC) as well as the reluctance of government, civil society and the religious groupings that has resulted in a "frozen conflict" in the current South African society. He therefore proposes a contextual pastoral approach to address the vacuum this has caused. **Benaya Niyukuri** examines the ethnic conflicts that have been a cause of the political unrest in Burundi in order to emphasise the role of Practical Theology in peacebuilding and the church in reconciliation in Burundi. **Oholiabs D. Tuduks** examines the praxis of reconciliation among the religious groups in Northern Nigeria with the intention of finding the factors that affect the success of reconciliation. Nigeria is known for its periodic religious crises among Christians and Muslims. Through a pastoral care hermeneutical approach the chapter suggests a number of ways for effective reconciliation. Some of these include a focus on inter-religious understanding and learning, inter-religious hospitality, healthy inter-religious dialogue, and tolerance that promotes interest in diversity.

In the concluding chapter **Wilhelm Verwoerd** invites the reader to commit to the complex, and arduous task, of reconciliation that is coupled with justice. He does so by sharing aspects of his own journey towards reconciliation, and experience that he has gained from sharing in the journeys of others who are on this path. His contribution brings together insights from South Africa, the broader African context, and some lessons learned in Ireland. Verwoerd emphasises the importance of an authentic, and textured, spirituality as a foundation for biblical, theological, and practical embodiment of reconciliation and justice in Africa.

We are grateful to each of the colleagues for their hard work that makes this collection of essays such a diverse disciplinary, and contextually varied, contribution on the themes related to reconciliation, forgiveness and violence in Africa. We are particularly grateful to Dr Lee-Anne Roux who did a superb job of proof-reading and editing the text. The volume is dedicated to the memory of H Russel Botman. It was Professor Botman's commitment to human dignity that was the genesis of this project. The process out of which this volume comes was supported by the HOPE funding that he secured for the Stellenbosch University. We trust that the scholarship contained in these chapters will invite conversation, deepen reflection, and contribute towards our understanding of human dignity and the fostering of lasting hope for justice, peace, and flourishing in Africa.

After the completion of this manuscript, one of the contributors to the volume, Dr Alease Brown, passed away from a sudden illness. She was a promising and brilliant theologian, as you will see from her chapter in this book. We are deeply saddened by her untimely death. We hope that the work that she was so committed to will serve as an inspiration and invitation to others to think deeply and act courageously for justice. Alease will be missed.

Marius J. Nel
Dion A. Forster
Christo H. Thesnaar
Faculty of Theology, Stellenbosch University, February 2020.

# MATTHEW'S RECONFIGURING OF SALVATION IN A CONTEXT OF OPPRESSION

*Marius J. Nel[1]*

## INTRODUCTION

Socio-historically both the story of Jesus narrated by Matthew, and the community he wrote for, can be located within Rome's sphere of influence (Wainwright, 2017:30).[2] According to Jonker (2018:6), it is important to take both these contexts (the world in and behind the text) into consideration when interpreting the biblical text in Africa. In reading the biblical text simply with a comparative paradigm, as is often done in studies undertaken by African scholars, a direct relationship between the world(s) constructed in the text and various African contexts is often assumed. Jonker has instead argued for an analogical paradigm that relates the textual communication to its socio-historical setting of communication (the world behind the text). While both the setting of Matthew's story and that of Matthew's communication must therefore be taken into consideration, the point of departure should be the contextual engagement of the constructed realities with the social-historical circumstances of the time of textual formation (Jonker, 2018:12–13).

Matthew's story of Jesus (the world in the text) is primarily set in Roman-occupied Galilee and Judea with its protagonist, in the words of Sim (2012:73), ultimately "brutally executed in Roman fashion by Roman soldiers on the orders of the local Roman governor." The composition of the Gospel itself occurred approximately two decades after the disastrous Jewish revolt against Rome. In this period its audience would have been exposed to a relentless Roman propaganda campaign[3] that sought to humiliate the defeated Jewish people with which Matthew's community had a close association (Sim, 2012:63, 73). While it is a speculative enterprise to attempt to reconstruct the precise social history of a text like the Gospel of Matthew (the world behind the text) in terms of its patterns of scriptural citation, it remains important to read it in terms of the broad context of its protagonist and initial readers.

---

1    The author is presently an associate professor in New Testament studies at Stellenbosch University, and Chair of the Department of Old and New Testament.

2    If Matthew was written in Antioch, the seat of the provincial governor and the permanent posting of four legions, the presence of the Roman Empire would have been impossible to ignore (Carter, 2001:77; Sim, 2012:73).

3    Cf. The triumphal procession of Jewish captives and loot from the Temple in Jerusalem through Rome, coins minted especially to celebrate the capture of Judea, and the reallocation of the levy of the annual Temple tax for the restoration of the Temple of Jupiter Capitolinus (Sim, 2012:73).

It is clear from Matthew that they were subject to the economic exploitation, political oppression, military power and idolatry that characterised the Roman Empire (Hays, 2016:108; Sim, 2012:73).

## MATTHEW AS COUNTER-NARRATIVE

It has been argued by Warren Carter (2001:93-167) that Matthew can be read as a counter-narrative. As a counter-narrative it instructs its audience to live as an alternative community guided by a vision of a more just society than that embodied in the rhetoric and practices of the dominant Roman imperial culture.[4] While Carter focuses on the inherent conflict between Roman imperial theology and Matthew's description of Jesus as saviour, God's salvific agent, other recent studies have argued for a more ambivalent relationship between the Roman Empire and the Gospel of Matthew (Wainwright, 2017:33-34). This ambivalence is evident in Matthew's presentation of individual Romans as being either good or bad[5] and the Roman Empire as being both the instrument and object of God's wrath. It is important for African interpreters of the New Testament to note this ambivalence in the text instead of only interpreting it in line with a view that supports their particular interest (e.g. the church should follow the Matthean church in collaborating or confronting contemporary dominant power structures).

In terms of the first, the parable in Matthew 22:1-14 can be interpreted as a direct, metaphoric reference to the destruction of Jerusalem in 70 CE by Rome. In the parable, a king in response to the elite spurring his repeated invitations to attend his son's wedding, sends his troops to kill them and burn their city. The burning of cities was a common punitive imperial tactic. The parable's reference to a city specifically destroyed by fire (Matt 22:7) also matches Josephus's account of the burning of Jerusalem (Carter, 2001:82). Read in this manner the parable depicts Rome as God's chosen agent for punishing the Jerusalem elite for rejecting Jesus just as he had used the imperial powers, Assyria (Isa 10:1-7) and Babylon (Jer 25:1-11), as his punitive agents in the past (Carter, 2001:83). Instead of Jesus saving his people from the Roman Empire, his rejection by the Jerusalem elite had thus three decades later resulted in their punishment by God through Rome's destruction of their city.

Other sections of Matthew can, however, be read as referring to the specific eschatological fate of Rome in the final battle between the forces of evil and the righteous. Leading up to this battle there will be a great tribulation (Matt 24:15-27) perpetrated by those who end up being "a corpse where eagles gather" (Matt 24:28).

---

4    Satan's third attempt to test Jesus in Matthew is to show him all the kingdoms of the world, which assumes that Satan controls their fate. The power of Rome over others is thus implicitly due to Satan (Sim, 2012:74). The community of Matthew was therefore to resist both the power of Rome and the Evil One who gave it its power.

5    Positive depictions of individual agents of the Roman Empire are that of the centurion of Capernaum (Matt 8:5-13), Pilate's wife who describes Jesus as righteous and innocent (Matt 27:19). Negative depictions include Pilate (Matt 27:11-26) and the soldiers who guard the tomb of Jesus (Matt 27:62-66; 28:4, 11-15) (Sim, 2012:74).

Sim (2012:75) translates the plural of ἀετός in Matthew 24:28 not as "vultures," which are usually drawn to carrion, but as 'eagles.' The gathering of eagles at a corpse for Sim represents the legions of the Roman Empire, who had the eagle as their standard, that have been vanquished by the Son of Man. The arrival of the Son of Man and his angels, which brings the great tribulation to its conclusion, is thus understood as being described in military terms (Matt 24:29-31). The sign of the Son of Man can be interpreted as his military standard (Matt 24:30) in view of it being accompanied by a trumpet (σάλπιγξ), which was commonly used by Roman legions for battlefield signals, being sounded (Matt 24:31). These images, according to Sim, therefore evoke the eventual military defeat of Rome. After its defeat, God will furthermore judge Rome along with all the nations (Matt 25:31-46). God's universal vengeance and eternal punishment will thus also befall them (Sim, 2012:75).

While the abovementioned interpretations of Carter and Sim need not be accepted without critique, they illustrate what Botha (2011:21-48) has convincingly argued, namely that the Roman Empire provides a complex context for interpreting early Christianities, in that they not only resisted its power but also often imitated its imperial practices and imagery (cf. The depiction of God as a ruler who judges and punishes his enemies). It is thus important for the church in Africa to attempt to understand the fine line walked by communities like Matthew's between resistance and accommodation, protest and negotiation (Carter, 2006:24) when engaging with their own communities' context when appropriating the sacred texts of Israel.

It is not just Matthew's relationship with the Roman Empire that is complex. Its relationship to Jewish hope is also unclear because the precise nature of this hope itself is often vague. After surveying four different types of literary evidence,[6] Wright (1992:319) comes to the conclusion that while there was no fixed view of the Messiah in the first century, messianic themes and ideas based on Hebrew biblical passages and motifs were current. While explicit references to a messianic figure are comparatively rare therein, a common theme is that of a great reversal in the future which would result in their vindication with the defeat of their enemies. Liberation from Rome, the restoration of the temple, and a life of enjoying the fruits of their land are common elements congruent with this hope (Wright, 1992:300). Furthermore, though a Messianic hope in Judaism is commonly expressed in symbolic language it often has a very this-worldly notion of a ruler, or judge, who would arise from within Israel and who would enact the divine judgement and vengeance on Israel's oppressors. This enactment of judgement often involved military action.

It is important to note that forgiveness and national restoration are at times causally linked in Israel's Messianic hope (Wright, 1992:300) and that the antithesis between national and individual, and "political" and "spiritual" salvation is therefore an anachronism in view of the available literary evidence (Wright, 1992:322). It is thus a question if the same hope for the national-political liberation of Israel is evident in Matthew's extensive use of the Old Testament, or if he had deliberately deleted

---

6    Wright (1992:319) surveyed the Psalm of Solomon, as well as various texts from Josephus, Qumran and selected apocalyptic writers.

references to political deliverance. In order to attempt to answer this question, this chapter will, after a brief overview of intertextual references related to Matthew's hope for political salvation, focus on Matthew 1:21 to ascertain how he envisions his community's hope for salvation while living under the yoke of the Roman Empire.

## Matthew's use of the Old Testament

Intertextuality understood, in line with Richard Hays (1989:15), as "the imbedding of fragments of an earlier text within a later one" plays an important role in clarifying the salvific intent of the Matthean Jesus. Intertextually Matthew is permeated with Old Testament passages and motifs due to the Jewish practice of thinking in scriptural categories (Hartman, 1970:133).

This intertextual link with the Old Testament is crucial for understanding Matthew's engagement with the Roman Empire. Carter (2001:202–203), for example, refers to the following intertextual references which all evoke a context of imperial oppression:

- (a) Two fulfilment texts in Matthew 1:22-23 and 4:15-16 evoke Isaiah 7-9 and suggest that almost all fulfilment texts derive from and evoke imperial situations.
- (b) Isaiah is quoted in Matthew 8:17 (Isa 53:4); 12:17-21 (Isa 42:1-4, 9) and 21:5 (Isa 62:11, in part). Matthew thus regularly uses texts from the context of Babylonian imperialism in his narrative of the work of Jesus.
- (c) Matthew 2:23 may be citing or alluding to Isaiah 4:3, which refers to God's reign being restored in Jerusalem, which is an imperialist vision. Matthew 2:23 may recall Judges 13 and with it the context of Israel's imperialist struggle with the Philistines.
- (d) Two quotes from Zechariah 9-11 (9:9 in Matt 21:5; 11:13 in Matt 27:9-10) anticipate the defeat of all of Israel's enemies and the establishment of God's reign or empire.
- (e) In Matthew 2:17-18, Jeremiah 31:5 is cited from Jeremiah's ministry in the context of the growing Babylonian imperial threat.
- (f) Hosea 11:1 is cited in Matthew 2:15 and recalls the exodus liberation in the context of Assyrian imperialist rule.
- (g) Matthew 13:34 cites Psalm 78 that surveys Israel's unfaithfulness and God's contrasting faithfulness that results in their deliverance from Egypt by him.

Carter (2001:202–203) proposes that these inter-texts, shaped by different experiences of various imperial threats in the history of Israel, address Matthew's community's experience of Roman imperialism. Similarly, Zacharias (2017:18–19) has shown how Matthew's interaction with Davidic messianism through the use of typology, formula quotations, allusions, and clustered echoes at major junctures of his narrative both evoke the restoration of Israel as a nation, and reconfigures the hope associated with it. While the Son of David is, for example, portrayed as a violent messiah in both Ps Sol 17 and the Dead Sea Scrolls, Matthew's Davidic messiah is instead presented as a humble king and a healing shepherd (Zacharias, 2017:191).

In the light of this reconfiguring of Israel's hope in the Son of David typology, it is a question if a similar process is evident in Matthew's references to salvation. Has he in other words deliberately reconfigured the hope of Israel by toning down the references to political liberation contained therein? Along with John the Baptist's calling for the confession of sins (Matt 3:6) and Jesus forgiving sins (Matt 9:2, 5, 6), three texts are often singled out by commentators (Davies & Allison, 1988:210; France, 2007:54; Nolland, 2005:98) as clearly articulating Matthew's understanding of the salvific work of Jesus (Matt 1:21, 20:28 and 26:28). The focus of this chapter will be on Matthew 1:21 as a test case for how Matthew appropriated Israel's hope for salvation as it is articulated in the Old Testament. This is important since the dynamic of appropriating authoritative traditions in an African context should be done in an analogical manner to how these traditions were appropriated in biblical times in text like Matthew (Jonker, 2015:299).

## THE ONE WHO WILL SAVE HIS PEOPLE FROM THEIR SINS

The announcement of the angel in Matthew 1:21 programmatically describes Jesus as the one who will "save his people from their sins" (αὐτὸς γὰρ σώσει τὸν λαὸν αὐτοῦ ἀπὸ τῶν ἁμαρτιῶν αὐτῶν) thereby marking the importance of the theme of salvation[7] in the Gospel of Matthew.

### Interpreting the nature of Jesus' mission

The interpretation of the nature of the announced salvation has usually been conducted along two lines of interpretation.

The first line of interpretation is that the announcement of imminent salvation envisions the spiritual renewal of Israel. For example, according to France (2007:54), the angel's words signal that any political expectations evoked by the Davidic theme of his prologue is not in line with Jesus' true mission. His ministry, which begins with a call to repentance from sin (Matt 3:2, 6; 4:17), instead focuses on teaching, healing and exorcism, and forgiving sins (Matt 9:6) and culminates in his death "as a ransom for many" (Matt 20:28), "for the forgiveness of sins" (Matt 26:28). Jesus as the son of David thus does not conform to the popular messianic expectation in that there is no mention of freedom from the oppression of the governing powers (in contrast to Ps. Sol. 17) which indicates the religious and moral, instead of political, character of the messianic deliverance brought about by Jesus (Davies & Allison, 1988:210). According to Davies and Allison (1988:174), who follow this line of interpretation, "His kingship neither involves national sovereignty nor does it restore Israel to good political fortune. Jesus' kingdom is instead one which can be present even in the midst of Roman rule. The Messiah's first task is to save his people from their sins (1:21), not deliver them from political bondage."[8]

---

7    Even though Matthew does not use salvation language to the extent Luke does he does refer to the saving role of Jesus in Matthew 8:25; 9:21–22; 14:30; 27:42 (Nolland, 2005:98).

8    Davies and Allison (1988:210) emphasise that the deliverance accomplished by Jesus is religious and moral in nature since it removes the wall of sin between God and the human race and that Matthew says nothing about the liberation of Israel from the governing powers that were oppressing them. It thus differs in this regard from Ps. Sol. 17 which addresses both the sin which separates people from God and their political liberation (Carter, 2001:192).

The second line of interpretation supports the opposite view that Matthew 1:21 expects the political liberation of Israel. In this approach Israel's national-political salvation, involving their deliverance from Roman imperialism is taken as the most natural meaning of "saving his people" (Hagner, 1993:19) in view of it being linked to the etymology[9] of Jesus' name which recalls the conquest of the promised land by Joshua. Novakovic (2003:73–75) has argued in this vein that "salvation from sins" should be understood as the undoing of the consequences of sins (e.g. illness).[10] Since the ultimate consequence of Israel's sins was her continued exile (i.e. the Roman occupation) her political deliverance should therefore be seen as part of her salvation. This is evident in the reference to the Babylonian exile in the preceding genealogy (Matt 1:1-17) which reminds the reader that the sin of Israel had in the past caused a rift with God. By linking Jesus to the Babylonian exile (the deportation to Babylon and not their return) Matthew indicates that he, as the saviour, is Emmanuel, the one who restores God's presence as the son of David and the son of Abraham (Repschinski, 2006:257). Through him God will bring the exile of Israel to an end (Charette, 1992:64–77).

According to Charette (1992:20, 61–62), the theme of recompense is an integral part of Matthew's story of socio-political salvation which is impossible to understand without recalling the similar story in the Old Testament. The Old Testament scheme of recompense is centred on the land in that the covenants of Abraham, Sinai and David all relate to the promise, entrance and ruling of the land (Luomanen, 1998:26). For Matthew, the Sinai covenants are of special importance since it links blessing and curse to obedience of the law with the latter resulting in the conquest of Israel and her subsequent exile. Even though the nation had set a wrong course, the prophets expressed the hope that a righteous remnant would remain and that they would be restored in the promised land (Luomanen, 1998:26). Carter (2001:76, 84) has therefore argued that Matthean soteriology includes deliverance from all forms of bondage as was expected of the coming Messiah. The Matthean Messiah would thus enact God's political, socio-economic and military salvation of Israel since moral, political and social salvation are entwined with each other in Jesus' genealogy (Carter, 2001:79, 84). All that changed for Matthew is that the according to him Jesus does not save his people through military means (Carter, 2001:85).[11]

While it would be anachronistic[12] to assume that Matthew's reference to salvation from sins implies that he envisioned Jesus' mission as being solely to save individuals

---

9   The name, the Greek form of Yeshua, is according to popular etymology related to the Hebrew verb עשׁי ("to save") and noun העושׁי ("salvation"). It should be noted that despite Jesus' name meaning "Yahweh is salvation" Matthew ascribes the salvation from sins to Jesus and not God (Novakovic, 2003:64)

10  Notice that Matthew does not refer to the forgiveness *of* sins but rather to the salvation *from* sins (Novakovic, 2003:72).

11  His second coming in Matthew 24:29-31 can, however, according to Sim (2012:75), be described in military terms.

12  It is anachronistic because it assumes a division between the religious and the political spheres which was not made in the ancient world (Carter, 2001:75–76).

from their moral and spiritual failings[13] (Charette, 1992:87) it is evident that Jesus, according to Matthew, had not saved his people from political oppression. When Matthew continues the Old Testament story through his genealogy the hope for the restoration of a remnant was still unfulfilled (Luomanen, 1998:26). Even if the intent of Jesus' ministry announced by the angel in Matthew may have been the political liberation of Israel (the second line of interpretation outlined above) it had not happened in practice for Matthew's readers. While the people of Jesus' (τὸν λαὸν αὐτοῦ) sins had been atoned for they had not been saved from its consequences. Not only in Matthew's narrative of Jesus' life, but also in his own context, Israel remained in exile. Luz (1989:95) therefore observes that the statement that he will save the people "from their sins" does not reflect the usual Jewish hope that the Messiah will eliminate sinners (Ps. Sol. 17.22–25) or that he judges the sinners and lawless (1 Enoch 62.2; 69.27–29) but that it instead reflects the Christian experiences with Jesus.

The experience of Matthew's community was that a spiritual and not political liberation had occurred (Charette, 1992; Luomanen, 1998:27). The national-political deliverance of Israel would also not easily have been accomplished in the period after the destruction of the Temple in 70 CE. This reality necessitated Matthew to reinterpret the messianic hope of his community. The great reversal would, according to him, now occur at the end of this age when the meek shall inherit the land (cf. Ps 37:11 [Ps 36:11 LXX]). The inheritors are, furthermore, no longer only the physical descendants of Abraham, nor is the land to be identified with Canaan. In line with the expected cosmic renewal (Matt 19:28), already expressed by Isaiah 60-66, the new people of God will instead inherit a renewed creation and not just the land promised to Moses. While the future coming of the Son of Man in Matthew would thus irrevocably transform the world, Matthew's message for a community living in the interim period under Roman occupation needs to be reflected on.

## While under Rome

In dealing with representatives of the Roman Empire the Matthean Jesus encouraged his disciples to be as accommodating as possible in that they were to walk a second mile if commanded to walk a single one (Matt 5:40-41), love their enemies (Matt 5:44), and pay all taxes due to Caesar (Matt 22:21). It further appears that Matthew intends the reference to a mile as a metonymic for the legitimate demands of Roman soldiers within the power-structure of the Roman Empire (Baasland, 2015:236) and that the non-resistant attitude Jesus advocates is not to be restricted to this specific demand. It is also noteworthy that while Jesus was embroiled in a fierce public conflict with the Jewish leadership he, according to Matthew, had a less combative relationship with the representatives of the Roman Empire. Not only did Jesus respond positively to the faith of the centurion whose servant had been ill (Matt 8:10), but is it another centurion who after Jesus' crucifixion confesses that he was the Son of God (Matt 27:54).

---

13    Matthew usually prefers to use the verb ἀφίημι to refer to the salvation of sins
      (Repschinski, 2006:255).

A possible explanation for this nuanced depiction of Jesus' relationship with the Roman military could be that the catastrophic events of 70 AD had convinced Matthew that resistance against Rome was futile. Therefore his community had to be very careful in their dealings with the functionaries of the Empire. This strategy allows Matthew to propagate an ethic of appeasement while waiting for the general and specific judgement of God. Rather that fighting on all fronts (Romans, Jews and internal opponents)[14] it is instead a case of carefully choosing the conflicts one gets caught up within Formative Judaism and waiting faithfully for God's judgement of those too powerful to challenge (Rome) in the present. This strategy of Matthew would necessitate that he redacts Israel's hope for political salvation based on the promises of the Old Testament. It is thus apparent that the world of Jesus and his ministry constructed by Matthew was influenced by his own context. It is, however, an open question if Matthew's redactional activity supports the proposal that he consistently reconfigured the hope of his community in order to temper the political aspects thereof. In order to investigate Matthew's redaction and appropriation of Israel's hope his interpretation of Psalm 129:8 (LXX) in Matthew 1:21 will be studied as a test case.

## Matthew's redaction of Psalm 129:8 (LXX)

The announcement by the angel in Matthew 1:21 has been described as a "deliberate echo" (France, 2007:53), "echo" (Carter, 2001:83) or an "allusive quotation"[15] that is wholly independent of the LXX (Gundry, 1967:128). It is therefore important to clarify what is meant by the terminology used to describe these different types of intertextual references. This is especially important since the presuppositions of interpreters often determines the identification and interpretation of intertextual references.

Quotation, allusion and echo may be understood as points along a spectrum of intertextual references with the first two being used intentionally (Hays, 1989:23, 29). Allusions are distinguished from echoes by their deliberate use by an author.[16] Quotations in turn are distinguished from allusions in that they can only apply to a text while the latter can allude to a particular passage, place, person, theme, action or event (Lucas, 2014:110). The higher "volume", to use the term of Hays (2002:53) for the degree of repetition of words and syntactical patterns, of quotations also

---

14    See Sim (2012:62–78).

15    Matthew 1:21 is, according to Gundry (1967:128), not a straightforward quotation of Psalm 129:8 (LXX) but rather an allusive quotation since it he has reconfigured its wording. According to Hartman (1970:138) it can be described as a "twisted" quotation that has the salient function of drawing attention to a new interpretation in line with how it has been redacted. It is thus a question if this new interpretation should be based on its "surface meaning," which any reasonable reader may grasp, or the deeper meaning thereof which only a reader with specialised knowledge can access (France, 1981:241). In this chapter the terminology of Hays will be followed and Matthew 1:21 will be simply described as an allusion.

16    Lucas (2014:110) defines echoes as unintentional references to a particular passage, place, person, theme, action, or event that are in principle capable of being recognised by the audience or author.

differentiates it from allusions. It is in terms of volume that Matthew 1:21 can be understood as an allusion of Psalm 129:8 (LXX).

In order to understand an allusion the readers (or hearers) of a text must recognise it as such (Hartman, 1970: 134–135). Furthermore, for communication to take place a common interpretive tradition or contextual guideline is necessary to indicate how the author understood the text (Hartman, 1970:142). In this regard, France (1981:233) has asked how sophisticated readers need to be to understand the formula quotations in Matthew 2. The same can be asked of Matthew 1:21 as an allusion. This is especially important if it is also to be understood as an example of metalepsis,[17] or metonymy (Carter, 2001:83), in that its partial allusion to Psalm 129 (LXX) evokes the whole thereof.

Metalepsis is a literary device that establishes an intertextual connection between two texts through what is explicit in the citation or allusion of one text by another, as well as an implicit connection thanks to the unstated resonances between them (Lucas, 2014:95). In the words of Hays (1989:20) metalepsis "functions to suggest to the reader that text B should be understood in light of a broad interplay with text A, encompassing aspects of A beyond those explicitly echoed." Metalepsis is thus a powerful device for evoking the message of a text by only explicitly engaging with a part of it. By quoting a fragment of a text which as a whole expresses the hope for political liberation, that is not apparent in the fragment quoted, an author may also conceal what is evoked by it from readers unfamiliar with the intertext. At the same time it would strengthen the hope of informed readers or hearers.[18] In interpreting the salvation intended by Matthew 1:21 it is, therefore, important to ascertain if it is an instance of metalepsis.

Hays (2002:53) has suggested seven criteria (availability, volume, recurrence, thematic coherence, historical plausibility, history of interpretation and satisfaction), as "modestly useful rules of thumb," for detecting metalepsis in a text.[19] Applied to historically orientated studies like this one only two of these criteria, availability and

---

17    The work of Richard Hays (1989, 2014, 2016) has called attention to the occurrence of metalepsis in both the letters of Paul and in the Gospels.

18    Hays (2016:370) has remarked in this regard that sometimes it is the most important things that are unsaid and that the intended reader or hearer would therefore need to have the text referred to stored in their memory in order to "hear" what is unsaid.

19    Hays (2002:53) defines them as follow: (a) Availability – The suggested source had to be available for both author and reader. (b) Volume – The degree of repetition of words and syntactical patterns must be sufficient for the intertextual relationship between the texts to be recognised. (c) Recurrence – It has to be determined how often the possible intertext is alluded to. (d) Thematic coherence – does it fit the argument of the text? (e) Historical plausibility – could the author and readers have understood the meaning of the supposed metalepsis? (f) History of interpretation – have others understood it as metalepsis? (g) Satisfaction – how satisfying is the metaleptic proposal? While Hays' criteria have been criticised by Porter (1997:82–84) they have been defended by Lucas (2014:93–111) and used by scholars like Eubanks (2013) and Beetham (2010). Porter links Hays' criteria of availability with an audience-orientated approach in that the cited text must also be available to the audience. Porter (1997:82–84) himself has chosen for an author-orientated approach instead of an audience-orientated approach.

historical plausibility, are important (Lucas, 2014:100).[20] In terms of Matthew 1:21 it is clear that the text of some Psalms were available to Matthew (as well as his intended readers) and that it is historically plausible that he utilised it and therefore the verse can be understood as an allusion to Psalm 129:8 (LXX) and an example of metalepsis.

As an example of metalepsis, Matthew 1:21 evokes both the salvation of individuals and that of Israel in that Psalm 129 (LXX) not only refers to the salvation of individuals in its opening six verses, but also to national salvation since Israel is called upon to "hope" in God and are reassured that he would redeem her in the final two verses.[21] It is, however, unclear if Matthew alludes to this nationalistic hope in Psalm 129:8 (LXX), that is only accessible to informed readers through metalepsis, to affirm it or if he intends to amend it. It is therefore necessary to have a closer look at his redaction of the Psalm.

## Redacting the hope of Israel

When Psalm 129:8 LXX (καὶ αὐτὸς λυτρώσεται τὸν Ισραηλ ἐκ πασῶν τῶν ἀνομιῶν αὐτοῦ) is compared to its allusion in Matthew 1:21b (αὐτὸς γὰρ σώσει τὸν λαὸν αὐτοῦ ἀπὸ τῶν ἁμαρτιῶν αὐτῶν) it is readily apparent that the allusion has been redacted by Matthew.

Two redactional changes are especially noteworthy. Matthew has, firstly, replaced "will redeem" ((λυτρώσεται) with "to save" (σώσει), possibly to create a closer link with the etymology of Jesus' name in that its Hebrew root ישע is in the LXX usually translated as σῳζω (Gundry, 1982: 23; Novakovic, 2003: 65). It is, however, not clear if Matthew has not also intentionally removed the allusion to Israel's political salvation from their present occupation by Rome (contra Carter 2001:84).

While the noun λύτρον (and its cognate verb λυτρόω) has a strong connotation with the end of Israel's exile,[22] the verb σῳζω can refer to a broad range of phenomena from which one can be saved (Keener, 1999:97) and does thus not specifically allude to Israel's political liberation. The broader meaning of σῳζω is evident in the manner in which Matthew uses it in his narrative. While it is only used in Matthew 1:21 in reference to sins as the phenomena from which subjects are to be saved, it is often used by Matthew in Jesus' eschatological speeches (10:22; 19:25; 24:13, 22) and in the context of his miracles (8:25; 9:21, 22; 14:30) and crucifixion (Novakovic, 2003:67).[23]

---

20  The other criteria have a poetic or aesthetic nature. Identifying an occurrence of metalepsis is therefore primarily a qualitative and secondly a quantitative one (Lucas, 2014:100).

21  "O Israel, put your hope in the Lord, for with the Lord is unfailing love and with him is full redemption. He himself will redeem (λυτρώσεται) Israel from all their sins" Ps 130:7-8 (129 LXX).

22  The verb "redeem" (λυτρόω) is, for example, used in the LXX for Israel's redemption or return from Egypt, Babylon and Assyria (Carter, 2001:84).

23  Repschinski (2006:257–258) has noted that after the announcement in Matthew 1:21c, Matthew does not link σῳζειν and ἁμαρτία again. With the exception of Matthew 3:6, he instead usually uses the noun ἁμαρτία in conjunction with the verb ἀφίημι (9:2, 5, 6; 12:31; 26:28). (Novakovic, 2003:67–68). Matthew also uses σῳζω in reference to physical affliction and eschatological salvation. It is, for example, used in regard to physical affliction in 8:25; 9:21; 9:22 (2x)

It can thus be argued that the programmatic statement in Matthew 1:21 anticipates Jesus' healing ministry and atoning death, which were not part of what is known of contemporary Jewish messianic expectations (Novakovic, 2003:74), and that in contrast to a Jewish nationalistic understanding of the son of David, Matthew instead depicts Jesus as the healing and dying son of David.[24] It is, however, unlikely that Matthew is thereby also intentionally removing all references to Israel's hope for political salvation, or that he wanted to conceal this hope from ordinary readers, by changing λυτρώσεται to σώσει in that he does not do this consistently in his narrative. Matthew has, for example, no qualms about using λύτρον in Matthew 20:28 which allude to various Old Testament texts.[25] The metalepsis between these texts and Matthew 20:28 makes it apparent that Jesus is, for Matthew, the promised Messiah who would remit Israel's sin and restore her as a nation. The literary context (the last supper of Jesus) of this allusion to the restoration of Israel, however, makes it clear that this restoration task of Jesus as the Messiah is for Matthew linked to his death and not to his Galilean ministry.

The second important redaction is the change of Ἰσραήλ (LXX) to τὸν λαὸν αὐτοῦ (Repschinski, 2006:255) which could be intended to indicate that Jesus has come to save his new people (the church) from their sins in that the pronoun (αὐτός)[26] indicates that those who follow him are in view. This would be in line with the shift in Jesus' focus from Israel to the nations that occur in the narrative of Matthew (cf. 4:18-22; 16:18; 18:18; 28:16-20). This interpretation is, however, implausible since neither the salvation of sins, nor the church has been a focus of Matthew in his narrative up to this point. Matthew also does not avoid referring specifically to Israel as the focus of Jesus' salvific activity since he explicitly uses Ἰσραήλ in Matthew 15:24 to describe the mission of Jesus. It is thus a question if it does not instead refer to Israel (Repschinski, 2006:255–256). The textual context of God's faithfulness to Israel (Matt 1:1-17), and the reference to Jesus being the shepherd for Israel (Matt 2:6), can in this regard be seen as support for taking Israel as the referent of τὸν λαὸν αὐτοῦ (Carter, 2001:79).

Novakovic (2003:66), however, argues that Matthew has used ὁ λαὸς αὐτοῦ in place of the Ἰσραήλ (LXX) in order to "refer to Jesus' church composed of both Jews and Gentiles." This is in line with the genealogy of Jesus (Matt 1:1-17) introducing him as the son of David and Abraham with the first representing the nationalistic covenant with the house of David[27] and the second the universalistic tradition in

---

(Repschinski, 2006:257). Luomanen (1998:38) adds 14:30; 27:40; 27:42 (x2); 27:49 to this list. The verb σῴζειν is in turn used in 27:39-43 (Repschinski, 2006:264) to link the cross to salvation just as forgiveness of sins had been linked to it. For example, Jesus is ironically mocked as being able to save others (27:42-ἄλλους ἔσωσεν) but not himself.

24　In Matthew Jesus is called the "son of David" by those in need of healing (9:27-31; 20:29-34) and release from being possessed (15:22; 21:14-16) (Carter, 2001:78-79).

25　Cf. Jeremiah 31:15 [38:15 LXX] and Isaiah 40:2-10; 50:1.

26　The two personal pronouns (αὐτός) also have different antecedents (God in Ps 129:8 LXX and Jesus in Matt 1:21).

27　The reference to David as "king" (1:6) and his successors (1:6-11) recalls God's promise to him that his descendants would constitute an eternal kingdom (2 Sam 7:14; Ps 89:3-4) (Carter, 2001:78).

Second Temple Judaism[28] (Repschinski, 2006:252–253). If Matthew had intended to refer only to Israel as an national entity in Matthew 1:21 it is thus unclear why has he changed Ισραήλ (LXX) to τὸν λαὸν αὐτοῦ at all (Novakovic, 2003:65). The Gospel of Matthew thus presents Jesus as the fulfilment of both covenants. He is the saviour of Israel and the nations which reflects the situation of the Matthean church which was comprised of an increasing number of gentiles.

## CONCLUSION

In conclusion Matthew's intent with his allusion to Psalm 129:8 will be summarised before a few hermeneutical remarks will be made about the interpretation of the biblical text in Africa.

### The function of Matthew's allusion to Psalm 129:8

The redactional changes made in the allusion to Psalm 129:8 (LXX) in Matthew 1:21 appear to be influenced by the etymology of Jesus' name (λυτρώσεται to σώσει) and the passage's literary context (Ισραήλ to τὸν λαὸν αὐτοῦ) rather than Matthew's political ideology. This conclusion is supported by the observation that it does not appear as if Matthew intentionally wanted to deny all hope for the national salvation of Israel by changing specific words in Matthew 1:21 since they occur in the rest of his Gospel (e.g. λύτρον in Matt 20:28). The changes made in the allusion to Psalm 129:8 (LXX) are, however, in line with the shift that occurs in Matthew's narrative in his understanding of the nature and scope of the salvation to be hoped for. While the Matthean Jesus does not confront the agents of the Roman Empire in his Galilean ministry to effect political salvation through a military victory, his healings and exorcisms demonstrate God's power to restore all of creation. There is also a fundamental change in the way in which this all-encompassing victory was to be accomplished in that it is brought about by the death, and not victory, of the Messiah. Matthew has, furthermore, modified Israel's hope for salvation by the Messiah into a two-step process, enlarged the scope of his ultimate victory (from the Promised Land to a renewed creation),[29] and broadened the beneficiaries thereof (from Israel to all nations). It is also clear that for Matthew the church should not seek to be an agent of judgement since it is the sole prerogative of God to judge. This redefining of the geo-national scope and eschatological timing of Israel's hope for the Matthean community can possibly be ascribed to its new, mixed, ethnic composition and their experience of the Jewish war.

---

28  The genealogy refers three times to Abraham (1:1, 2, 17) recalling God's promise to through him bless all the people of the earth (Gen 12:1-3) (Carter, 2001:78).

29  In view of Matthew's broader narrative the nature and scope of salvation it proclaims has been expanded to include all of creation (Matt 19:28). Matthew thus defies a narrow, purely spiritual or nationalistic, understanding of salvation.

## The interpretation of the biblical text in Africa

It, finally, has to be asked what the engagement with Matthew's hope for salvation alluded to in Matthew 1:21 can contribute to the process of interpreting the biblical text in Africa?

It firstly, serves as a reminder that the church must always be aware of the difference between the hermeneutical presuppositions it brings to the text as its interpreter and the intent of the author thereof (Wainwright, 2017:34). While the inherent ambiguity of intertextual relations in the Bible necessitates that an interpretative choice has to be made as to their meaning interpreters must, however, be aware of their own ideology which influences these choices. The biblical text can thus serve as mirror for the church in Africa in which to examine its own ideology and susceptibility to the lure of power if it allows a rigorous critique of its own interpretation thereof (e.g. by noting which texts in Matthew are given prominence in the proclamation of the church). This is vital since Matthew, along with other biblical text, have in the past been used to provide an ideological basis for the Christendom which has itself often functioned as an empire (Wainwright, 2017:38). The text of Matthew is thus not just a counter-narrative to the Roman Empire or a text propagating non-violence that can be directly applied to any context but also a narrative which potentially can be used to subjugate others.[30]

Secondly, Matthew's appropriation of Israel's hope serves as a warning against being too dogmatic in our description of the intention of Matthew's numerous intertextual quotations, allusions and echo's. In this regard Hartman (1970:152) is correct in his assessment that interpreters should not expect too lucid answers to the question how Matthew uses quotations and allusions as communication, for our ears can only with some difficulty catch these faint nuances of the voices that reach us through the centuries.[31] Interpreters should thus be careful of only hearing the voices which support their political agenda. A reading of the biblical text along with a diversity of readers is therefore essential for hearing its full message.

Thirdly, noting the manner in which text like Matthew have appropriated their sources to address their own context can help contemporary interpreters to undertake analogical interpretations to address their own contexts.

---

30  Matthew 1:21 can, for example, be used to justify the church's active involvement in the violent overthrow of governments in the present.

31  We also do not even know if we have the same Vorlage as Matthew with which to compare his use of the LXX, or how consistent he is in his theology or approach to the LXX. It has been suggested by Gundry (1982:23), for example, that Matthew is following the tradition behind Luke 1:77 in changing his text to "his people" and to "from their sins" (in the place of "from all his iniquities"). In response Novakovic (2003:65) has noted that there are, however, differences between Matthew 1:21 and Luke 1:77 in that Luke speaks about John and not Jesus, and that his people denotes God's, not Jesus' people. Furthermore, sins are linked to forgiveness and not salvation (it should, however, be kept in mind that Matthew has no qualms in shifting utterances of John to Jesus – cf. the reference to the forgiveness of sins during the last supper by Jesus in Matthew 26:28 which Mark 1:4 uses to describe the ministry of John the Baptist).

Finally, Matthew's appropriation of the Jesus tradition and the Old Testament in his context reminds the church in Africa that while there are many strategies in the New Testament for engaging with oppressive powers none allows the church to resort to violence. The church is instead called to suffer for God's righteousness (Matt 5:6, 10-12). The reality of God's eschatological judgement allows the church to witness to all through its words and deeds that are in line with the righteousness demanded by God (Matt 6:33), while avoiding a judgemental attitude in the present (Matt 7:1-2). Ultimately for Matthew it is God who will punish the wicked and reward the righteous, and not the church (Matt 25:31-46).

# REFERENCES

Beetham, C.A. (2010). *Echoes of Scripture in the Letter of Paul to the Colossians.* Atlanta: Society of Biblical Literature.

Carter, W. (2001). *Matthew and empire: initial explorations.* Harrisburg, PA: Trinity Press International.

Carter, W. (2006). *The Roman Empire and the New Testament an essential guide.* Nashville: Abingdon.

Charette, B. (1992). *The theme of recompense in Matthew's Gospel.* Sheffield: JSOT Press.

Davies, W.D. and Allison, D.C. (1988). *A critical and exegetical commentary on the Gospel according to Saint Matthew 1-7.* Edinburgh: T & T Clark.

Eubank, N. (2013). *Wages of cross-bearing and debt of sin: the economy of heaven in Matthew's gospel.* Berlin: De Gruyter. https://doi.org/10.1515/9783110304077

France, R.T. (1981). The formula-quotations of Matthew 2 and the problem of communication. *New Testament Studies,* 27(2):233–251. https://doi.org/10.1017/S0028688500006184

France, R.T. (2007). *The Gospel of Matthew.* Grand Rapids: Eerdmans.

Gundry, R.H. (1967). *The use of the Old Testament in St. Matthew's Gospel: with special reference to the Messianic hope.* Leiden: E.J. Brill.

Gundry, R.H. (1982). *Matthew: a commentary on his literary and theological art.* Grand Rapids: Eerdmans.

Hagner, D.A. (1993). *Matthew 1-13.* Dallas: Word Books.

Hartman, L. (1970). 'Scriptural Exegesis in the Gospel of St. Matthew and the Problem of Communication,' in Didier, M. (ed.) *L'Evangile selon Matthieu: redaction et theologie.* Gembloux: J. Duculot, pp.131–152.

Hays, R.B. (1989). *Echoes of the scriptures in the letters of Paul.* Yale University Press.

Hays, R.B. (2002). '"Who has Believed our Message?" Paul's Reading of Isaiah,' in J.M. Court (ed.) *New Testament Writers and the Old Testament: An Introduction.* London: SPCK, pp.46–70.

Hays, R.B. (2014). *Reading backwards: figural Christology and the fourfold gospel witness.* Waco: Baylor University Press.

Hays, R.B. (2016). *Echoes of scripture in the Gospels.* Waco: Baylor University Press.

Jonker, L.C. (2015). *From adequate biblical interpretation to transformative intercultural hermeneutics: chronicling a personal journey.* Elkhart, Indiana: Institute of Mennonite Studies.

Jonker, L.C. (2018). 'Further Interrogation of the Comparative Paradigm in African Biblical Scholarship: Towards an Analogical Hermeneutics for Interpreting the Old Testament in Africa,' in Punt, J. and Nel, M.J. (eds.) *Reading writing right.* African Sun Media, pp.1–28.

Keener, C.S. (1999). *A Commentary on the Gospel of Matthew.* Grand Rapids: Eerdmans.

Lucas, A.J. (2014). Assessing Stanley E Porter's objections to Richard B Hays's notion of metalepsis. *The Catholic Biblical Quarterly,* 76(1):93–111.

Luomanen, P. (1998). *Entering the kingdom of heaven: a study on the structure of Matthew's view of salvation.* Tübingen: Mohr Siebeck.

Luz, U. (1989). *Matthew: A commentary.* Minneapolis: Augsburg.

Nolland, J. (2005). *The Gospel of Matthew: A commentary on the Greek text.* Grand Rapids: Eerdmans.

Novakovic, L. (2003). *Messiah, the healer of the sick: a study of Jesus as the Son of David in the gospel of Matthew.* Tübingen: Mohr Siebeck.

Porter, S.E. (1997). 'The Use of the Old Testament in the New Testament: A Brief Comment on Method and Terminology,' in Evans, C.A. and Sanders, E.P. (eds.) *Early Christian interpretation of the scriptures of Israel: investigations and proposals.* Sheffield: Sheffield Academic, pp.79–96.

Repschinski, B. (2006). "For he will save his people from their sins" (Matthew 1:21): a Christology for Christian Jews. *The Catholic Biblical Quarterly,* 68(2):248–267.

Sim, D.C. (2012). 'Fighting on all Fronts: Crisis Management in the Gospel of Matthew,' in Sim, D.C. and Allen, P. (eds.). *Ancient Jewish and Christian texts as crisis management literature.* London: T & T Clark, pp.62–78.

Wainwright, E.M. (2017). *Matthew: an introduction and study guide: Basileia of the heavens is near at hand.* London: Bloomsbury T & T Clark.

Wright, N.T. (1992). *The New Testament and the people of God.* London: SPCK.

Zacharias, D. (2017). *Matthew's presentation of the Son of David: Davidic tradition and typology in the gospel of Matthew.* T & T Clark Biblical Studies. London: Bloomsbury.

# CONQUERING EVIL

## Engaging Violence from the Perspective of Paul's Letter to the Romans

*Endale Sebsebe Mekonnen*[1]

## INTRODUCTION

The scholarly definition of violence has created conceptual complexity across disciplines. It is not possible to deal with all proposed definitions of violence in this brief chapter and therefore it will only focus on a number of interdisciplinary definitions which might contribute as a conceptual framework for understanding Paul's letter to the Romans' view of violence.

The Norwegian sociologist, John Galtung (1969:168), conceives violence in terms of influence and defines it as *"the cause of the difference between the potential and the actual, between what could have been and what is"* (italics in original). For Galtung (1969:168), violence is the cause for the increase in the distance between the actual and the potential and "impedes the decrease of this distance". Violence can either be personal (direct) or structural (indirect) and it can happen intentionally or unintentionally with or without an object either at physical or psychological level (Galtung, 1969:173). The anthropologist, David Riches (1986:8), however, defines violence differently as "an act of physical hurt deemed legitimate by the performer and illegitimate by (some) witness". Riches' definition is important because it provides room for cross-cultural studies. Symbolic interactionist, Norman Denzin (1984:488), also proposes a definition of violence as "the attempt to regain through the use of emotional and physical force, something that has been lost". For political philosophers such as Raymond Geuss (2001:21), violence is "best understood by focusing on adverbial expressions such as 'to act violently'". Hence, for Geuss, violence is to inflict pain or to injure other human beings. Willem Schinkel (2010:45), a theoretical sociologist, defines violence ontologically as a *"reduction of being"* (italics in original). He argues that violence as a reduction of being is essential to social life and denying it is due to the fear of violence. Violence is inevitable in social life, and in some cases, it is constructive. The New Testament scholar Jeremy Punt (2012:24) has comprehensively described violence as "action and everything that restricts, damages, or destroys the integrity of things, living beings or people, or of cultural or social entities through superior power, in short, the 'violation of personhood'".

1    Dr. Endale Sebsebe Mekonnen is a Research Fellow in the Department of Old and New Testament at Stellenbosch University, and the President of Shiloh Bible College, Ethiopia.

These diverse definitions indicate that there is no standard definition of violence. All these attempts at defining violence contribute to explicate different facets of violence as well as its complexity. It, however, appears as if the intricate connection between violence and power underlies all of them. Whether it is physical, psychological, ontological, verbal, personal, structural or ideological violence and its different aspects, the concept of violence can be understood as the exertion of power upon a person or an object for a specific result – usually negative – for the receiver. In this chapter, however, care will be taken not to read Romans anachronistically since the ideological and conceptual understanding of violence by the different disciplines surveyed are foreign to Paul and his audiences. For example, some of the questions that have been raised by modern literature in the area of violence were not known in the time of Paul and his readers. Therefore, a concept more or less equivalent to violence might be conveyed in Paul's terms such as wickedness, unrighteousness and evil.

Particularly, the concept of evil (κακός) in Romans presents an opportunity to understand Paul's view on violence. Although the word is usually used to refer to wrong acts in general, it is used in Romans in relation to violence.[2] Paul contrasts evil against good in Romans 3:8 while he later argues that no one does good (Rom-3:12). Paul describes evil as being characterised by deception, vilification, murder and rejection of the ways of peace. Evil, for example, robbing, killing, and stealing, is what the Law prohibits. The cumulative concept of evil in Romans is verbal, ideological and physical in nature which is analogous to our modern understanding of violence.

It will be argued that Paul in the Letter to the Romans speaks to the Christ-believing community in the context of the Roman Empire, and he believes that violence (evil) continues until God's redemptive work is completed. Nonetheless, in the interim, Christ-believing communities who are under the realm of the Spirit are encountering evil (violence) and are reminded to aggressively and perseveringly engage and conquer it through faith in the Messiah and obedience to the commandments of God which are holy, good and just. Hence, the discussion follows the following steps: first a discussion on the concept of violence in the Letter to the Romans will be provided, then, a discussion on the means to conquer it will be undertaken, and finally, a conclusion will be provided followed by a brief overview of the implications thereof.

## THE CONCEPT OF VIOLENCE IN THE LETTER TO THE ROMANS

Violence was endemic in the Roman Empire in that "to the largest extent the history of the Roman Empire is a grim chronicle of military despotism in the name of law and order, cringing servility on the part of the senate and irresponsible opportunisms by the armies" (Africa, 1971:21). Mass killings of slaves, deserters, rebels and captured enemies along with their leaders, the execution of cowardly captains, harsh imprisonment and private revenge were deeply embedded in Roman daily life (Lintott, 1969:38, 42–44, 50). The purported *Pax Augusta* with its results, whether reform, peace, or education, was established "on violence, killing,

RECONCILIATION, FORGIVENESS AND VIOLENCE IN AFRICA

---

2    Cf. Matt 27:23, Mark 15:14, Luk 23:22, Joh 18:30, Act 9:13; 16:28; 23:9.

and preoccupation with death, sometimes repressed and sometimes bubbling in blood to the surface" (Zanker, 1988:289). Even the emperors themselves were victims of the violent systems of the empire (Nimgade, 2016:616). Criminals were exposed and executed and their corpses left to be viewed by the public for the sake of imposing power and fear on them (Barry, 2008:222–246). The city of imperial Rome was rife with housebreakers, pickpockets, petty thieves, and muggers; and the common people admired the bloody and dehumanising gladiatorial games. Riots about food shortages and injustice were common (Africa,1971:3–21). The populace also often expressed their anger against the authorities by demolishing statues (Barry, 2008:234).

Punt (2012:28–29) rightly states "violence bred violence, and the violent setting of the first century CE influenced and contributed to the shaping of the NT documents' appropriation of violence-related issues". In short, the means to triumph in the Roman Empire whether at the authoritarian or popular levels was simple: *war*. The Letter to the Romans is also replete with the vocabulary of violence. In the next section the concept of violence and engaging, resisting and conquering it will be studied in the Letter to the Romans. First, God and the concepts and words for violence will be studied. Next, there will be a discussion on violence in relation to human beings, and then the means to engage violence will be analysed before a conclusion is offered.

## VIOLENCE IN RELATION TO GOD: DISHONOURING GOD

In the first chapter of the letter, Paul presents God and God's gospel in relation to power (δύναμις) (Rom 1:4). Jesus' appointment as king by God is in δύναμις (Rom 1:3-40). It is worth noting that Paul's mention of the power of God counters the situation of νεκρός (the deceased). The word νεκρός here is connected to his humiliating death by a violent act of imperial Rome. The power of imperial Rome was established by military might that humiliated, killed and abused countless victims. Paul seems to argue that the violent power of imperial Rome is defeated through the power of God. Such a reading can also be substantiated from Romans 1:16 where Paul claims that the Gospel is the power (δύναμις) of God to bring salvation. In the cultural context of Romans, the priestly, military, and administrative powers are effective means to salvation. Augustus and Nero were, therefore, celebrated as saviours and benefactors of the entire world (Jewett & Kotansky, 2007:139). Their gospel is a dehumanising power promising peace, security, and wealth for Rome through violence that included killing, abusing, subjugating, and confiscating other nations. Paul, however, announces that he is not ashamed of the Gospel because it promises to rescue the nations from the power of unrighteousness.

Paul argues that the power of God is revealed to the whole world through creation (Rom 1:20). In Romans 1:19, Paul contends that unlike the Roman Emperors, God has shown God's glory and the honour of God's eternal power through the things God created – not through violence. God's splendour and glory is revealed by providing humanity with all the necessities of life. Roman populace used to revolt when there was a shortage of food; Paul in contrast claims that it is not the Roman Emperors who sustain life, but God.

However, this creative power of God is consciously rejected by the nations. In so doing, they have opposed God. They are God's enemies (Rom 5:10), and they oppose God by suppressing the truth (Rom 1:18). The word suppress (κατέχω) connotes "violence"; here it is suppressing the truth about God and replacing it with a lie through ἀσέβεια (impious and a prescribed crime) and ἀδικία (wrongdoing, injustice and law-breaking) (Jewett & Kotansky, 2007:152). God is dishonoured, for God's personhood is replaced by mortal human beings, animals and birds, or created beings. If our definition of violence as the violation of personhood is kept in view, God's personhood is violated; or to borrow a part of Schinkel's definition of violence, God's person is negatively affected when it is replaced by images of the emperors being honoured, worshiped and served as gods (Rom 1:23, 25).

However, God has resisted violence against God's personhood through the manifestation of God's wrath. The wrath of God did not manifest through bloody military action, murder, or dehumanising actions but by delivering God's opponents to their own desire, passions (Rom 1:24, 26) and debased mind (Rom 1:28). God freed those who rebelled from God's control and left them to experience the consequences of their own decisions. Such a godless life, argues Paul, brought dishonour to humanity and chaos to its societal life (Rom 1:24-32). Deliverance into the tyranny of desire and a debased mind is not the reason for God's wrath but the result of it (Jewett & Kotansky, 2007:167–168). The heart's desire, passion and a debased mind are personified as if they were powers to control and dominate persons to do things that violate their own personhood in terms of their bodies and conduct. Paul thus argues that freedom from the control of God's kingship results in violence either in the form of violating one's own personhood or that of others.

Paul again discusses God's power and wrath in Romans 9:17 and 22. God contested with Pharaoh to manifest God's power. Pharaoh is the symbol of obdurate and oppressive kingdoms which refuse to acknowledge God and who use their power to abuse and violate their subjects (Jewett & Kotansky, 2007:583). Paul clearly states the purpose of raising Pharaoh to power is to bring glory to God over all the earth (Rom 9:17). God's conflict with Pharaoh was to demonstrate how the power of a human kingdom is weak when compared to God's power. The analogy of the potter makes it clear (Fitzmyer, 1993:569) since the function of the clay is different based on the purpose of the potter (Rom 9:21). Hence, the kingdom of Pharaoh seems to be assigned to lead and to promote oppression and violence, which had already been installed as a system and a culture against the Jews' God. Paul's argument seems to be anchored in the traditional Jewish concept of God who can use evil leaders to serve God's purpose (Wagner, 2003:73). The victory over the power of Pharaoh is the archetypical manifestation of God's power in Jewish literature in this regard. Paul's understanding of God's power is positive because it brought deliverance to the Israelites who were suffering violence.[3] The power of God is not only for

3    Since the interest of this study is on the concept of violence, I will not enter into the traditional debate over predestination and exegetical discussion related to it. However, Wagner's reading of 9:22 and 11:28 is adopted, i.e. if God endures Pharaoh with much patience, then he will be much more patient with Israel until they repent; however, they are enemies at present (Wagner, 2002:77).

deliverance. It also punishes and destroys the evil-doers. However, according to Romans 9:22, God is patient with the vessels of wrath, which echoes Romans 2:4-9. If Paul is thinking of what he wrote in Romans 2:4-11 then those who disobey the truth, but obey wickedness because of the hardness of their heart, will be destroyed. Hence, they determine their own destiny.

Paul makes the point very clear in Romans 2:5 that the wrath of God is the righteous and impartial judgment of God against those who do evil and that such evil is defined by the Law of God (Rom 2:12). The judgement against those who do evil is tribulation, distress, destruction and wrath and fury (Rom 2:8-9). Such judgement is based on one's actions and is not done arbitrarily, but with patience after giving ample room for the possibility of change on the side of the evil-doer. Doing good results in peace, honour and glory (Rom 2:9). However, Paul argues that such judgement is not the prerogative of fellow human beings; rather, it belongs solely to God.

Nonetheless, in relation to imperial Rome, Paul seems to argue that God in God's sovereignty appointed the Roman Empire as an instrument to execute God's wrath according to Romans 13:4, as opposed to Pharaoh, who was the object of God's wrath. Romans 13:1-7 has been considered as an anomaly in the letter, generating a variety of speculation ranging from its authenticity to its historical situation. There is no question that Paul had a specific situation in mind while writing this exhortation, although it is impossible to reconstruct it accurately. Elliott (1997:195) has observed that Paul's use of subjection in Romans 8:20, 11:25-32 and 13:1-2 is not positive. The subjection in Romans 8:50, according to Jewett (2010:91–105), is the result of Adam's disobedience. Hence, it can be related to the wrath of God. The Christ-believing community shares the particular suffering due to their allegiance to Christ and as part of the universal family of creation. If Elliott's understanding of subjection as being negative could be maintained, then subjection to the Roman Empire's system could also be interpreted as a Christ-believing community sharing in the suffering of creation. However, unlike the subjection in Romans 8:17-23 where creation is subjected to futility which cannot be avoided, the Christ-believing community could avoid the brutal imperial system by doing good (Rom 13:3). The brutal system of the Roman Empire is part of God's wrath that will be executed against wrong-doers (Rom 13:5), for the Christ-believing community is not allowed to take revenge, instead they should leave it to God (Rom 12:19-20). The Roman Empire is the servant of God for the benefit of the Christ-believing community for it punishes the evil-doers (Rom 13:4a). The paradox, however, is that they suffered and were also persecuted by the empire itself like Jesus did (Rom 8:17, 31-39).

In Romans 5:6 and 10, Christ-believing communities were also enemies before their reconciliation to God. The word καταλλάσσω basically means exchanging one thing for another and is used in the sphere of conflict. For example, Dio Cassius refers to Antony's desire to be reconciled to Caesar, similarly Caesar desires to be reconciled to Folvius and Lucius, and Otto's wish to be reconciled to Vitellius (Dio Cassius *Hist.* Rom 39.6; 55:21; 64.9.3.15). Thucydides also speaks about the reconciliation of common people with each other and a city with another (Thucydides *Hist.* 4.61.2).

The reconciliation of alienated marital partners is also referred to by Josephus (*Ant* 7.185, 196, 1.195). The language of reconciliation is imported from the political sphere of creating peace between warring parties (Jewett & Kotansky, 2007:366). Hence, the word reconciliation is used in the context of violence. The initiative as well as the necessary prerequisite for the creation of peace is not taken by the enemies who violated the being of God, but by God, who is being violated. The paradox is that the means of reconciliation and the creation of peace is violence – the death of the Messiah at the hands of imperial Rome (Rom 5:6-11). Furthermore, the rejection of the one is the cause of the reconciliation of others (Rom 11:13).

Paul presents the death of the Messiah from two viewpoints. One viewpoint is from the symbolic world of Jewish sacred cults – atonement (Rom 3:25-26) and the other from the context of imperial violence (Rom 8:31-39). Romans 8:32 is particularly revealing regarding violence. Paul says God delivers up the Messiah for "us all". Paul does not explicitly say to whom the Messiah was given up. The verb παραδίδωμι can be translated as "to deliver up to custody", "to be judged", "condemned", "tormented", and "to be put to death" (Mark 9:31; 10:33; 15:1). The context of Romans 8:31-39 seems to be the encounter between the Messiah and the enemies of God and later between the Christ-believing community and the enemies of God. Gaventa (2013:65), in her analysis of the word παραδίδωμι, has concluded that it is used in a military context for surrendering to the enemy. It appears that the Messiah, being on the side of God, is engaging evil, but as a soldier of righteousness he is captured, defeated, and put to death by the power and violence of imperial Rome. God's act of delivering up the Messiah is expressed in terms of not being willing to spare him until imperial Rome exhausts its power of violence and know its limit in order that God may manifest God's supreme power and glory by raising the Messiah from death, the result of violence, and thus not just sparing him from the act of violence. Schinkel (2010:56) argues that violence also has a positive aspect. Punt's (2012:23–42) analysis of violence in the New Testament concludes that at times violence is "necessary to effect positive change." From God's side, the violent suffering and death of the Messiah is positive enough to create peace between God and God's enemies.

In sum, God's wrath is directed at those who reject the truth about God and God's commandments and have therein committed violence against God's personhood and God's Messiah. This includes Israel, who was once the vessel of mercy. The wrath of God can be understood as God's righteous and impartial judgement against evil and evil-doers. Human beings are not entitled to such a prerogative, as it is solely God's prerogative to pass such judgement. Although God's power is constructive in some respect as God positively uses God's power to create nature to sustain humanity and to bring salvation, God also uses it to destroy and punish the wicked. Such a violent use of power is understood positively in the letter to the Romans because it destroys evil. Hence, for Paul, God's power not only creates and provides but also crushes and destroys God's enemies unless otherwise, they reconcile and do good, which is the basis for peace, honour and glory.

In the Letter to the Romans, Paul categorises humanity into at least two groups, namely: Those outside of the community of Christ and those who are of the community of Christ. The outsiders are enemies of God but are also potential friends. Galtung's (1969:168) definition of violence as the distance between actualised violence and the potential for it, while the necessary condition is at one's disposal for actualising the potential, could be applied to the outsiders. The outsiders have all the necessary reasons and conditions to realise their potential of being God's reconciled friends. If this is not the case, then they exercise self-imposed violence against themselves.

Such self-imposed violence is the result of being under the power of one's own evil passions and desires, which is the result of God's wrath. These evil passions result in (1) Violating one's own personhood: dishonouring (ἀτιμάζω) one's own body (Rom 1:24), exercising dishonourable (ἀτιμία) passion (Rom 1:26) and shameless acts (ἀσχημοσύνη); (2) Violating another's personhood: this involves both physical and verbal violation, such as envy, murder, strife, deceit, malignity, gossip, slander, insolence, being haughty, boastful, inventing evil, disobedience to parents, and ruthlessness. Although such a violent way of life was ubiquitous in imperial Rome, Paul exposes the violent life of the Jews as well in his discussion of the Jews' unfaithfulness in Romans 2:17-24 and 3:9-20. The Jewish teacher steals, commits adultery, robs temples and therefore dishonours (ἀτιμάζω) God by breaking the Law. This is elaborated on in Romans 3:13-17, which deals with verbal and physical violence. Verbal violence includes deception and cursing, whereas physical violence refers to the shedding of blood.

Paul argues that such a violent way of life is the result of humanity being slaves of violent kings, namely Sin and Death. In Romans 5:12-21, Sin and Death (θάνατος) are two cosmic ruling forces. Jewett and Kotansky (2007:377) find no parallel concept either in Greek or biblical literature (i.e. Death exercising kingly power). Therefore, it is Paul's distinct conception of Death. If Sin and Death are understood in the light of aggression or invasion and domination of another nation by power, Paul is making an analogy between the violent dominion of the Roman Empire and the power and dominance of Sin and Death in the world of humanity. Sin and Death invaded the human world and exerted their power over humanity to execute their desire. Paul provides a specific example from the life of the Jews under the Law regarding how powerful these kings are (Mekonnen, 2017:63-64). Paul portrays Sin as a violent force because it kills (Rom 7:11). Such killing might be understood ontologically. However, Paul uses terms that explicitly describe violent action. Sin not only kills. It also makes one a slave. In the Roman Empire, slavery was a violent system and business (Gaventa, 2013:67). Paul, however, used slavery in a positive sense in Romans 1:1-2 and Romans 6:12-23 despite the Roman Empire's killing of masses of slaves. Others died of diseases and maltreatment (Gaventa, 2013:67). Paul is not ignorant of this in that he describes slavery as a life of fear (Rom 8:15). Hence, Sin and Death are violent powers (Gaventa, 2013:66) from which enslaved persons would desperately need someone who might free them of their grip.

The kind of slavery Paul is speaking about is that of being a prisoner of war. In Romans 7:11 and 23; Paul uses three important words that illuminate the nature of the slavery: ἀφορμή, ἀντιστρατεύομα, and αἰχμαλωτίζω. The noun ἀφορμή means a place from which a movement or attack is made, i.e. a base of operations. It could generally mean "opportunity" but it is often used with its military meaning (Gaventa, 2013:64). The verb ἀντιστρατεύομα is to undertake a military expedition, or take the field, against anyone. It means to oppose, and to war against. The verb αἰχμαλωτίζω means to lead away the captive. In light of these words, Romans 7 indicates that there was conflict between the Jews and the Sin that the commandments of the Law revealed to them (Mekonnen, 2017:63-64). Paul uses violent military language to explain the power of Sin. The power of Sin not only defeats its opponent, but also kills or destroys them.

Paul's analysis of human violence is that it is the result of opposing God, suppressing God's truth and rejecting God's commandments and therefore human beings are handed over to a tyranny that powerfully enslaved them under its grip. Paul thus argues that humanity is living under a cruel tyrannical kingdom that violated human freedom and reduced their personhood to that of being a prisoner to Sin. Thus, Paul's analysis of human violence is that it is the result of opposing God, suppressing God's truth, and rejecting God's commandments, which resulted in obtaining freedom to serve unrighteousness and wickedness.

## ENGAGING EVIL: CONQUERING THE VIOLENT KING

Unlike the traditional interpretation, the Letter to Romans has received a different characterisation from the perspective of reading it within the context of the Roman Empire. For example, it can in this context be understood as a political declaration of war on Caesar and as an "ideological intifada" against Roman imperial ideology (Elliott, 2010:61). The opposition that God declares through the Messiah, although it is implicitly against the thought and ideology of imperial Rome as Elliott claims, is against all ἀσέβεια (ungodliness) and wickedness (ἀδικία) of human beings outside of the community of Christ (which includes the Caesars) (Rom 1:18). Paul seems to be looking at this warfare in different stages. First the Messiah was defeated, victimised by the power of the Caesars, but God triumphs over the violent power of the Roman Empire by raising the Messiah and appointing him as King to bring about the obedience of the nations through faith in him. For God, this is good news. Second, God freed those who believe in the Messiah from evil and established them as a Christ-believing community in order to engage the same foe.

Paul argues that for such a community not only faith and reconciliation with God is needed (Rom 5:1-11) to resolve the enmity between God and the wicked, but also participation in the death and resurrection of the Messiah through baptism (Rom-6:4). Participation in the violent death of Jesus and the defeat of Death through the resurrection of Christ consists of the sacramental submission to the kingship of Jesus and the declaration of freedom from the tyranny of ungodliness and wickedness. Paul declares that for those who united with the death and resurrection of the Messiah their old self (the enemy) is killed (crucified) in order to: (1) Destroy the sinful body of those who believe (Rom 6:6). Paul used the verb καταργέω which could mean to disarm (Jewett & Kotansky, 2007:404) or to deprive of force, influence and power or to destroy; (2) Prevent the believers from becoming slaves again to wickedness and ungodliness. Baptism as union with the violent death of Christ is used as a means of killing the wicked personhood in order to free the believer from the slavery of sin (Rom 6:1-11). Paul declares that the violent death of the Messiah at the hands of the empire of Rome, in which the believers must participate through baptism, is God's mysterious strategy of engaging all the power of ungodliness and wickedness. It is the method of destroying the violent king through his own violent act by breaking and disarming his power in the life of those who believe in the Messiah.

However, those who are freed should maintain their freedom and should not succumb again to the enemy – i.e. wickedness (Rom 6:13). Placing oneself under the dominion of Sin is understood in terms of military domination. Particularly, yielding one's limbs and organs to the desires of wickedness is to participate willingly in the opposition against God and the Messiah. The limbs and organs are ὅπλον, which can be translated as "weapons". The bodies of the believers must thus not be made available to oppose and engage righteousness but must be presented to God as weapons of engaging wickedness.

Not only limbs and organs are important but also the mind of the Christ community is as important as the members of the body (Rom 12:1-3). In Romans 8:7, Paul warns that setting one's mind on the things of the flesh (wickedness) can be seen as hostility to God. The mental life of the community should be influenced by the things of the Spirit. Such exercises are a matter of life and death. It is saving oneself from death. One has to kill in order to live! Kill the works of the flesh by the Spirit; otherwise death is the only option (Rom 8:13). Paul uses the metaphor of war and violence and seems to affirm that violent power is a necessary measure to stop not only evil action but also evil thought. Unlike imperial Rome, Paul declares a spiritual combat that positively affects one's moral behaviour. Paul believes that peace is the result of the destruction of one's enemies. These enemies, however, are not physical but cosmic, namely: Sin, Death and Satan (Rom 16:20). Nevertheless, Paul uses the analogy of war in imperial Rome to help him drive his point home to his audience about the kingdom of God, which is righteousness, peace, and joy in the Holy Spirit (Rom 14:17).

However, Paul understands that opposing evil involves physical suffering similar to that of the Messiah and the killing of the flesh attracts physical violence towards the believing community (Rom 8:17). The enemy is aiming at separating the community from the Messiah by releasing a physical and psychological assault against the believing community such as tribulation, distress, persecution, famine, nakedness, peril, and the sword. The encounter against the community is carried out by an allied army of imperial Rome and cosmic forces. Paul describes this assault of the enemy against the believing community as unceasing killing (cf. "we are being killed daily" – Rom 8:37). It is a paradox that the community is daily assaulted and killed by the system of imperial Rome but never dies – instead conquers through the Messiah with whom the community shares his resurrection life. Since the people are loved by him, every evil thing will be thwarted, to work out for the good of the community. Paul also describes the cosmic forces that allied with the Roman Empire, such as death, life, angels (evil angels), principalities, and powers. Yet, even all these creations cannot separate the community from their Messiah and God. Instead, the believing community are "super victors" (ὑπερνικάω). Jewett and Kotansky (2007:549) observe that the word ὑπερνικάω "brings Paul's discourse within the scope of divinely inspired warriors and kings who win total victories over their foes… [It is not just] "prevailing but supervictor." Hence, the community along with its Messiah crushes its enemy completely.

Paul, thus, sees violent power as part of daily life in the Christ-community. The enemies are both spiritual (i.e. Sin, Death, and spiritual beings) and physical, which comes through the imperial system of Rome. The community is expected to endure and engage violence until the peace that comes through the destruction of their foes is realised.

## THE WEAPONS FOR ENGAGING EVIL: DOING GOOD

Paul's vocabulary for violence could be stated as ἀσέβεια and ἀδικία. The Messiah comes to remove ἀσέβεια (Rom 11:20), which is impurity that might relate to worshiping idols. The word ἀδικία includes all kinds of sins (Rom 1:28) and is not limited to injustice. Rather, it is disobedience to the revealed truth of God, therefore it is the opposite of truth (Rom 2:8); it is to be unfaithful by breaking the commandments of the law (Rom 3:5) and it is a way of life or system opposing and engaging the ways of God (Rom 6:3). Paul, however, uses one key word that represents ἀσέβεια and ἀδικία, namely: κακός. The catalogue of ἀσέβεια and ἀδικία in Romans 1:18-32 and the ones in Romans 13:11-14 are stated as κακός in Romans 2:9. Paul in Romans 12:17 and 21 explicitly prohibits using evil (κακός) as a means to defeat evil (κακός). He also opposes the concept of using evil to bring good (Rom 3:8). But κακός is so powerful that one cannot resist doing it (Rom 7:19) because it dwells inside of a person (Rom 7:21) and it is the source of fearing authority (Rom 13:3).

The preferred weapon for engaging κακός is doing ἀγαθός. For Paul, doing ἀγαθός results in glory, honour and peace (Rom 2:7-10). However, ἀγαθός must be done by persevering (Rom 2:7). Perseverance is the language of war that refers to not losing one's ground in a battle. Doing ἀγαθός is an instrument for engaging wickedness and unrighteousness which is a comprehensive term for evil. However, who or what defines ἀγαθός? Paul argues that the commandments of the Law is ἀγαθός and opposes κακός and by nature it is holy and righteous (Rom 7:12-13). Violence against the personhood of God is the result of breaking the commandments of God. God's wrath against ἀσέβεια and ἀδικία of human beings is because it is breaking the very first commandments of the Decalogue, the worship of idols and suppressing the truth which is dishonouring God (Rom 1:21-23). Malina and Pilch (2006:227-232) have also observed that Paul is evaluating the acts and behaviour of the Gentiles in accordance with the Ten Commandments.

Paul declares that the Law is the embodiment of knowledge and truth which makes the will of God known and it is a way of honouring God (Rom 2:17-24) (Mekonnen, 2017:65). The commandments of the Law are against all κακός that exists inside a person (Rom 7:7-20). The Christ-believing community must have a transformed mind that discerns the will of God, which is acceptable, perfect, and good (ἀγαθός) (Rom 12:2). The will of God is embodied in the Law. The hallmark of those who walk according to the Spirit is obedience to the commandment of the Law (Rom 2:25-29 and 8:1-8). Thinking about the flesh is hostility to God because it results in disobedience to the Law and displeases God (Rom 8:7). If walking in the Spirit and not walking according to the flesh means fulfilling the Law (Rom 8:4), then walking in the Spirit does ultimately mean obeying commandments of the Law after the freedom from Sin and its condemnation is experienced in Christ. If this is granted, the commandments of the Law in the realm of the Spirit area means to kill the flesh (Rom 8:13).

In Romans 7, Paul depicts a Jewish community engaging Sin but, by being in the realm of the flesh, was defeated and killed through the commandments of God, and enslaved by an undesired king, whereas in Romans 8:1-16, he depicts a community which is in the Spirit and strong, alive, a killer of the flesh and obedient to the commandments of the Law which is an expression of friendship with God and honouring God. Once the commandments of the Law was an instrument in the hands of Sin to kill the one who desires to keep it, but now in Christ, it is reversed, those who are free and are walking in the Spirit (which implicitly means obedience to the commandment of God) use it to kill the enemy – Sin.

Paul calls the Christ-believing community to put on the weapons of light (Rom 13:12), as opposed to the physical weapon sworn by the Roman Empire, which attempt to bring order through fear (Rom 13:1-7). In Romans 13:1-7, Paul is not speaking about being simply subservient to the violent imperial system, rather Paul insists that a Christ-believing community should do good (ἀγαθός). The good Paul is speaking of in Romans 13:1-7 is not the civil laws of the imperial system because "good" (ἀγαθός) should be understood in terms of Paul's usage of the word in the letter. The commandments of God are the weapons of light which defeat evil through the Spirit. Furthermore, the Roman Empire's army is the servant of the God of the Christ-believing community (Rom 13:4). The Christ-believing community is not the servant of the Roman Empire; rather the community is the slave of righteousness or of God (Rom 6:19, 22). The ways in which the community submits to the empire are indirect, i.e. through obeying the commandment of the Law and the teaching of Paul (i.e. doing good and avoiding evil). However, Paul argues that the empire channels the wrath of God upon those who do evil (Rom 1:18-32). Disobeying the commandments of God and the teaching of Paul exposes one to the brutal and violent system of the empire. However, Paul argues that life and peace are not in the hands of Roman Empire and cannot be attained through its system since it is the result of obeying God through the Spirit (Rom 8:6-7).

Paul explicitly commands the Christ-believing community to overcome evil (κακός) with good (ἀγαθός) (Rom 12:21). Doing good ἀγαθός) is a weapon against all violence that they experienced. It is obvious that the community experienced evil (κακός), which can be called violence, from the imperial system (Rom 12:14, 17), but they are called to do good (ἀγαθός) in return and not to retaliate, but instead to strive to foster peace through obedience to God (Rom 12:17-19). The good that Paul enumerated in Romans 12:9-21 is inclusive in the sense that it is the opposite of evil which also includes all aspects of evil. It is described in the language of love in Romans 12:9 as hating evil and holding fast to good. A more elaborate description of love is given in Romans 13:8-10. Loving one's neighbour means not doing wrong to one's neighbour (Rom 13:10). What is wrong is defined by the commandments of the Law, which embodies the knowledge, truth and will of God (Rom 13:9; 2:17-20). Similarly, what is good is also defined by the commandments of the Law (Rom 7:12-13, 18-19). Doing ἀγαθός to one's enemy is not only Jesus' teaching but it is also one of the commandments of the Law (Exod 23:4-5; Prov 17:13; 20:22). For example, Deuteronomy insists that retaliation and judgement belong to God alone (Deut 32:35). The Law discourages taking revenge by one's own hand (Deut 32:35). Therefore, ultimately loving one's neighbour is obeying the commandments of the Law (Mekonnen, 2017:ii-iii). The Christ community is called to conquer evil (ἀγαθός) with good (ἀγαθός), but what is evil and what is good cannot be arbitrarily defined. It needs to be defined by God through God's commandments. Hence, for the community of Christ, the weapon against violence is the commandments of God.[4]

For Paul, Christ believing communities are the righteous army of God who are engaging wickedness (Rom 6:12-23). All opposition against the proclamation of the reign of the Messiah of God must be resisted and repelled by doing good (Rom 2:7 and 8:31-39) until the salvation of God fully comes (13:11-14 and 8:18-26). All of the cosmos will experience violence until God's final redemption of the world is manifested. Till then engaging evil continues. The ways of life of the Christ-community is as an imitation of the Messiah, their King who suffered under the imperial system. They are destined to share in his suffering and glory (Rom 8:17), and to be formed in his image (Rom 8:29). The Christ-community is denied the right to judge others and retaliate against their enemies, as this is the sole prerogative of God. However, the Christ-believing community conquers the evil they encounter through the proclamation of the good news and actively engaging themselves in doing good as defined and prescribed in the commandments of God.

## CONCLUSION

In the Letter to the Romans, Paul presented God as a wrathful God (Rom 1:18-32), an impartial judge (Rom 2:5-16), rejecter of the disobedient (Rom 11:14), stern (Rom 11:22), and as an avenger (Rom 12:17-20), warrior (Rom 16:20), as well as saviour (Rom 1:16-17), kind, forbearing, patient (Rom 2:4), loving (Rom 5:1-11),

---

4   Whether such commandments are the Ten Commandments or Paul's elaborated teachings on them which traditionally called exhortation does not make significant difference – they are all commandments of God.

deliverer (Rom 8:1-39), initiator and performer of the reconciliation of the world to himself (Rom 11:15), as well as merciful (Rom 12:1). If Schinkel's theory of violence as the reduction of being is taken into consideration, Paul seems to be very careful not to reduce God to just a loving and merciful God. Further, considering violence in terms of exerting power and in light of God's character presented in the Letter to the Romans, violence is an inevitable phenomenon in the realm of the created world. But the question is who is using the power and for what purpose? Paul argues that the power of God is for deliverance by crushing ungodliness, wickedness, corruption and the spiritual foe – Satan – to bring freedom to those willing to believe the Messiah, and to the whole creation in order to restore honour to God's name and God's community. Power used for dehumanising, humiliating and fabricating social chaos is understood as being the result of God's wrath upon those who reject and break the commandments of God. But the wrath of God is God handing them over to the freedom of exercising their own desire and ways of life. However, such persons or communities are not free but under the kingship of Sin and Death.

On the other hand, the Christ-believing community is called and destined to share the suffering and mission of its Messiah and is devoid of the right to judge others and retaliate against its enemies, despite experiencing violence either from the system they live in, or from individuals who do evil against them. Instead, these people are called to live in the realm of God's Spirit in Christ, although insignificant in number, they engage perseveringly and engage evil by doing good through obedience to the commandments of God. This is how they live until the redemption of the whole creation, which is now subjected in hope, is completed by the God of peace by crushing Satan under their feet and making them super victors.

## Implications for the Ethiopian evangelical church

My understanding of violence comes from first-hand experience and witness of the persecution of evangelical churches in Ethiopia under the Marxist-Leninist ideology junta, which confiscated church properties, and tortured and imprisoned Christians and their leaders. In addition to the communist cruelty towards Christians in the country as a whole, before and after the fall of the communist regime, evangelical Christians, in particular, are ridiculed, vilified, insulted, ostracised, and persecuted by communities who are adherents of the Ethiopian Orthodox Church as well by Muslims, animists, and their close relatives. However, the Churches' response to such violence has been non-violent in nature. The paradox is furthermore that the evangelical churches came out stronger in faith and unity after the period of official persecution and today they have increased in number and influence.

From the churches' experience of persecution, I can deduce that the persecutor's understanding of 'good' is to protect and defend one's own country, religion, culture, honour, ideology and influence from a rival. To date, on the popular level the evangelical churches are considered to be the enemy – a Western religion invading and weakening the established religion, culture, ideology and values of the country. Their members are labelled as weak, timid and enemies of the country because of their non-violent ideology. They are thus considered as unfit for military and political responsibilities.

The concept of 'good' and 'evil', for the evangelical churches, while it is biblically understood is not clearly defined and articulated. However, at the practical level, doing good is seen as obedience to the Word of God and doing evil is equivalent to transgressing the Word of God, therefore engaging evil through the means of evil is abhorred and denounced. Hence, for Ethiopian evangelical Christians, the biblical concept of doing good to overcome evil is a challenge given that the normative practice has been to use violence to defend one's honour, country, religion, culture, and ideology. My reading of Romans articulates the cause of violence, and identifies the ways in which the evangelical churches in Ethiopia can overcome violence, and it explicates God's role as a righteous judge of evil and a vindicator of the victims of violence which gives them hope and a reason for continuing to do good. It also underscores the reason for the non-violent feature of the Ethiopian evangelical churches' response to violence and the means used by its members who were able to conquer it through non-retaliation, non-judgmental persuasion and actively and perseveringly doing good as defined in my reading of the Letter to the Romans.

# References

Africa, T.W. (1971). Urban Violence in Imperial Rome. *The Journal of Interdisciplinary History*, 2(1):3–21. https://doi.org/10.2307/202441

Barry, W.D. (2008). Exposure, Mutilation and Riot: Violence at the "Scalae Gemoniae"in Early Imperial Rome. *Greece & Rome*, 55(2):222–246. https://doi.org/10.1017/S0017383508000545

Denzin, N.K. (1984). Toward a Phenomenology of Domestic, Family Violence. *American Journal of Sociology*, 90(3):483–513. https://doi.org/10.1086/228114

Elliott, N.(1997). 'Romans 13:1-7 in the Context of Imperial Propaganda,' in Horsley, R.A. (ed.) *Paul and Empire: Religion and Power in Roman Imperial Society*. Harrisburg, PA: Trinity, pp.184–204.

Elliott, N. (2010). *The Arrogance of Nations*. Minneapolis, MN: Fortress Press.

Fitzmyer, J.A. (1993). *Romans*. New York, NY: Bantman Doubleday Dell Publishing Group.

Galtung, J. (1969). Violence, Peace, and Peace Research. *Journal of Peace Research*, 6(3):167-191. https://doi.org/10.1177/002234336900600301

Gaventa, B.R. and Krans, J.(2013). 'The Rhetoric of Violence and The God of Peace in Paul's letter to the Romans,' in Mitchell, M. and Moessner, D.P. (eds.) *Paul, John, and Apocalyptic Eschatology: Studies in Honour of Martinus C. de Boer*. Leiden: Brill, pp.61–75. https://doi.org/10.1163/9789004250369_006

Geuss, R. (2001). *History and Illusion in Politics*. Cambridge: Cambridge University Press.

Jewett, R. (2010). Interpreting Romans 8:18-23 within Imperial Context. *Biblica et Patristica Thoruniensia*, 3:91–105. https://doi.org/10.12775/BPTh.2010.004

Jewett, R. and Kotansky, R.D. (2007). *Romans: A Commentary*. Second Impression edition. Epp, E. J. (ed.) Minneapolis, MN: Fortress Press.

Lintott, A.W. (1969). *Violence in Republican Rome*. London: Oxford University Press.

Malina, B.J. and Pilch, J.J. (2006). *Social-science Commentary on the Letters of Paul*. Minneapolis, MN: Fortress Press.

Mekonnen, E.S. (2017). *The Torah and Community Formation: A Comparative Study of Romans 13:8-14 and Matthew 22:34-40*. Viewed from http://scholar.sun.ac.za/handle/10019.1/101181 [Accessed 3 May 2017].

Nimgade, A. (2016). Instability and violence in Imperial Rome: A "laboratory" for studying social contagion? *Complexity*, 21(S2):613–622. https://doi.org/10.1002/cplx.21839

Punt, J. (2012). 'Violence in the NT and The Roman Empire: Ambivalence, Othering, Agency,' in de Villiers, P.G.R. (ed.) *Coping with Violence in the New Testament*. Leiden: Brill, pp.23–42. https://doi.org/10.1163/9789004221055_003

Riches, D. (1986). 'The Phenomenon of Violence,' in Riches, D. (ed.) *The Anthropology of Violence*. Oxford and New York: Blackwell Pub, pp.1–27.

Schinkel, W. (2010). *Aspects of Violence: A Critical Theory*. New York, NY: Springer. https://doi.org/10.1057/9780230251342

Wagner, J.R. (2003). *Heralds of the Good News: Isaiah and Paul "In Concert" in the Letter to the Romans*. Leiden: Brill. https://doi.org/10.1163/9789004268197_007

Zanker, P. (1988). *The Power of Images in the Age of Augustus*. Ann Arbor, MI: University of Michigan Press. https://doi.org/10.3998/mpub.12362

# The Reconciliation of Lepers in Luke 5:12-15 and its Implications for Human Dignity

## An African Perspective

*Godwin Etukumana*[1]

## Introduction

Reconciliation is an important topic in contemporary political, social, economic and religious spheres since it has the ability to redefine human relationships therein. Without the possibility of reconciliation it would be impossible for humanity to live together in the modern world. The same was true of the ancient world in which the New Testament was written.

The focus of this chapter[2] is on the various ways in which the Gospel according to Luke describes the reconciliation of those who had become estranged from their communities with special reference to the case of lepers[3] in Luke 5:11-16. Based on Luke's account, this estrangement directly deprived the sufferer from having contact with the community of people and thereby denied him or her, in a violent manner, the right to liberty and human dignity. By using a socio-historical hermeneutics this chapter will investigate whether the metaphors used in Luke are similar to those used in African[4] society's engagement with lepers.

## Methodology

In order to understand how reconciliation was effected in the social world of Luke a socio-historical hermeneutics, which is a combination of sociological exegesis and

---

1    Dr. Godwin Etukumana is a Research Fellow at the Department of Old and New Testament, Stellenbosch University, South Africa, and is currently the Provost of ECWA Theological Seminary, Aba (ETSA), Abia State, Nigeria.

2    I would just like to express my deepest gratitude to my academic advisor, Professor Marius Nel, for all his input and wise counsel in the writing of this chapter.

3    The use of the word 'leper(s)' to refer to one living with leprosy or a leprosy patient is no longer acceptable within the academic or medical fields. The usage in this paper is, however, based on its meaning within its historical context (Manton, 2011:127).

4    The use of Africa in this chapter refers to the ancient African society, particularly Southern Nigeria. The available literature indicates that black Africans have many things in common irrespective of environment and location. While references may be made to the African society in general, the focus in this study is on the context of Southern Nigeria.

the historical critical method, will be used to investigate the Gospel of Luke. A good example of sociological exegesis is that of Gerd Theissen (1992:33) who states that the function of this method is to "investigate the relation between the written text and human behaviour" while the historical critical method focuses on the place of history in the interpretation of the biblical text (Aune, 1969:94). In the context of this study, the historical critical method helps an interpreter to deal with authorial intent, issues that prompted the creation of the text, and the situation of the text (Aune, 2010:105-108). The historical critical method thus embraces many facets that are crucial to the interpretation of a text. It also helps to prevent the present being read into the text (Barton, 2007:179).

The synthesis between sociological exegesis and the historical critical method provides a more balanced interpretation of a given text. This synthesis results in what might be called "socio-historical interpretation" (or hermeneutics) which intends to guard against reductionism from affecting the interpretation of a text (Van Staden, 1991:178). One of the results of using socio-historical hermeneutics is that its analysis enables the interpreter to draw tentative conclusions in regard to the origin, the setting, the author and the social context of the text as well as the social issues that emanates from the text (Theissen, 1992:34).

By using a socio-historical hermeneutics this chapter will attempt to analyse the different metaphors that refer to reconciliation in Luke 5:11-15 by considering both Greco-Roman and Jewish perspectives on reconciliation that is reflected in their respective literature (Porter, 1994:60-62). This chapter will also provide an African perspective on metaphors for reconciliation and the actions that bring about the process of reconciliation and the restoration of the dignity of people (Bediako, 1992:16).

## Healing as metaphor for reconciliation in Luke

In the Gospel of Luke there are sixteen healing episodes and four exorcisms (Wahlen, 2004:144). Some of the healing episodes are unique to Luke's Gospel. Luke thus specifically introduces his readers to the healing power of Jesus as a means through which the sick were able to find relief. The Lukan emphasis on Jesus as a healer is a direct allusion to the expected Isaianic *gô'ēl* (לֹאֵג).[5] Casting out demons and healing the sick were clear signs in Luke that the kingdom of God (ἡ βασιλεία του θεου) had come near to the people through Jesus. The coming of Jesus, according to Luke, was thus nothing less than the arrival of the salvation promised by God.

Healing in the New Testament incorporates different social and cultural phenomena[6] than what it is associated with in the modern world, since sickness was not seen as

---

5   The meaning of this word is well explained by Paul in Romans 11:26. Paul uses ὁ ῥυόμενος to explain the meaning of *gô'ēl* in Isaiah 59:20 (MT). The gô'ēl or ὁ ῥυόμενος (LXX) is the expected redeemer who will take away iniquity from Jacob and restores the fortune of Israel. The opinion of this chapter is that the Lukan Jesus fulfils this expectation through his action on the leper.

6   Paul John Isaak (2006:1214), in reference to healing using an African lens, emphasises that, "For such an individual being healed means being restored to one's extended family, friend and community." He

the result of environmental, physical or pathological problems.[7] Sickness, in both ancient Israel and Greco-Roman society, was regarded as a bad omen that came upon the sufferer as a result of punishment from the gods. Some of these sicknesses called for ostracising the sick person from his or her community. In Judaism lepers were, for example, expelled from their communities. They were regarded as being dead, with funeral services even being held on their behalf.

Lepers were, furthermore, not ostracised because their sickness was understood as being contagious, but because it was seen as bringing pollution into a community (Weissenrieder, 2003:136-139). The community therefore determined the contaminating nature of the sickness and how to deal with it (Pilch, 2000a:67-68). The healing of lepers was furthermore the only way through which the ostracised could be reconciled with their community.[8] This is in line with healings in the Gospel of Luke which often refer to the integration of healed persons back into their community. It is, therefore, important to note that the work of reconciliation carried out by Jesus in the Gospel of Luke would not have been completed if the sick were not healed and the captives set free from their bondage of suffering and sin. In the words of Pilch (2000b:14), "Jesus reduces and moves the experiential oppressiveness associated with such afflictions. In all instances of healing, meaning is restored to life and the sufferer is returned to purposeful living."[9] In other words, since the

---

further adds that, "Health, therefore, implies safe integration into the life of the society."

7    Annette Weissenrieder (2003) in her book, *Images of illness in the Gospel of Luke: insights of ancient medical texts*, emphasises the importance of understanding the ancient socio-historical understanding of illness and how it was constructed based on specific social and cultural parameters. Weissenrieder (2003:3) elucidates that: "Illnesses only ever exist for us in the form of a socially imposed image that reflect both the knowledge and the judgments and expectations of particular eras and cultures. Objective manifestations such as medical and social evidence are nearly always the cornerstones on which images of illness are built. However, the meaning that people attribute to these manifestations is a constructivist issue rather than a natural one."

8    The case of the outbreak of Ebola in recent time may be likened to that of a person that suffered leprosy in the ancient world. In the case of Ebola, sufferers are separated from their families and the community of people, but if they recover they will be reintegrated into their families. This differs from HIV/AIDS, which often has negative socio-cultural values attached to it, and therefore people see anyone suffering from it as being immoral. In the *Priesterschrift*, leprosy is seen as pollution that created socio-cultural oppressiveness in the life of whoever suffered from such a disease. The two cases of leprosy in the Old Testament are treated as cases of pollution and sin (Num. 12:10, 15; 2 Chron. 26:17, 20), which Israel was to be mindful of. The same socio-cultural understanding in ancient Israel of some sicknesses as pollution is evident in Num. 5:1-4. The emphasis here is to remind the people what happened to Miriam, the prophetess and elder sister of Moses, when she sinned against God and Moses. Hence the people were called to remember *rkz* (μνήσθητι) the punishment associated with crossing such a boundary. This established the matrix through which the subsequent socio-cultural dynamic was interpreted.

9    It is noteworthy that sickness was perceived to be a sign of sin in the Old Testament, and in order to be healed the person had first to be forgiven and reconciled to God. This forgiveness and reconciliation did not end with the person concerned and God, but also impacted society in order to enable the person to be accepted back into the community. For this to be carried out, the deity provided humanity with two options, which are prayers and sacrifice, as the means through which reconciliation could be effected (Mbabzi, 2013:69-71).

restoration of the sick to their community is concomitant with the removal of the estrangement that caused their separation, it implies enacted reconciliation.

## THE λέπρα TEXTS AND RECONCILIATION IN LUKE

The leper text in 5:12-16 occurs in all the three Synoptic Gospels. However, despite the text being found in all three Synoptic Gospels, Luke has a unique addition (Plummer, 1922:151)[10] in that he adds another pericope on lepers in 17:11-19. Due to the different settings in which the two stories (5:12-16 and 17:11-19) occur in Luke, the two accounts and their implication for the Lukan community will be examined separately. Luke's inclusion in his narrative of the issue of leprosy[11] also raises questions concerning the nature of leprosy and how those who suffered from the disease were treated in the ancient world.

### Leprosy in the ancient world

The actual meaning of the term λέπρα is not clear. Some scholars believe that the disease comprised a number of different ailments associated with the skin. They argue that the biblical nomenclature for what is today called leprosy does not denote what was known as leprosy in biblical times. Scholars such as Pilch (2000b:39-56), Weissenrieder (2003:35) and Edmond (2006:37-42) follow the argument that was first put forward by Bateman, who argues that leprosy was mistranslated by those who translated the works of Arabian writers into Latin. Bateman notes that the Greek meaning of leprosy is similar to that of the Hebrew word, but that the muddled translation came about with the misappropriation of the nomenclature after the translators had already used words for other tubercular diseases for leprosy.[12] The first misappropriation of this name probably came from Aretaeus, who used ελέφας and ελεφαντίασις, which were tubercular diseases, for λέπρα (Bateman, 1813:294). Bateman, in trying to end the misappropriation of the use of "leprosy" for the Greek (*Lepra Graecorum*), divides the category *lepra* into *Lepra vulgaris*, *Lepra alphoides*, and *Lepra nigricans*. Based on his description, leprosy was a scaly skin disease (Bateman, 1813:25-36; Edmond, 2006:37-44).

Bateman's description of leprosy does not however offer any solution to the understanding of the term as used in the ancient texts, like the Old Testament's Uzziah, and its conceptualisation in the Lukan text. All the varieties of leprosy listed by him, for example, are believed to be non-contagious and do not fit the description of the Old Testament texts such as Numbers 12:10-15 and 2 Chronicles 26:17-20. The Old Testament describes leprosy as a whitish disease that covers the whole body. The cases of Miriam and King Uzziah are typical examples. The Lukan

---

10  Scholars such as Taylor and Fitzmyer see Mark as Luke's source for his leper texts, while some argue that Luke had an independent source. Fitzmyer (1985:571) acknowledges that the context of the story is part of the Synoptic Triple Tradition, but argues that the sources available to each of them might have been different from each other. The addition of the polis by Luke aims at describing wondering nature of those that suffered from leprosy in the ancient world.

11  Luke alludes to lepers in several places in his Gospel (4:27; 5:12-16; 7:22; and 17:11-19).

12  Tubercular diseases are caused by bacteria (e.g. tuberculosis).

language is in line with that of the Old Testament description of leprosy. In 5:12, Luke uses the Greek term πλήρης "full" or "covered with" to describe the nature and the extent of the disease, which none of Bateman's descriptions fit. Viewing the disease of leprosy through the modern lenses of its *non-contagious effect* in essence reduces the meaning and the implication of the text in the socio-historical context of Luke's time, since what the modern world calls non-contagious disease does not apply to the ancient world's understanding of λέπρα, especially when sacred and non-sacred spaces were involved. Consequently, the modern description of leprosy as Hansen's disease, psoriasis, pityriasis or ichthyosis (Bateman, 1813:25), may not actually convey what in the Lukan text is meant by leprosy. The reason for this is that the expression in Luke differs from the understanding of the disease based on the notions of modern medicine.[13] It must thus be understood in terms of its socio-cultural and religious implications for the sufferers and their community within the socio-historical context in which it occurred. For example, Luke emphasises the need of purity for leprosy sufferers, which necessitated rituals and sacrifices in order to enact reconciliation as an integral part of their healing. The ancient world regarded leprosy as a serious disease that had the power to contaminate the presence of the holy. It was not just a contagious disease, which easily spread to other persons, but was regarded as defilement and pollution that invoked the idea of diminishing the presence of the sacred or divine.

Little is known of how Greco-Roman society treated those who suffered from leprosy. However, the works of the Cappadocian Fathers—Aretaeus, Gregory of Nyssa, and Gregory Nazianzus (Or. 43.63-64)—provide information regarding the social stigmatisation of lepers in Greco-Roman society in the period 200 to 400 CE. The Cappadocian fathers heavily depended on the previous works of Aretaeus, who was a medical practitioner in Rome. Their works thus shed some light on the way in which lepers were treated in the earlier Roman period. As a result, Susan R. Holman (1999:285) concludes that:

> As with the ancient Israelite leper, those who contracted leprosy in the Greek and Roman worlds of late antiquity also faced the threat of social exile, destitution, and lingering self-destruction. Yet, at least in these texts, contagion is not defined in terms of ritual purity and pollution, but in terms of social terror of catching this dreaded sickness. Leprosy was, above all, a social disease. Its manifestations were most notable for their power to exile the afflicted from that religious identity which for Greek-speaking Christians and Greek and Roman religions was inseparable from civic life...

The situation of those suffering from leprosy was thus dire from ancient Egypt and Israel to the Greco-Roman period, since they were subjected to social stigmatisation and ostracism. The harsh treatment of the lepers in antiquity is reflected in the derogatory statement found in an ancient Egyptian papyrus document dated from 2500 BC and a Greek text from about 327 BC as well as a Roman one from about 62 BC. The dignity of the lepers as human beings were in essence stripped off them

---

13    Shellberg (2012:49-51) observes that the "modern judgments about the severity of an illness tend to influence interpretations toward enhancing the miraculous aspect of healings."

in ancient Greco-Roman society. This unwholesome treatment of lepers causes Holman (1999:286) to state that "Graeco-Roman culture was satisfied to exile this threatening group to the fringes of social existence," where they would live and beg for shelter. Holman thus comes to the conclusion that the treatment of those who suffered leprosy during late antiquity was similar to those received in ancient Israel. In other words, their dignity as humans was stripped off them, and that they were separated from the rest of society. This is also evident in the writings of Josephus. In his writing *Against Apion*, Josephus's argument against Manetho reflected on the way in which the lepers were treated in the ancient world, beginning from ancient Egypt to the Roman Empire. Josephus's argument is based on the writing of Manetho who explained that the reason why the Egyptians drove the Israelites from their land was because they were leprous. He further added that the leprous Israel, after being saved from Egypt, went into the desert and sought the face of the gods through fasting and supplication, as is told by Josephus (*Ag. Ap.* 1.308):

> Hereupon the scabby and leprous people were drowned, and the rest were gotten together, and sent into desert places, in order to be exposed to destruction. In this case they assembled themselves together, and took counsel what they should do; and determined, that as the night was coming on, they should kindle fires and lamps, and keep watch; that they also should fast the next night, and propitiate the gods, in order to obtain deliverance from them (νηστεύσαντας ἱλάσκεσθαι τοὺς θεοὺς περὶ τοῦ σῶσαι αὐτούς).

The argument of Josephus against the accusation of Manetho that the Jews were lepers, and that this caused them to be driven away from Egypt, thus sheds some light on how deeply lepers were despised in the ancient world. However, in Greco-Roman society, Asclepius was always available to effect healings in the lives of those that were afflicted with diseases including leprosy (Etukumana, 2016:74-76). The Lukan perspective provides an additional framework through which one could view the way lepers were treated during his time. The *Lepra Pericopae* in Luke 5:12-16 and 17:11-19 suggest that the people who suffered from leprosy in his time were given the same treatment as prescribed in the Mosaic code, in that they were excluded from their communities.

## Purity and reconciliation in Luke

In the biblical narrative, and in the ancient Near East, it can be argued that whenever the issue of reconciliation occurs it is always viewed from the perspective of purity. One of the reasons for seeking reconciliation in the Old Testament and in Greco-Roman society was to deal with the defilement brought about by humans' pollution of the sacred. The command of YHWH to the house of Israel in Leviticus 20:24-26 to be holy unto him provided the rationale for the rituals and sacrifices that were intended to deal with the estrangement that had come about as a result of the defilement of both sacred and communal spaces (Dunn, 2002:450).

The precise nature of the relationship between the purity code and the Gospel has, however, been "an ongoing debate" according to Dunn (2002:450-451). It was initially mainly between E.P. Sanders and Jacob Neusner before Bruce Chilton and Craig

A. Evans and others entered the debate (Dunn, 2002:499-453). All of these scholars believe that the purity code is very important for understanding the Gospel of Luke and Acts. James Dunn, for example, argues that the purity code is enshrined in both Lukan texts, but especially in the Acts of Apostles. According to Dunn (2002:451-453), Peter's behaviour towards others in Acts depicts the role of the purity code in his time. Neusner (1993:222-224) in turn believes that what determines the action of Jesus in Luke is tied to the purity code that was inherent in the Jewish religion from the time of Moses. Citing cases in Luke, such as the cleanings of leper(s) (5:12-16; 17:11-19) and the prohibition against touching unclean things (7:32-50), he states that such actions presuppose the continued functioning of the purity code in Luke. Suffice to say the ongoing debate on the precise function of the purity code in the time of Luke is beyond the scope of this study. It is sufficient for this study to note that the purity code plays a crucial role in Luke and therefore delineates how its author understood the reconciliation process, since defilement in the Old Testament, according to him, called for reconciliation in the house of Israel.

Jonathan Klawans (2000:137) in this regard argues that impurity defiles every boundary and space, and as such it must be atoned for. The same picture emerges in the Lukan text (e.g. 7:36-50; 15:1ff) (Evans, 1997:371). It was mentioned earlier that sickness and diseases were seen in antiquity as being caused by sin, and in turn caused pollution or impurity, which resulted in the sick being estranged from God and their communities (e.g. those suffering from leprosy). The idea of reconciliation is thus implicit whenever impurity as a boundary is removed. The way Jesus dealt with impurity in the Lukan text identifies him as the Messiah who had compassion and mercy on sinners and the sick amidst their impurity so as to bring about their reconciliation with God. The remission of their sin by Jesus was thus an important way through which reconciliation with God and their communities was enacted (22:19-20; cf. 5:20; 7:48).

## Socio-cultural boundaries in Luke 5:12-16

Based on the *Priesterschrift's* prescription, a leper in Israel was not allowed to have contact with other people, since impurity was seen as being highly contagious, it therefore caused those who came into contact with it to be polluted. Separation from the people around them was understood to be important.[14] People suffering from leprosy were thus regarded socially, religiously, economically and culturally as unfit to be a part of a healthy human society. They lived on the fringe of society and as such were regarded as being marginal in the ancient world.[15]

---

14   The treatment of a leprous person was similar to that of the scapegoat in that both a leper and the *azazel* were sent away from the inhabitants of Israel. In the purifying sacrifice for a leper the birds used for the sacrifice were also sent away like the *azazel* (Finlan, 2005:34-35).

15   Luke 5:12-16 contains "a constellation of stereotypical characters: entities on the outer edges of social and religious systems" (Spencer, 2007:152), who were readily responding to Jesus' benefaction.

## Λέπρα and ostracism in Luke 5:12-13

Luke's use of the word λέπρα (5:12-13) to refer to the nature of the sickness that was suffered by the man poses a number of problems in terms of its pathological nomenclature. Luke's writing implies an understanding of leprosy based on the procedures of the diagnostic apparatus provided and sanctioned by the *Priesterschrift* (Fitzmyer, 1985:573), instead of that of modern medicine. The Lukan use of the term thus invokes the notion that the disease is associated with impurity and that it was contagious in the sense that it could pollute the whole community (Weissenrieder, 2003:136-137). Since contact with lepers could make people unclean, to have leprosy was to face ostracism in accordance with the Mosaic prescription and the priestly legislation (Bock, 1994:472). Importantly, verse 12 reveals the leper to be an Israelite,[16] and not a foreigner, a son of Abraham who despite this still faced ostracism (Spencer, 2008:128).[17] The infinitive of the verb καθαρίζω, used by Luke means "to cleanse," in the LXX is used for the cleansing or purification ritual of unclean people (Nolland, 1989:227). Wherever the word is used in the LXX and other Hellenistic writings, it invokes the idea of pollution and defilement. It also implies a sense of estrangement in the relationship between humans and the divine that needs to be removed through cleansing. The cleansing also necessitated the physical declaration by a priest that the affected person was free of the pollution (Taylor, 1980:187). This is the reason why Jesus decided to send the healed man to a priest for a physical examination (Luke 5:14).

In the Levitical code the use of καθαριζομένου (Leviticus 14) and καθαρίσαι (Leviticus 16) all focus on sin as the cause of the impurity and estrangement. It is used in Psalm 51:2 (LXX 50:4), where David cried out to God to καθάρισόν him from his sin (καὶ ἀπὸ τῆς ἁμαπτίας μου καθάρισόν με). Josephus (*Ant.* 5.42) presupposes that the term καθαίρω had a similar usage in classical Greek,[18] especially in ritual purification which was necessary for a relationship to be restored with God and humanity. The notion is also evident in another of Josephus's works (*Ag. Ap.* 2.205), where he uses καθαίρω (first person active indicative of καθαίρειν) as a prescription ritual for those who were defiled by contact with dead bodies.

16 The setting of the event poses many interpretive questions, since Luke does not mention the name of the city where it took place. Hans Conzelmann (1960:43) asserts that Luke does not mention the exact location the event took place in since it was his intention to narrate the mission tour of Jesus to his community in Judea, or as Fitzmyer (1985:573) puts it, "the country of the Jews." Marshall (1978b:208), Bock (1994:472) and Green (1997:236) place the event within the jurisdiction of the "other cities" in the ministry of Jesus, as earlier mentioned. This unspecified *polis* in the Lukan text may figuratively describe the hopelessness of those found with such a disease in ancient Jewish society, since leprous people were living without a city, and therefore without human rules and regulations, being seen as dead people. Taylor (1980:186) alleges that for Luke to remove the name of the city where the event took place means that he was critical of Mark's historical record.

17 In the Greek context of the *polis*, citizens were expected to have equal rights as well as an existence without discriminatory practices, since they believed that the *polis* was a gift from the gods (Garrison, 1997:59). Unfortunately this notion was far from those that suffered disease such as leprosy. The ostracised individual suffered violent treatment from his or her people.

18 Deissmann's (1927:216-217) conjecture is that the use of καθαρίσαι by the λέπρα is derived from the Hellenistic Greek use of καθαρίζω, which is in agreement with the LXX.

The Hebrew word for καθαρίζω is *kipper*, which means "to cleanse." It played an important part in describing the special sacrifices that deal with the issue of impurity in the Old Testament (Lev 14:10-32). In the Old Testament the mediating figure between an impure person and the divine was ὁ ἱερεὺς. His role was to carry out the physical purification of the defiled people of God, thereby removing the barrier between God and his estranged people. The removal of this barrier through purification, rituals and sacrifice invokes the idea that God had forgiven his people and restored them back to fellowship with him and with one another. The usage of καθαρίζω in the Lukan text thus implies that there was impurity and sinfulness in the life of the λεπρός which is congruent with the view in Judaism that sickness was a result of moral contamination. His separation from the community of people also resulted in him being separated from the divine presence. Therefore, he was not qualified to be counted as a person in Israel's confederation. He needed to be cleansed of his impurity for his right as son of Israel to be restored to him. The Old Testament thus points to καθαρίζω as being one of the ritual actions that embodied reconciliation, and as an event that was particularly important within the ambit of communal worship.

The λεπρός calling the Lukan Jesus κυριε goes beyond just identifying him as a mere "lord." He understands him as the Lord who is capable of restoring his estranged relationship with his God and his community. From this point in the passage, Jesus functions as a mediator between the leprous and God and thus he goes beyond the stipulation of Leviticus 14. *The touching of the leper by Jesus* is a cultic (Hughes, 1998:170), cultural (Bovon, 2002:175) and emotional act (Bock, 1994:474) by which Jesus transferred his purity to the unclean to make him pure again (Hughes, 1998:170-171).[19] The lordship of Jesus in this text denotes him as a mediator between two groups that had been estranged by disease. The ancient Greek and Roman societies witnessed similar demonstration of healing power through the work of Asclepius (Etukumana, 2016:74-75).[20] Here the Lukan Jesus is the Lord of reconciliation, with the authority to remove boundaries and bring good news to the afflicted (Green, 1997:237-238). This δύναμις and ἐξουσία that the Lukan leper found in the Lukan Jesus are the power and authority through which an outcast could be reconciled to society. The nature and manner in which Jesus engaged the leprous in the text shows that Jesus treated him with dignity as a human contrary to the procedure prescribed by the Mosaic code.

---

19   Marshall (1978b:209) states that the stretching out of the hand of Jesus is reminiscent of the hand of God and his accomplishment in history, as well as the action of Moses in delivering Israel from captivity.

20   My intention of using Asclepius alongside Jesus is not to equate the two personalities but to ostentatiously indicate both as demonstrating healing power that effected reconciliation in the ancient world. Scholars such as H. Remus (1983), R.J. Rüttimann (1986), J.L. Wolmarans (1996), and L. Nogueira (2017) believe that there are similarities between Asclepius of the ancient Greco-Roman world and Jesus of the Gospel. F.S. Tappenden and C. Daniel-Hughes (2017:1-15) while acknowledging the existence of these similarities in Asclepius and Jesus, they further add that Jesus of the Gospels is far superior to that Asclepius.

The invocation of the name of Jesus was thus a medium through which this estranged leper found cleansing and reconciliation (Nolland, 1989:227). The longing of the man was to be "restored to his family and community" (Bratcher, 1982:79), thereby bringing to an end his unbearable ostracism.

## Legal and cultic prescripts for reconciliation in Luke 5:14-16

Wright (2001:57) states that the intention of Jesus for the healed leper was for "him to re-join his family, his village and his community as a full and acceptable member." It is noteworthy that in order to accomplish this Jesus followed the Mosaic code by commanding the leper to act according to the law (Fitzmyer, 1985:575; 1989:180) so as to be "officially reintroduced into social discourse" (Green, 1997:238).

Λεπροί in Israel were required to be certified or given a "clean bill of health" (Wright, 2001:57) before they were allowed access to people and their community. It was mandatory that no λεπρός was allowed to have any contact with other people before ritual purification took place. Fulfilling the requirements of the law as stated in Leviticus 14:2-57, would enable all the necessary processes to be completed for the certification of the leper as being healed (Ravens, 1995:86). The Lukan Jesus' use of προέταξεν implies unconditional obedience to the law, which was necessary for reconciliation to be enacted within Israel's legal jurisdiction. This is an allusion to Isaiah 42:3-4 (LXX),[21] and was not understood as merely a suggestion that one could decide to obey or not. It was a κέλευσμα that must be kept in Israel and any disobedience to it was punishable by death (Lev 14:2-57). The Lukan Jesus thus wanted the man to act based on the law in order for him to be accepted back into Israel's confederation.

Luke's retention of the Markan phrase εἰς μαρτύριον αὐτοῖς (Mark 1:44) may be explained based on his understanding of the Old Testament concept of ritual purification and sacrifice, which was geared towards reconciliation.[22] The Priestly Code prescribed a two-in-one ceremony for a healed leper. The first aspect of the ceremony was a ritual purification that prepared the leper to make the actual sacrifice which was to take place in the temple, and which would enable him to be welcomed back to the community of God and his people. The two-in-one ceremony was performed as a witness (εἰς μαρτύριον αὐτοῖς) to both the priest and the household of Israel that the person who had at one time been estranged from the confederacy of Israel and economy of God had now been reconciled, and the evidence for this was the ritual-sacrifice carried out by the priest. This is where ritual and sacrifice were acted out as means through which an estranged person (leper) could be reconciled

---

21   There is a possibility that Luke was influenced by the prophecy of Isaiah in 42:3 and that Luke here depicts Jesus as the one who fulfilled the law without breaking a "reed" κάλαμον as was spoken by the prophet Isaiah. By implication the Lukan Jesus thus fulfils all the legal requirements of the law. Luke's presentation of Jesus' instruction to the λέπρα is thus a succinct description of the Mosaic legal legislation for purification and reconciliation of a healed leper with Israel's community.

22   He thus sees that the only way reconciliation could be accomplished in Israel was through a ritual cleansing contra Fitzmyer (1989:575) who believes that Luke did not understand the meaning of the phrase.

to God and his people in Israel. The authority to do this rested on the priests, who were the custodians of the Mosaic legislation (Marshall, 1978b:209-210).

This procedure that the healed person had to undertake underlines the importance of ritual action in the process of reconciliation in antiquity. In other words, Luke upholds the premise that action was a valuable tool in the reconciliation process in ancient Israel. The rituals and sacrifices that were specified in the Law of Moses are actions that were expected to act as means of reconciling the estranged Israel with YHWH, as is stated by Mbabazi (2013:70), who acknowledges that God has provided to humanity prayers and sacrifices as means of achieving forgiveness and reconciliation. Rituals and sacrifices are tangible means that differentiated reconciliation from any other similar process. That Luke is aware of this is evident in his emphasis on the importance of ritual and sacrifices as actions of reconciliation in his narrative (5:14; 17:14; 22:19-20; 23:30-40). The Lukan Jesus does not downplay the assessment of the leper by the priests, who were trained both in cultic and socio-cultural ways to undertake this task, as it was the prerogative of the priest to carry out such an examination and certification (Nolland, 1989:228). Such action was also in agreement with the law as a *code of conduct* in Leviticus 13 and 14 (Esler, 1987:114-115).

## AN AFRICAN PERSPECTIVE

The treatment meted on those that suffered from leprosy in the past, based on the available documents, shows that the ancient African society was not different from its counterparts in the Jewish and Greco-Roman worlds as observed by El Hassan, Khalil and El-Hassan (2002:21). The stories of social stigmatisation of lepers and their degrading statuses are well documented in many parts of Africa, e.g. Tanzania (Van den Broek, O'Donoghue, Ishengoma, Masao & Mbega, 1998:57-74), Sudan (El Hassan, Khalil & El-Hassan, 2002:21-28), Ethiopia (Teckle-Haimanot, Forsgren & Gebrre-Mariam, 1992:157-168) and Nigeria (Manton, 2011:126).

### Social exclusion

The treatment of those with leprosy in African countries was characterised by social stigmatisation and exclusion. How this stigmatisation started is not readily apparent from ancient African literature (Manton, 2011:127). Derogatory language used in describing those that were affected by some illnesses however supports the inference that the people were highly stigmatised and excluded from day to day activities of society. Chinua Achebe (1958:59) has, for example, pointed to the derogatory words that his people, in Igbo land, used in describing a leper. Derogatory in the sense that a leper, according to Achebe (1958:59), was called "white-man" and "the polite name for leprosy was 'the white skin'" or what J. Manton (2011:126) termed in the context of Southern Nigeria as "colonial skin." This stigmatisation led to the lepers in many countries in Africa, especially the Igbo communities in South Eastern Nigeria being excluded from their communities (Manton, 2011:126). Even the name "colony" used in reference to where the lepers lived is itself derogatory and highlights the separation between the affected and unaffected persons (Edmond, 2006:180). Their exclusion from their communities was nothing other than violence that demeaned their human dignity.

## Ancestral curse

The general belief of the people in the South Eastern Nigeria in regard to leprosy sufferers was that such people were cursed. The disease, according to the traditional people, as observed by the work of T.F. Davey in 1938, was understood as a terrible disease caused by the gods. One of the effects of this disease was that the sufferer would not be allowed to join the glorious reign of the ancestors after death (Manton, 2011:129-130). The socio-historical interpretation of leprosy in many African communities in Nigeria also indicates that those that suffered from the disease would not reincarnate. Nor would they be welcomed into the spirit world of the ancestors. The initial separation started with the separation of the leprous from the physical world to colonies and this separation continued unless healing is effected before his or her departure from the world of the living to the world of the dead. The insight from Rod Edmond (2011:180), who believes that "Leper and penal colonies were places of forcible exile in which any productive activity was always compulsory," applies in to the African perspective on leprosy. The exile of lepers continues even in the world of the dead and that is why Davey concludes that the African people believe that anyone that dies without being healed from leprosy would never resurrect since "the leper is denied that right of resurrection into the spirit world which other mortals share ...' (Manton, 2011:130).

## Healing

The only plausible way of living a normal life with dignity or humanness in some of these communities was through healing. Just as in the biblical understanding of healing in reference to leprosy where a healed person was allowed to go back to their community, the same notion occurred in African society. Healing as a means of reconciliation for the leprosy affected person allowed integration and re-socialisation of the individual who was affected by the disease (Barton & Taylor, 2016:265). The social, religious, and cultural stigmatisation that ravaged the life of the sufferer was removed upon his or her healing. The removal of this stigmatisation overcame the estrangement that was caused by the disease and therefore brought reconciliation of the healed person with his or her family and community. Reintegration and reconciliation became possible in many communities for those who were affected by the sickness.

## CONCLUSION

This chapter has emphasised that there was ostracism, violence, and the denial of human dignity for those that suffered from leprosy in the ancient world. An argument can be made that healing as an action serves as the enactment of reconciliation in Luke's Gospel. Several actions that Luke believes that Jesus carried out were intended to transform human relationships so as to enable humanity to live with one another in peace. The effectiveness of some of these actions was expressed in the process of healing the sick person. Reintegration and socialisation thereby became effective tools in the process of the reconciliation of humanity with one another and to God. The healed person in Luke's Gospel was able to reintegrate into his society because of the healing that the Lukan Jesus made possible. The desire of the sick man was to be cleansed by Jesus and his desire was met and this brought about reconciliation with his community and God. Without healing his reconciliation would not have been possible.

Different methods for effecting reconciliation were practiced in Greco-Roman and Jewish societies. In Greco-Roman societies healing was carried out by Asclepius, the god of health. His duty was to heal all manners of diseases and illnesses and thereby bring re-integration, re-socialisation and re-union to those that were affected by sickness including leprosy. The same notion is evident in the ancient Jewish society where YHWH was the great healer of his people. While YHWH healed, the priest mediated in the process of this healing through atonement, sacrifice and cleansing. All these activities and processes were aimed at making sure that the afflicted people were reconciliation to God and the community of people.

On the African continent, where sickness is rampant, some of those that suffered from skin diseases were ostracised and stigmatised. The only solution to their plight was to regain their freedom through healing. The terms used in describing those that were afflicted by sickness were not based on how contagious the disease was medically, but instead on how contaminating the disease was socially, culturally and religiously. It, therefore, resulted in the sufferer of such disease being stigmatised based on social, cultural and religious ideologies while the healing of the disease conversely implied re-integration, re-union, and re-socialisation of the person to his or her community. Therefore the processes that aid in the removal of barriers that stood between the sufferer and his or her community are all enacted metaphors that imply reconciliation, which in turn restore their human dignity.

The Lukan Jesus exemplified this and was able to touch the leprous man providing his followers with an example to touch and heal those that have been devastated by sickness and human ideologies. The church in Africa can learn from the example of Jesus by touching the lives of those that are suffering from diseases and maltreatment that alienate them from others so as to heal and to restore their dignity as humans.

# REFERENCES

Achebe, C. (1958). *Things fall apart.* London: Heinemann.

Aune, D.E. (1969). Early Christian biblical interpretation. *The Evangelical Quarterly*, 41(2):89-96.

Barton, B. and Taylor, L.K. (2016). *Life application New Testament commentary.* Wheaton, IL: Tyndale House Publishers.

Barton, J. (2007). *The nature of biblical criticism.* Louisville, KY: Westminster John Knox.

Bateman, T. (1813). *Practical synopsis of cutaneous diseases.* London: Richard and Author Taylor.

Bediako, K. (1992). *Theology and identity the impact of culture upon Christian thought in the second century and in modern Africa.* Carlisle, Cumbria: Regnum.

Bock, D.L. (1994). *Luke.* Downers Grove, IL: Inter Varsity Press.

Bovon, F. (2002). *Luke 1: A Commentary on the Gospel of Luke 1:1-9:50.* Minneapolis, MN: Fortress.

Bratcher, R.G. (1982). A translator's guide to the Gospel of Luke. London: United Bible Society.

Conzelmann, H. (1960). *The theology of St. Luke.* London: Faber & Faber.

Craddock, F.B. (1990). *Luke: A bible commentary for teaching and preaching.* Louisville, KY: John Knox Press.

Culy, M.M., Parsons, M.C. and Stigall, J.J. (2010). Luke: A handbook on the Greek Text. Waco, TX: Baylor University Press.

Davey, T.F. (1938). 'A study of leprosy in South Eastern Nigeria (with special reference to the Owerri Province),' Unpublished Dissertation. Manchester: Manchester University. https://doi.org/10.5935/0305-7518.19380020

Deissmann, A. (1927). *Light from the ancient east or the New Testament illustrated by recent discovered text of the Graeco-Roman world.* London: Hodder & Stoughton.

Dunn, J.D.G. (2002). Jesus and purity: An ongoing debate. *New Testament Studies*, 48(4):449 467. https://doi.org/10.1017/S0028688502000279

Edmond, R. (2006). *Leprosy and empire: A medical and cultural history.* Cambridge: Cambridge University Press. https://doi.org/10.1017/CBO9780511497285

El Hassan, I.A., Khalil, E.A.G. and El-Hassan, A.M. (2002). Socio-cultural aspects of leprosy among the Masalit and Hawsa tribes in the Sudan. *Leprosy Review*, (73):20-28.

Esler, P.F. (1987). *Community and Gospel in Luke-Acts: the social and political motivations of Lukan theology.* Cambridge: Cambridge University Press. https://doi.org/ 10.1017/CBO9780511554933

Etukumana, G.A. (2016). 'Reconciliation in the Gospel of Luke: a socio-historical.' *PhD dissertation*. Stellenbosch University: Stellenbosch.

Evans, C.A. (1997). "Who touched me?" Jesus and the ritually impure, in Chilton, B. and Evans, C.A. (eds.). *Jesus in context: Temple, purity, and restoration*. Leiden: Brill, pp.353-376. https://doi.org/10.1163/9789004332478_022

Farmer, W.R. (1976). *The synoptic problem: A critical analysis*. Macon, GA: Mercer University Press.

Finlan, S. (2005). *Problems with atonement: The origins of, and controversy about, the atonement doctrine*. Collegeville, MN: Order of Saint Benedict.

Fitzmyer, J.A. (1985). *The Gospel according to Luke I-IX*. New York, NY: Doubleday.

Gardiner, F. (1871). *A harmony of the four Gospels in English, according to the Authorized Version*. Edinburgh: Warren F. Darper.

Garrison, R. (1997). *Greaco-Roman context of early Christian literature*. Sheffield: Sheffield Academic Press.

Green, J.B. (1997). *The New International Commentary on the New Testament: The Gospel of Luke*. Grand Rapids, MI: Eerdmans.

Gundry, R.H. (1994). *Matthew: A commentary on his handbook for a mixed church under persecution*. Grand Rapids, MI: Eerdmans.

Holman, S.R. (1999). Healing the Social Leper in Gregory of Nyssa's and Gregory of Nazianzus's "περίφιλοπτωχίας". *The Harvard Theological Review*, 92(3):283-309. https://doi.org/10.1017/S0017816000003400

Hughes, R.K. (1998). *Luke*, Vol. 1. Wheaton, IL: Crossroad.

Isaak, P.J. (2006). 'Luke,' in Adeyemo, T. (ed.). *Africa Bible Commentary*. Nairobi: Word Alive Publishers, pp.1203-1250.

Jeremias, J. (1971). *New Testament Theology*. London: SCM Press.

Josephus, F. (1987). *The works of Josephus: Complete and unabridged*. (Translated by Whiston, W.). Peabody, MA: Hendrickson Publishers.

Klawans, J. (2000). *Impurity and sin in ancient Judaism*. Oxford: Oxford University Press. https://doi.org/10.1093/acprof:oso/9780195132908.001.0001

Knight, K. (ed.). (n.d.). Gregory of Nazianzus. *Oration 43: Funeral Oration on the Great S. Basil, Bishop of Cæsarea in Cappadocia*. New Advent. [Online]. Viewed from http://www.newadvent.org/fathers/310243.htm (Accessed 13 March 2015).

MacDonald, M.Y. (1988). *The Pauline churches: A socio-historical study of institutionalization in the Pauline and Deutero-Pauline writings*. Cambridge: Cambridge University Press. https://doi.org/10.1017/CBO9780511470455

Manton, J. (2011). Leprosy in Eastern Nigeria and the social history of colonial skin. *Leprosy Review*, (82):124–134.

Marshall, I.H. (1978b). *The Gospel of Luke a commentary on the Greek text: New international Greek Testament commentary.* Exeter: Paternoster.

Mbabazi, I.K. (2013). *The significance of interpersonal forgiveness in the Gospel of Matthew.* Eugene, OR: Pickwick Publications.

Neusner, J. (1993). *Judaic law from Jesus to the Mishnah.* Atlanta, GA: Scholars Press.

Nogueira, L. (2017). 'Pool of Bethesda as an Asclepius-Pagan Temple in a Hellenistic Jerusalem: How Would this Understanding Contribute to the Interpretation of John 5 as a unit.' A seminar Paper. Andrew University. Grand Rapids, MI: Andrew University.

Nolland, J. (1989). *Word biblical commentary Vol 35A: Luke 1-9:20.* Dallas, TX: Word Books.

Novakovic, L. (2003). *Messiah, the healer of the sick: a study of Jesus as the Son of David in the Gospel of Matthew.* Tübingen: Mohr Siebeck.

Pilch, J.J. (2000a). Improving Bible translations: The example of sickness and healing. *Biblical Theology Bulletin. A Journal of Bible and Theology*, 30(4):129-134. https://doi.org/10.1177/014610790003000403

Pilch, J.J. (2000b). *Healing in the New Testament: insights from medical and Mediterranean anthropology.* Minneapolis, MN: Fortress Press.

Plummer, A. (1922). *A critical and exegetical commentary on the Gospel of S. Luke 5th ed. International critical commentary.* Edinburgh: T & T Clark.

Porter, S.E. (1994). Καταλλάσσω *in ancient Greek literature, with reference to the Pauline writings.* De Cordoba: Ediciones El Amendro.

Remus, H. (1983). *Pagan-Christian conflict over miracle in the second century* (Vol. 10). Macon, GA: Mercer University Press.

Rüttimann, R.J. (1986). 'Asclepius and Jesus: the form, character and status of the Asclepius cult in the second-century CE and its influence on early Christianity.' Th.D. dissertation. Harvard University. Microfilms International.

Shellberg, P. (2012). 'From cleansed lepers to cleansed hearts: The developing meaning of katharizō in Luke-acts.' PhD Dissertation. Marquette University: Marquette.

Spencer, F.S. (2008). *The Gospel of Luke and Acts of the Apostles.* Nashville, TN: Abingdon.

Spencer, P.E. (2007). *Rhetorical texture and narrative trajectories of the Lukan Galilean ministry speeches: hermeneutical appropriation by authorial readers of Luke-Acts.* London: T & T Clark.

Stein, R.A. (1992). *Luke: An exegetical and theological exposition of Holy Scripture. Luke*, Vol. 24. Nashville, TN: B & B Publishing.

Swanson, R. (1995). *New Testament Greek Manuscripts: Luke*. Sheffield: Sheffield Academic Press.

Tappenden, F.S. and Daniel-Hughes, C. (2017). 'Coming Back to Life in the Ancient Mediterranean: An Introduction,' in Tappenden, F.S. and Daniel-Hughes, C. (eds.) with the assistance of Bradley N. Rice, *Coming Back to Life*, Montreal, QC: McGill University Library, pp.1-15. https://doi.org/10.2307/j.ctvmx3k11.7

Taylor, V. (1980). *The historical evidence for the virgin birth*. Ann Arbor, MI: UMI.

Teckle-Haimanot, R., Forsgren, L. and Gebrre-Mariam, A. (1992). Attitudes of rural people in central Ethiopia towards leprosy and a brief comparison with observations on leprosy. *Leprosy Review*, (63):157-168. https://doi.org/10.5935/0305-7518.19920021

Theissen, G. (1992). *Social reality of the early Christians*. Minneapolis, MN: Fortress Press.

Van den Broek, J., O'Donoghue, J., Ishengoma, A., Masao, H. and Mbega, M. (1998). Evaluation of a sustained 7 year health education campaign on leprosy in Rufiji District in Tanzania, *Leprosy Review*, (69):57-74. https://doi.org/10.5935/0305-7518.19980007

Van Staden, P. (1991). *Compassion – the essence of life: a social-scientific study of the religious symbolic universe reflected in the ideology/theology of Luke*. Pretoria: HTS.

Wahlen, C. (2004). *Jesus and the impurity of spirits in the synoptic Gospels*. Tübingen: Mohr Siebeck.

Weissenrieder, A. (2003). *Images of illness in the Gospel of Luke: Insights of ancient medical texts*. Tübingen: Mohr Siebeck

Wolmarans, J.L. (1996). Asclepius of Epidaurus and Jesus of Nazareth. *Acta Patristica et Byzantina*, 7(1):117-127. https://doi.org/10.1080/10226486.1996.11745877

Wright, N.T. (2001). *Luke for everyone*. London: SPCK.

# Towards an (Im)possible Politics of Forgiveness?

## Considering the Complexities of Religion, Race and Politics in South Africa

*Dion A. Forster*[1]

## Introduction

This chapter engages the complexity of a politics of forgiveness in South Africa some 24 years after the end of political apartheid. We shall do so by considering contested understandings of forgiveness among Black and White South Africans in relation to the trauma and history of apartheid. Why do White South Africans want forgiveness? Is it to find freedom from the guilt of apartheid, or possibly also to be set free from the responsibility to make reparations for the past? Could forgiveness be a weapon that further wounds Black South Africans by expecting them not only to live with the social, political and economic consequences of apartheid, but also to stop calling for justice? In his poem, 'Fiction en estrangement,' Nathan Trantraal speaks of how the Christian religion calls Black South Africans to forgive their White perpetrators. Yet this call doesn't always count the cost of the call for forgiveness. He speaks of "die gif in vergifnis", the poison (gif) in forgiveness (vergifnis) (Trantraal, 2017).

This chapter draws upon a four-year qualitative empirical study on how Black and White South African Christians understand the processes and notions of forgiveness in the light of South Africa's complex economic, social and political context. The project is entitled 'The (im)possibility of forgiveness?'

We begin by considering the notion of the (im)possibility of forgiveness in present day South Africa. Why does the research focus on forgiveness (and not mercy, reconciliation, or indeed retribution or redistribution)? Next, we shall spend some time looking at the relationship between social identity complexities and notions of forgiveness among Black and White South African Christians. We shall end with some considerations of what may contribute towards making (im)possible forgiveness possible, and meaningful, among South Africans.

---

1     Dion A. Forster is Associate Professor of Systematic Theology and Ethics, and also Chair of the Department of Systematic Theology, at Stellenbosch University. He is also Director of the Beyers Naudé Centre for Public Theology, Stellenbosch University.

## Why (im)possible forgiveness?

Forgiveness, as a theological and social discourse in South Africa, is deeply contested. Numerous South African scholars and activists have raised concerns about the transactional nature of the concept of forgiveness (cf. Gobodo-Madikizela & Van der Merwe (eds.), 2009; Vosloo, 2015; 2012). As has already been noted, there are concerns about the expectation that the concept places on persons who have been wronged. Is it morally acceptable to expect a person, or community, that has undergone harm to choose to forgive the perpetrator? If there are certain instances in which this may be acceptable, or desirable, to do so, what are the expectations for the perpetrators of harm?

In surveying a range of views on this subject one soon comes to the realisation that forgiving another for wrongdoing is a complex and difficult process. Theological understandings of forgiveness vary a great deal among Christians. This is particularly so when persons hold different understandings of the concept based on their social identity and current contextual reality. It will be shown that social identity shaped by notions such as race, culture, economic reality, theological beliefs, and current experience, play a significant role in understandings of forgiveness.

Moreover, interpersonal socio-political factors such as the nature of the historical offence, whether reparation has been made (or attempted), the political identities of the parties involved, expectations and conditions for the self and for the other, also play a role in understandings of forgiveness.

At this point it is necessary to make a brief discursus on an aspect of terminology. In my writing, and whenever I speak, I encourage colleagues not to use the phrase "post-apartheid South Africa" (cf. Botha & Forster 2017:2, Footnote 7). Although political apartheid ended in South Africa with the first democratic elections in 1994, the reality is that in the daily experience of most South Africans, apartheid remains very real and present. As we shall see, economic segregation, racial and spatial geographic segregation, racism, and the politics of identity are worse today than they were in 1994 (cf. Hofmeyr & Govender, 2015:1). Recent work that I have been doing with young Black activists (many of whom were born into freedom after 1994) has led me to the conviction that the use of the term "post-apartheid South Africa" is disingenuous. It compounds the suffering of the poor and disenfranchised by using language that suggests that their daily experience of the slow violence of poverty, inequality, and identity politics is not valid or real. Hence, we shall not use that term in this chapter.

Returning to the importance of studies on forgiveness, some persons have suggested that forgiveness is a necessary condition for moving forward to a better future for all South Africans (Mandela, 1995:617; 2012:44; Thesnaar, 2008:53–73; 2014:1–8; Tutu, 2012:47–48, 74, 218). Yet, some of the entrenched theological, social, racial, economic and political challenges that South Africa faces seem to suggest that forgiveness is almost impossible at present. The 2015 Institute for Justice and Reconciliation (IJR) report found the following:

> While most South Africans agree that the creation of a united, reconciled nation remains a worthy objective to pursue, the country remains afflicted by its historical divisions. The majority feels that race relations have either stayed the same or deteriorated since the country's political transition in 1994 and the bulk of respondents have noted income inequality as a major source of social division. Most believe that it is impossible to achieve reconciled society for as long as those who were disadvantaged under apartheid remain poor within the 'new South Africa' (Hofmeyr & Govender, 2015:1).

Recent events in South Africa, such as the #FeesMustFall protests against economic inequalities and economic injustice in higher education (Baloyi & Isaacs, 2015), the spate of racial slurs and denials of Black pain on social media, for example, Penny Sparrow and Hellen Zille (Herman, 2017; Makhulu, 2016:260; Nhemachena, 2016:411–416; Surmon, Juan & Reddy, 2016:1–2), and the re-racialisation of society through identity politics (Mbembe, 2015), seem to support the validity of the IJR's findings.

South Africa faces significant challenges with regards to dealing with the 'sins' of its past and the complexity of our present life. How do persons understand forgiveness in such a context? What may authentic, and acceptable, forgiveness mean for Black or White South Africans? Is forgiveness in South Africa (im)possible?

The use of the phrase "(im)possible" is deliberate. The notion is predicated on Jacques Derrida's use of im-possible in his lecture, *A Certain Impossible Possibility of Saying the Event* (Derrida, 2007:441–461), and also Richard Kearney's discussion of this concept in relation to forgiveness in, *Forgiveness as the limit: Impossible or possible* (Kearney, 2013:305–320). The concept is discussed in greater detail elsewhere (Forster, 2017a:16, b:1–3, 8–9; Ricoeur & Brennan, 1995:7; Vosloo, 2015:360–378). What is of importance in the usage of the term in this chapter is the tension that the phrase creates between what is impossible, and so possible (i.e. the bracketing of the what makes the (im)possible, possible) (Vosloo, 2015:365–368). As it will be shown, the impossibility of forgiveness (the fact that true forgiveness is not possible in an economic or practical sense in South Africa), is what makes true forgiveness, as an act of impossible grace both necessary and possible.

How could one ever attach a price to compensate for the violence of apartheid? What possible act, or gesture, could truly account for the dehumanising experiences and consequences of this social and political system? Of course, this does not mean that such acts are unimportant; indeed, they are essential and have to be undertaken! However, it does question the contingent relationship that some political actors place on mere political, economic, or social recompense. For example, when Black South Africans 'own' the land and the economy of South Africa, would this have dealt with all of the horror and brokenness of apartheid? Would it have sufficiently re-humanised both victim and perpetrator for mutually interdependent flourishing? No, this is a necessary beginning, but the intended aim of forgiveness requires these transactions and more (Gobodo-Madikizela, 2013:119–120, 172). Narrow transactional views of forgiveness, as shall be shown, are not only theoretically inadequate; they also do not meet the expectations and understandings of what is required among Black and White South African Christians.

In this sense, we can claim that forgiveness is both theological and political in nature – it is a politics of forgiveness. So, let's move on to consider how Black and White South African Christians conceptualise the politics of forgiveness.

## A POLITICS OF FORGIVENESS IN SOUTH AFRICA

As was mentioned in the introduction, this chapter draws on the process and findings of a recently completed four year long project in empirical intercultural biblical ethics (cf. Forster, 2017a). That project was predicated upon the notion that complexifying and texturing understandings of how individuals and groups from two racially and culturally diverse Christian communities in South Africa understand forgiveness in their interpretation of Matthew 18.15-35. Stated differently, the project considered social identity complexity at the intersection of political and theological identity in relation to the hermeneutics of forgiveness among contemporary readers of the biblical text.[2]

Before we discuss the findings of the project it is worth clarifying why forgiveness was chosen. Why not mercy, or retribution, or redistribution, or compensation, or reconciliation? Why such a deeply religious and theologically textured, even contested, concept such as forgiveness?

## The politics of forgiveness and the South African religious social imaginary

In part, the answer to the previous question can be related to earlier discussions on the recognised inadequacies of mere transactional engagements between those who have been harmed, and those who harm them. Political and economic transactions, while necessary, are inadequate to re-humanise both parties for mutual flourishing and shared humanity (Gobodo-Madikizela, 2013:119–120, 172). However, there are some further reasons for the choice of forgiveness as a concept. South Africa remains a deeply religious nation. Religion plays a very significant role in the formation of South African values and political identities.

---

2    In the research project, Black and White Christians read Matthew 18.15-35. They first read it in their homogenous 'in-group' setting (i.e. a predominantly Black group reading on their own, and a White group reading on their own). This allowed the participants in each group to express their understandings, beliefs and convictions in a safe cultural and social setting. Next, the two communities were brought together. In these intercultural sessions they read the text together as a mixed group of Black and White readers. This intercultural dynamic changed their engagement with the text, and with one another, in significant ways. Finally, the two groups met separately on another occasion. In these last meetings they once again read the text in their homogenous 'in-group' cultural and racial setting. The intention was to see how much the members adapted their understandings of forgiveness between the first and last sessions. In particular, the research wanted to see if reading the text in a setting of positive intergroup contact (an intercultural Bible study) changed their understandings of forgiveness.

The most recent survey of the South African population conducted by Statistics South Africa was done in 2013. This survey shows that 84.2% of South Africa's citizens self-identified as Christians (*General Household Survey 2013, 2014; Schoeman, 2017*:3).

**Table 3**   General Household Survey 2013 religious affiliation

| Religion | N | % |
|---|---|---|
| Christian | 44 602 155 | 84.2 |
| Muslim | 1 042 043 | 2.0 |
| Ancestral, tribal, animist, or other traditional African religions | 2 626 015 | 5.0 |
| Hindu | 529 471 | 1.0 |
| Buddhist and Bahai | 16 992 | 0.0 |
| Jewish | 101 544 | 0.2 |
| Atheist and agnostic | 112 972 | 0.2 |
| Something else | 48 084 | 0.1 |
| Nothing in particular | 2 916 049 | 5.5 |
| Refused and do not know | 154 569 | 0.3 |
| Unspecified | 832 097 | 1.6 |
| Total | 52 981 990 | 100.00 |

*Source:* Statistics South Africa 2014

This is an increase of 4.4% from 79.8% in 2001 (Hendriks & Erasmus, 2005; Schoeman, 2017:3). The largest percentage of Christians belong to a diverse conglomeration of churches and Christian groupings which are collectively categorised as "African independent" (40.82%) and "Other Christian" (11.96%). The Methodist Church of Southern African is the largest mainline Christian denomination (9.24%) followed by a collective grouping of Reformed Christian churches (Uniting Reformed Church, Dutch Reformed Church, Presbyterian Church, etc.), at 9.04%.

**Table 2**   Census 2001

| Denomination | Total | % Christian | % Total |
|---|---|---|---|
| Reformed | 3 232 194 | 9.04 | 7.21 |
| Anglican | 1 722 076 | 4.82 | 3.84 |
| Methodist | 3 305 404 | 9.24 | 7.37 |
| Lutheran | 1 130 986 | 3.16 | 2.52 |
| Presbyterian, Baptist | 1 687 668 | 4.72 | 3.77 |
| Roman Catholic | 3 181 336 | 8.90 | 7.10 |
| Pentecostal, Charismatic | 2 625 830 | 7.34 | 5.86 |
| Africa Independent | 14 598 922 | 40.82 | 32.57 |
| Other Christian | 4 275 942 | 11.96 | 9.54 |
| Total Christian | 35 760 358 | 100.00 | 79.79 |
| Jew | 75 555 | - | 0.17 |
| Hindu | 551 669 | - | 1.23 |
| Muslim | 654 064 | - | 1.46 |
| Eastern faith | 7 395 | - | 0.02 |
| Other faith | 417 864 | - | 0.93 |
| Total other religions | 1 706 547 | - | 3.81 |
| No religion, refused or not specified | 7 352 875 | - | 16.41 |
| Total South African population | 44 819 780 | - | 100.00 |

*Source:* Hendriks 2005:30-31

So, in a nominal sense at least, South Africans have a self-identified religious identity. However, what role does religion play in their public (political) lives? A 2010 Pew-report found that 74% of South Africans "indicated that religion plays an important role in their lives" (Lugo & Cooperman, 2010:3; Schoeman, 2017:3–4).

The Global Values Survey (GVS) helps us to gain a qualitative insight into the "important role" of religion in the lives of South Africans. The survey shows that religious organisations remain among the most trusted institutions in society, enjoying higher levels of public trust and confidence than either the state or the private sector (Winter & Burchert, 2015:1). The report notes that "while trust in political institutions recedes. In contrast, civil society organisations [including religious organisations][3] enjoy growing trust" (Winter & Burchert, 2015:1). Hennie Kotzé, the lead researcher on the GVS for South Africa, explains this sentiment when he comments that, "Religion in general, and churches in particular, plays an important political socialisation role [for South Africans]" (Kotzé, 2016:439–440; Kotzé & Garcia-Rivero, 2017:33).

From this overview of the statistics in the recent General Household Survey (2013) and the Global Values Survey on South Africa (2013), at least two things can be concluded:

- First, that South Africa remains a deeply religious nation with almost 85% of the population self-identifying as members of the Christian faith.[4]
- Second, that South Africans place a great deal of trust and confidence in their religious convictions, religious leaders, and faith communities, as these remain among the most trusted personal and social institutions in South African at present (Kotzé, 2016:439–440; Kotzé & Garcia-Rivero, 2017:33). This is particularly so for the Christian population, Christian leaders, and Christian Churches and Faith Based Organisations.

The Church is clearly a significant social institution that garners a great deal of respect and trust among South African citizens. Moreover, religion plays an important role in shaping social and political ideals.

As mentioned earlier, some persons have argued that forgiveness is too contested and contingent a concept (or process) to allow for constructive social engagement toward change in South Africa (cf. Gobodo-Madikizela & Van der Merwe, 2009; Lephakga, 2016; Vosloo, 2015; 2012). For example, John Brewer[5] has advocated for the use of "mercy" instead of forgiveness (Brewer & Hayes, 2016). His contention is that discourses of forgiveness are too contingent on the actions of the offending party, and the expectation of grace on the part of offended party is frequently unreasonable. Brewer suggests that mercy only requires a decision, or act of will, on the part of the offended party (i.e. the person who has been injured). This may

---

3   In this report, the Church is classified within the 'civil society' grouping.
4   The General Household survey has further interesting information on attendance at religious ceremonies, the age, race and gender breakdown of South Africa's religious population, and the decline and growth of different religions and Christian denominations (cf. *General Household Survey 2013, 2014; Schoeman, 2017:1–7*).
5   John Brewer is Professor of Post Conflict Studies at Queens University, Belfast.

indeed, be true, and Brewer's results for Ireland tend to support his findings for that context. However, in South Africa the language of forgiveness, and the associated discourses seem to be more widely accepted for two reasons.

First, after the transfer to democratic rule in South Africa, Nelson Mandela initiated a process of 'healing' and 'forgiveness' that merged the political and religious – the Truth and Reconciliation Commission (TRC). Mr Mandela appointed Archbishop Desmond Tutu, a trusted religious leader who garnered political respect and general social acceptance at the time, to head this process. The TRC sought to create a space, and opportunity, for South Africans to tell of the atrocities of apartheid, in a safe environment where victims of apartheid (or their relatives) could engage with the perpetrators of abuse (Cochrane, De Gruchy & Martin, 1999; Gobodo-Madikizela, 1998; Meiring, 2014; Villa-Vicencio & du Toit, 2006). The intention was to facilitate a measure of truth telling, where forgiveness, and the possibility of reconciliation, could be facilitated.[6] The TRC strengthened the social currency and social imaginary[7] of political forgiveness in South African society for some years. Although, it must be noted that the TRC is being reconsidered and challenged in recent years (cf. Bundy, 2000:9–20; Landman, 2001; Lephakga, 2016; Statman, 2000; Van der Merwe & Chapman, 2008).

Second, the South African political, social and economic history has contributed to an untenable social reality that would seem to necessitate tangible acts of change, restitution, and remorse, on the part of the offending parties (i.e. White South Africans) (Bowers du Toit & Nkomo, 2014; Lephakga, 2016). The expectation for compensation and redistribution is a significant aspect of the discourse of transformation and reconciliation in South Africa; this might be different from what is expected in Ireland. For example, in my work with 'born free' activists, there is very little patience with discourses of forgiveness or reconciliation that do not require the perpetrators of economic violence, spatial politics, and privilege, to make tangible and significant contributions to transformation. These young activists want land and access to the formal economy, not just social harmony, national cohesion and a lack of racial enmity (Forster, 2016). What they are calling for is an ethics of responsibility more than a theology of mercy.

Hence, as we shall see in the empirical findings in the next section, Black South Africans tend to favour the language of tangible forgiveness over mercy since it has religious and social familiarity. In addition, it has the requirement and expectation of compensatory action on the part of the beneficiaries and perpetrators of apartheid.

---

6    For a powerful narrative of the establishment, work, and outcomes of the TRC please see, *Chronicle of the Truth and Reconciliation Commission: A Journey through the Past and Present into the Future of South Africa* (Meiring, 2014:90). For a critical appraisal of the work of the TRC please see, Villa-Vicencio, C. and du Toit, F. (2006). *Truth & Reconciliation in South Africa: 10 Years on.* Cape Town: New Africa Books, and Lephakga, T. (2016:1-10). Radical reconciliation: The TRC should have allowed Zacchaeus to testify? *HTS Teologiese Studies / Theological Studies,* 72(1).

7    For a discussion of the notion of the "social imaginary" please see, Taylor, C. (2004), *Modern Social Imaginaries.* Durham, NC: Duke University Press, pp.22-30.

## The politics of forgiveness and social identity in South Africa

Black and White South African Christians hold very different views on the concepts and processes of forgiveness as the findings in this research project (cf. Forster (2017a), Sections 6.11.1–6.11.3) and the literature show.[8] Vosloo notes that the unfinished business of forgiveness in South Africa reiterates that "forgiveness and related concepts regarding engagement with the past continue to be influential, albeit also highly contested, in public discourse" (Vosloo, 2015:363). This is particularly true for the public life and witness of Christian communities and Christian individuals in South Africa.

One significant problem that has been identified, and is evidenced in the findings of the aforementioned IJR research, is that these un-reconciled persons seldom have contact with each other because of the legacy of the apartheid system which separates persons racially, according to economic class, and geographically (Hofmeyr & Govender, 2015:1). The result is that, as inter-group contact theory[9] suggests, each group's own social views and religious beliefs (in-group identity) become entrenched, and the views and beliefs of the 'other' (out-group identity) are rejected or ignored because they are not understood or engaged across the socially separating boundaries of South African society (Bornman, 2011:411–414; Brewer & Kramer, 1985:219–223; Duncan, 2003:2, 5).

In at least one sense, this makes forgiveness nearly impossible – not only is it impossible for persons to forgive one another since they have no proximate or authentic social engagement with one another; forgiveness is also a theological impossibility because of deeply held and entrenched faith convictions about the nature and processes of forgiveness. In other words there is no willingness to 'translate' in-group understandings in relation to out-group understandings of the processes and requirements for authentic forgiveness to take place (Kearney, 2007:151–152). Thus, there is both a hermeneutic and a social barrier to forgiveness. Paul Ricoeur suggests that what is needed is an act of translation[10] that can bridge the differences in language (linguistic translation) and the very nature of the difference of experience between the self and the other (ontological translation) (Ricoeur & Brennan, 1995:7).[11] Kearney comments on the necessity for such acts of translation and forgiveness that it,

---

8   See, Byrne (2007); Chapman and Spong (2003:169); Daye (2012:8–18); Elkington (2011:5–35, 135–155); Gobodo-Madikizela and Van der Merwe (2009:vii–xi); Krog (2010); Thesnaar (2008; 2013:1–15); Tutu (2012:10–36, 47–60, 92–124); Villa-Vicencio and du Toit (2006:75–87); Vosloo (2015:360–378; 2012).

9   Inter-group contact theory is a well-developed and credible academic field. It is one of the two primary theories used in this research. Please see Forster (2017a:57–80) for a detailed discussion.

10  "Translation can be understood here in both a specific and a general sense. In the specific sense – the one in common contemporary usage – it signals the work of translating the meanings of one particular language into another. In the more generic sense, it indicates the everyday act of speaking as a way not only of translating oneself (inner to outer, private to public, unconscious to conscious, etc.) but also more explicitly of translating oneself to others" (Ricoeur, 2007:xiv–xv).

11  "The identity of a group, culture, people or nation, is not that of an immutable substance, nor that of a fixed structure, rather, of a recounted story" (Ricoeur & Brennan, 1995:7).

... is only when we translate our own wounds in the language of strangers and retranslate the wounds of strangers into our own language that healing and reconciliation can take place (in Ricoeur, 2007:xx).

De Gruchy says that in this sense the process of forgiveness, and even reconciliation, "is a work in progress, a dynamic set of processes into which we are drawn and in which we participate" (De Gruchy, 2002:28). The notion of participation in the process of forgiveness is important. It shows just how much we need one another – the 'self' and the 'other' – to discover what may make forgiveness possible. He goes on to say that forgiveness, in this shared relational sense, is more than a mere event or a goal for which we aim. Rather, it is a varied and multifaceted discovery that grows out of our togetherness. In the processes of encounter the opportunity for translation and discovery of new meaning among the participants becomes possible. The shared journey may even lead to the creation of new understandings of forgiveness that unsettle, or transcend, the previously held notions of the participants as they discover a new and possible future.

As mentioned earlier, the empirical intercultural Bible research project, which generated the qualitative data for this study, focussed on the hermeneutic perspectives of forgiveness among the Black and White Bible readers of Matthew 18:15-35.[12] An integral All Quadrant All Level (AQAL) social identity model was employed to gather rich and textured data on the participants' social identities and theological views in relation to concepts and processes of forgiveness (c.f. Forster, 2017a, chap. 2).

According to AQAL integral theory there are four irreducible perspectives that must be taken into account when attempting to understand an aspect of reality. They are, the subjective (I), the intersubjective (we), the objective (it) and the interobjective (its) (see Figure 1 below). In its most basic form, the integral theory expresses that everything can be considered from two basic distinctions: 1) An inner and an outer perspective, and also from 2) An individual and a collective perspective.

---

12   This chapter will not present the biblical exegetical element of the study since it is an extensive and complex body of work that is not central to the current argument. You can read it in chapter 4 of the book and in the following article (Forster, 2017b).

```
                    INTERIOR              EXTERIOR

                    UPPER LEFT            UPPER RIGHT

              I           I                   IT
              A
              U     Intentional          Behavioural
              D
              I     (subjective)         (objective)
              V
              I
              D
              N
              I
              _____

                        WE                   ITS
              E
              V     Cultural             Social
              I
              T     (intersubjective)    (interobjective)
              C
              E
              L     LOWER LEFT           LOWER RIGHT
              L
              O
              C
```

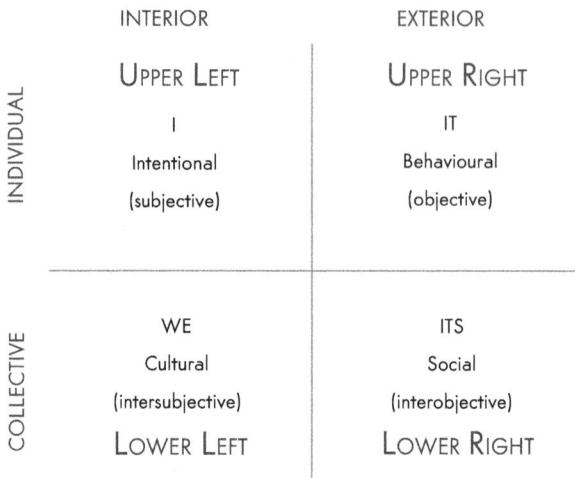

Figure 1 Four aspects of social and individual identity and meaning

This approach provided both language and a thought construct around which to develop a nuanced understanding of the multifaceted complexity of social identity and hermeneutics.

What we found in our study with these groups of Black and White Christians, was the following:

- In Group A, which is a predominantly Black / Coloured community, forgiveness was largely understood in a collective and social manner (cf. Forster (2017a), Sections 6.2.1-6.2.5). In other words, forgiveness was not only an individual concern; it had social consequences and social expectations within the community. Moreover, this group understood that forgiveness was not only a matter of spiritual restoration between the individual (or community) and God. Rather, it should be evidenced in the restoration of relationships and structures in the community. For this group, forgiveness can only be authentic if the conditions for forgiveness are evidenced in the community – in other words, forgiveness in South Africa would be contingent upon economic transformation, transfer of land ownership, a transformation of social power dynamics, and visible and tangible expressions of remorse on the part of the beneficiaries and initiators of apartheid in South Africa. A social understanding of community harmony is largely in keeping with notions of intersubjective identity that are more common in Black and Coloured South African communities (Adhikari, 2005; Cakal, Hewstone, Schwär & Heath, 2011; Forster, 2010a, b; cf. Shutte, 2009).

- An analysis of the results showed that Group B, which is an entirely White community, largely understood forgiveness in an individual and spiritual manner (cf. Forster (2017a), Sections 6.2.6-6.2.9). For the majority of participants in this group, the pre-intercultural engagement data showed that they viewed forgiveness as being primarily a matter of restoring their spiritual relationship with God. They did not initially consider that forgiveness may need to engage the party against whom the sin (or grievance) was committed. Forgiveness would have been enacted when God had set them free from the guilt and spiritual culpability of their actions. Such a view of forgiveness would not necessarily entail the restoration of relational harmony among members of the community or the restitution of social, political or economic structures in the community. Common expressions of this view would be statements such as, "Apartheid was wrong, but it is over. I confessed my part in it and I believe God has forgiven me. Now we need to move on and stop living in the past. We must stop talking about apartheid".

It is not too difficult to see how persons who hold these different views of the politics of forgiveness may struggle to understand one another, and may even face conflict with one another as a result.

## Towards the possibility of shared understandings of forgiveness?

The research reported on in this study was structured as a practice oriented research project (Forster, 2017a, chap. 5). In other words, it was initiated at the request of a problem owner (i.e. the Methodist Church of Southern Africa, Helderberg Circuit), and sought to address a problem in practice (i.e. that a Black and White Christian community were living with historical trauma and hurt as a result of racial strife expressed in spatial, economic, and social separation). The problem owner wanted to understand how the Black and White members of the community conceptualised notions and processes of forgiveness, but more importantly, might there be certain conditions under which they would be willing to engage one another towards the development of some shared understanding of forgiveness?

As was shown in the previous section, members of the respective communities (Group A and Group B) approached the biblical text from a hermeneutic perspective that was consistent with their primary social identity. Thus, it can be said that the participants displayed culturally and socially informed biblical hermeneutics. This being the case, the study postulated that when the participants engaged in biblical interpretation in an intercultural biblical setting that they will undergo some hermeneutical shifts in their understandings of forgiveness, and their perceptions of one another. The new intercultural setting would lead to a broader intercultural biblical hermeneutical perspective that would alter their theological understandings of forgiveness.

However, a positive intercultural shift can only take place if the intercultural group contact is facilitated as a form of "positive inter-group contact" (Forster, 2017a:9, 61–63). Mere contact between the participants from two different homogenous cultural, or race, groups is not sufficient to facilitate a positive integral shift in hermeneutic and theological-ethical understandings of forgiveness. Negative inter-group contact could lead to an increase in anxiety between the in-group and out-group participants (from both group perspectives). Rather than allowing for a positive, more integrated and culturally diverse biblical hermeneutics, it could lead to a closed, more entrenched, or more strongly held in-group perspective on the interpretation of forgiveness in the text (Forster, 2017a:137–139).

Thus, the study hypothesised that if the intercultural biblical reading process takes place under conditions in which the mechanisms for positive inter-group contact are introduced with care, the participants will experience a decrease in anxiety and an increase in affective empathy and cognitive empathy (Bornman, 1999:412; Forster, 2017a:139; Pettigrew, 1998:67–69; Pettigrew & Tropp, 2005:951–957).

These psychosocial states could facilitate the conditions under which participants are willing re-evaluate their own hermeneutic perspectives of forgiveness in the light of the perspectives of members from the other group, i.e. in relation to out-group perspectives.

To illustrate this, I would like to share just one story of an encounter between two participants in the study. The event that took place between two members of the groups exemplifies the complexity of forgiveness in the network of memory, emotion, politics, economics, race and class. Two male members of the groups, one Black the other White, were engaged in a heated discussion on economic inequality, White privilege, and the need for restorative justice and reparation as a pre-condition for forgiveness in South Africa. The White participant conceded that apartheid was wrong. He went so far as to say that he felt remorse and guilt over the past. Yet, he was quick to add that he could not agree with the Black participant that he was privileged, and that he should pay reparations (economic recompense, giving up land ownership, etc.) in order to make forgiveness a reality between them. He simply could not understand why the Black participant was framing his understanding of forgiveness in political and economic terms, when his primary focus for forgiveness was his faith, i.e. forgives as grace, mercy and hope. He said something like, "I have confessed my part in apartheid. It was wrong. I asked God to forgive me. I am not willing to live in the sin of the past. This is a new day. We need to move on. Anyway, I work hard and I was never given anything for free. Everything I have has been earned." The Black participant stopped the conversation and asked the White participant a question: "Do you have children?" To which the White participant replied, "Yes, I do." Then, he said, "When you dream about your children's future, what do you dream for them?" He replied, "I dream that they are safe, and happy, that their lives are full, that they don't have to suffer and can thrive". To which the Black participant replied, "Well guess what, I have the same dream". This encounter (affective empathy accompanied by cognitive empathy) (Forster, 2017a:199–201) allowed the two participants to encounter one another on a deeper and more constructive level. Because of this incident, the book which recounts the research findings is dedicated as follows: *For my children, Courtney and Liam, and for a more just future shared with all of South Africa's children.*

## Is forgiveness (im)possible among South African Christians?

As was explained earlier, the research process compared understandings of forgiveness before a facilitated intercultural Bible reading process, and after the process. The primary question that can be asked is whether the intercultural Bible reading process (facilitated under the conditions of positive intergroup contact) helps the Black and White Christians to adapt and change their understandings of forgiveness in relation to one another?

The findings of the post intervention research data and analysis shows that to a large extent (except for minor variations) the participants of the intercultural Bible reading intervention developed more integral (shared in-group and out-group) understandings of forgiveness. This means that participants were far more open to accepting understandings of forgiveness that were not initially held within their in-group but were more common among members of the out-group. For example, members of Group A (the predominantly Black and Coloured group) were willing to aggregate their social and political understandings of forgiveness with individual and spiritual understandings. In other words, while they held that forgiveness has social, political and economic aspects, it was also more than just a transaction. Re-humanisation required some theological and spiritual resources in dealing with their perpetrators. In Group B (the White group), members who had held almost exclusively individual and spiritual understandings of forgiveness, adopted understandings of forgiveness that had social and political implications and consequences. This means that they came to understand the importance of making tangible and sacrificial contributions towards the economic, political and social development of those who suffer under apartheid.

Hence, the data showed that the majority of participants underwent a shift in theological understandings of forgiveness between the pre-intercultural Bible reading engagements and the post-intercultural Bible reading engagements. The "extent" of the shift was significant both in the theological content of how understandings of forgiveness changed and in the number of participants that expressed such hermeneutic shifts (Forster, 2017a:178–189). Moreover, the "theological understanding" of forgiveness among the participants was more integrated for the majority of participants, i.e. the participants expressed theologically shared expressions of forgiveness that included the individual and the collective, the spiritual, and the political. This is in keeping with an AQAL reading of the possibilities of understanding forgiveness in Matthew 18.15-35 (cf. Forster, 2017b).

A second important set of findings in the research relates to the mechanisms of positive inter-group contact that were used among the participants. Allport's inter-group contact theory suggested that certain types of contact could contribute towards what is called an "optimal contact strategy" in which the prejudice between groups is reduced, and the possibility of social transformation and harmony is increased (Allport, 1954:264; Dixon, Durrheim & Tredoux, 2005:699). Since this was a case study with a limited number of participants and a limited number of inter-group contact sessions, the findings are not conclusive or normative in nature. In other words, they would need to be tested in other settings, with different groups, to see what aspects are valid or invalid among different sets of participants.

In summary, the study showed that more integral (shared) theological understandings of forgiveness were evidenced among the majority participants in this intercultural Bible reading process conducted under the conditions of positive inter-group contact. In this sense, the discovery of one another, and the willingness to engage one another's perspectives (at least in part) does speak of the possibility of forgiveness that is both gracious, and grounded. The evidence showed shared understandings of forgiveness that sets the other free, but also forgiveness that works for true social, political and economic freedom. Indeed, this is the work of recognising the other as human, and becoming more fully human in one's self as a result of the encounter.

## CONCLUSION

This chapter began with an acknowledgement that forgiveness is a complex and contested issue in South Africa. In particular, the point was made that while it is a necessary and important process for South Africans, our different hermeneutic understandings of what the Bible says about forgiveness, contribute towards our inability to forgive and be forgiven.

Does this mean that forgiveness is impossible?

This study showed that one could give content to, and explicate, the theological perspectives, and the hermeneutic informants, of Black and White readers of the biblical text. This helps the 'problem owner', i.e. the Methodist Church of Southern Africa, Helderberg Circuit, to understand what some of the barriers to shared understandings of forgiveness may be. Moreover, it allowed for the design of the intercultural Bible reading intervention under the conditions of positive inter-group contact that facilitated shared and textured understandings of forgiveness among the participants. The participants engaged in a process of theological translation that allowed for the emergence of a shared, and authentic, politics of forgiveness. Nussbaum suggests that such processes of hermeneutic translation remain important for social transformation. She writes:

> [T]he ability to imagine the experience of another – a capacity almost all human beings possess in some form – needs to be greatly enhanced and refined if we are to have any hope of sustaining decent institutions across the many divisions that any modern society contains (Nussbaum, 2010:10).

It is suggested that this project facilitated an act of translation, even if only in a modest form, between the two participating communities. So, to answer the previously stated question, "Is forgiveness impossible?" In a modest and limited manner, this study has shown that as far as theological understandings of forgiveness among culturally diverse readers of Matthew 18.15-35 is concerned, the journey toward shared politics of forgiveness may indeed be a possibility.

# References

Adhikari, M. (2005). *Not White Enough, Not Black Enough: Racial Identity in the South African Coloured Community*. Athens, OH: Ohio University Press.

Allport, G.W. (1954). *The Nature of Prejudice*. Boston, MA: Addison-Wesley.

Baloyi, B. and Isaacs, G. (2015). #FeesMustFall: What are the student protests about? - CNN.com. [Online]. Viewed from https://cnn.it/2wuHx8N [Accessed 20 November 2015].

Bornman, E. (1999). Self-image and Ethnic Identification in South Africa. *The Journal of Social Psychology*, 139(4):411–425. https://doi.org/10.1080/00224549909598401

Bornman, E. (2011). Patterns of intergroup attitudes in South Africa after 1994. International *Journal of Intercultural Relations*, 35(6):729. https://doi.org/10.1016/j.ijintrel.2011.06.006

Botha, J. and Forster, D.A. (2017). Justice and the Missional Framework Document of the Dutch Reformed Church. *Verbum et Ecclesia*, 38(1):1–9. https://doi.org/10.4102/ve.v38i1.1665

Bowers du Toit, N.F. and Nkomo, G. (2014). The ongoing challenge of restorative justice in South Africa: How and why wealthy suburban congregations are responding to poverty and inequality. *HTS Theological Studies*, 70(2):1–8. https://doi.org/10.4102/hts.v70i2.2022

Brewer, J.D. and Hayes, B.C. (2016). The quality of mercy: how religion and ethno-nationalism influence attitudes towards amnesty in Northern Ireland. *Democratic Audit Blog* [Online]. Viewed from http://eprints.lse.ac.uk/69058/ [Accessed 22 November 2016]. https://doi.org/10.1080/13537113.2016.1239444

Brewer, M.B. and Kramer, R.M. (1985). The Psychology of Intergroup Attitudes and Behavior. *Annual Review of Psychology*, 36(1):219–243. https://doi.org/10.1146/annurev.ps.36.020185.001251

Bundy, C. (2000). The Beast of the Past: History and the TRC. *After the TRC: Reflections on truth and reconciliation in South Africa*, pp.9–20.

Byrne, M. (2007). *Trauma and Forgiveness: Lessons from South Africa and East Timor*. Alexandria, NSW: Australian Catholic Social Justice Council.

Cakal, H., Hewstone, M., Schwär, G. and Heath, A. (2011). An investigation of the social identity model of collective action and the 'sedative' effect of intergroup contact among Black and White students in South Africa. *British Journal of Social Psychology*, 50(4):606–627. https://doi.org/10.1111/j.2044-8309.2011.02075.x

Chapman, A. and Spong, B. (2003). *Religion & Reconciliation in South Africa*. West Conshohocken, PA: Templeton Foundation Press.

Cochrane, J., De Gruchy, J. and Martin, S. (1999). 'Faith, struggle and reconciliation,' in Cochrane, J., De Gruchy, J. and Martin, S. (eds.) *Facing the truth. South African faith communities and the Truth and Reconciliation Commission*. Cape Town: David Philip Publishers, pp.1–11.

Daye, R. (2012). Political Forgiveness: *Lessons from South Africa*. Eugene, OR: Wipf & Stock Publishers.

De Gruchy, J.W. (2002). *Reconciliation: Restoring Justice*. London: Fortress Press.

Derrida, J. (2007). A certain impossible possibility of saying the event. *Critical Inquiry*, 33(2):441-461. https://doi.org/10.1086/511506

Dixon, J., Durrheim, K. and Tredoux, C. (2005). Beyond the Optimal Contact Strategy: A Reality Check for the Contact Hypothesis. *American Psychologist*, 60(7):697-711. https://doi.org/10.1037/0003-066X.60.7.697

Duncan, N. (2003). 'Race' talk: discourses on 'race' and racial difference. *International Journal of Intercultural Relations*, 27(2):135-156. https://doi.org/10.1016/S0147-1767(02)00095-0

Elkington, R. (2011). *Transformation: Race, Prejudice and Forgiveness in the New South Africa*. New York, NY: Lulu.com.

Forster, D. (2016). *Why the 'loss of faith' in heroes like Mandela may not be such a bad thing* [Online]. Viewed from http://bit.ly/2P8NJJU [Accessed 3 November 2016].

Forster, D.A. (2010a). A generous ontology: Identity as a process of intersubjective discovery – An African theological contribution. *HTS Teologiese Studies / Theological Studies*, 66(1):1-12. https://doi.org/10.4102/hts.v66i1.731

Forster, D.A. (2010b). African relational ontology, individual identity, and Christian theology An African theological contribution towards an integrated relational ontological identity. *Theology*, 113(874):243-253. https://doi.org/10.1177/0040571X1011300402

Forster, D.A. (2017a). *The (im)possibility of forgiveness? An empirical intercultural Bible reading of Matthew* 18:15-35. 1st ed. Vol. XI. (Beyers Naudé Centre Series on Public Theology). Stellenbsoch, South Africa: African Sun Media.

Forster, D.A. (2017b). A public theological approach to the (im) possibility of forgiveness in Matthew 18.15-35: Reading the text through the lens of integral theory. *In die Skriflig/In Luce Verbi*, 51(3):1-10. https://doi.org/10.4102/ids.v51i3.2108

*General Household Survey 2013*. (2014). (Statistical Information 1). Pretoria, South Africa: Statistics South Africa [Online]. Viewed from http://bit.ly/2HB53TN [Accessed 11 June 2015].

Gobodo-Madikizela, P. (1998). 'On Reconciliation and Reflecting on the Truth Commission,' in Will, D. (ed.) *The Global Citizen*. Needham Heights, MA: Simon and Schuster, pp.274-276.

Gobodo-Madikizela, P. (2013). *A human being died that night: Forgiving apartheid's chief killer*. Portobello Books.

Gobodo-Madikizela, P. and Van der Merwe, C.N. (eds.). (2009). *Memory, Narrative and Forgiveness: Perspectives on the Unfinished Journeys of the Past*. Cambridge: Cambridge Scholars Publishing.

Hendriks, J. and Erasmus, J. (2005). Religion in South Africa: 2001 population census data. *Journal of Theology for Southern Africa*, 121:88–111.

Herman, P. (2017). Official: Zille suspended from DA activities. *News24 / City Press.* 7 June. [Online]. Viewed from http://bit.ly/2SDxNBJ [Accessed 11 June 2017].

Hofmeyr, J.H. and Govender, R. (2015). *SA Reconciliation Barometer 2015: National Reconciliation, Race Relations, and Social Inclusion.* Cape Town: Institute for Justice and Reconciliation [Online]. Viewed from http://bit.ly/38EDjcY [Accessed 22 November 2016].

Kearney, R. (2007). Paul Ricoeur and the Hermeneutics of Translation. *Research in phenomenology*, 37(2):147. https://doi.org/10.1163/156916407X185610

Kearney, R. (2013). 'Forgiveness as the limit: Impossible or possible,' in F. O'Rourke (ed.) *What happened in and to moral philosophy in the twentieth century: Philosophical essays in honour of Alasdair Macintyre.* Notre Dame: University of Notre Dame Press, pp.305–320.

Kotzé, H. (2016). Shared values in South Africa? A selection of value orientations in the field of personal ethics. *Scriptura*, 75:437–448. https://doi.org/10.7833/75-0-1266

Kotzé, H. and Garcia-Rivero, C. (2017). Institutions, crises, and political confidence in seven contemporary democracies. An elite–mass analysis. *Journal of Public Affairs*, 17(1–2) [Online]. Viewed from http://onlinelibrary.wiley.com/doi/10.1002/pa.1642/full [Accessed 2 April 2017]. https://doi.org/10.1002/pa.1642

Krog, A. (2010). *Country Of My Skull.* New York, NY: Random House.

Landman, T. (2001). Publish Not Punish: The Contested Truth of the South African Truth and Reconciliation Commission. *Human Rights and Human Welfare*, 1(3):1–6.

Lephakga, T. (2016). Radical reconciliation: The TRC should have allowed Zacchaeus to testify? *HTS Teologiese Studies / Theological Studies.* 72(1):1–10. https://doi.org/10.4102/hts.v72i1.3120

Lugo, L. and Cooperman, A. (2010). Tolerance and tension: Islam and Christianity in sub-Saharan Africa. *Washington, DC, Pew Research Center*, pp.1–147.

Makhulu, A.M. (2016). Reckoning With Apartheid: The Conundrum of Working Through the Past, An Introduction. *Comparative Studies of South Asia, Africa and the Middle East.* [Online]. Viewed from: http://bit.ly/2SZnC9s [Accessed 5 December 2016].

Mandela, N. (1995). *Long Walk to Freedom: The Autobiography of Nelson Mandela.* 1st Paperback Ed ed. Boston, MA: Little, Brown and Company.

Mandela, N. (2012). *Notes to the Future: Words of Wisdom.* Simon and Schuster.

Mbembe, A. (2015). Achille Mbembe on The State of South African Political Life. [Online]. Viewed from http://bit.ly/2Hz2xNZ [Accessed 2 January 2016].

Meiring, P. (2014). *Chronicle of the Truth and Reconciliation Commission: A Journey through the Past and Present into the Future of South Africa.* Eugene, OR: Wipf and Stock Publishers.

Nhemachena, A. (2016). Rhodes Must Fall: Nibbling at Resilient Colonialism in South Africa. *Journal of Pan African Studies.* 9(4):411–416.

Nussbaum, M.C.C. (2010). *Not For Profit: Why Democracy Needs the Humanities.* Princeton, NJ: Princeton University Press.

Pettigrew, T.F. (1998). Intergroup contact theory. *Annual review of psychology.* 49(1):65–85. https://doi.org/10.1146/annurev.psych.49.1.65

Pettigrew, T.F. and Tropp, L.R. (2005). Relationships Between Intergroup Contact and Prejudice Among Minority and Majority Status Groups. *Psychological Science,* 16(12):951–957. https://doi.org/10.1111/j.1467-9280.2005.01643.x

Ricoeur, P. (2007). 'Introduction: Ricoeur's philosophy of translation,' in Paul Ricoeur (Translated by Eileen Brennan), *On Translation.* New York: Routledge, pp.vii–xx. https://doi.org/10.4324/9780203003831

Ricoeur, P. and Brennan, E. (1995). Reflections on a new ethos for Europe. *Philosophy & social criticism,* 21(5–6):3–13. https://doi.org/10.1177/0191453795021005-602

Schoeman, W.J. (2017). South African religious demography: The 2013 General Household Survey. *HTS Teologiese Studies / Theological Studies,* 73(2):1–7. https://doi.org/10.4102/hts.v73i2.3837

Shutte, A. (2009). 'Ubuntu as the African Ethical Vision,' in M.F. Murove  (ed.) *African Ethics: An Anthology of Comparative and Applied Ethics.* University of Kwazulu-Natal Press, pp.85–99.

Statman, J.M. (2000). Performing the truth: the social-psychological context of TRC narratives. *South African Journal of Psychology,* 30(1):23–32. https://doi.org/10.1177/008124630003000105

Surmon, K., Juan, A. and Reddy, V. (2016). Class over race: new barriers to social inclusion. *HSRC Review.* (9258) [Online]. Viewed from http://bit.ly/2uaCYj2 [Accessed 5 December 2016].

Taylor, C. (2004). *Modern Social Imaginaries.* Durham, NC: Duke University Press. https://doi.org/10.1215/9780822385806

Thesnaar, C.H. (2008.) Restorative Justice as a Key for Healing Communities. *Religion and Theology,* 15(1):53–73. https://doi.org/10.1163/157430108X308154

Thesnaar, C.H. (2013). Embodying collective memory : towards responsible engagement with the "other". *Scriptura,* 112(1):1–15. https://doi.org/10.7833/112-0-75

Thesnaar, C.H. (2014). Seeking feasible reconciliation: A transdisciplinary contextual approach to reconciliation. *HTS Teologiese Studies / Theological Studies,* 70(2):1–8. https://doi.org/10.4102/hts.v70i2.1364

Trantraal, N. (2017). *Alles het niet kom wôd: 'n digbundel.* Eerste uitgawe ed. Kaapstad: Kwela.

Tutu, D. (2012). *No Future Without Forgiveness.* New York, NY: Random House.

Van der Merwe, H. and Chapman, A.R. (eds.). (2008). *Truth and reconciliation in South Africa: Did the TRC deliver?* Philadelphia, Pennsylvania: University of Pennsylvania Press.

Villa-Vicencio, C. and du Toit, F. (2006). *Truth & Reconciliation in South Africa: 10 Years on.* Cape Town: New Africa Books.

Vosloo, R.R. (2012). Traumatic memory, representation and forgiveness: Some remarks in conversation with Antjie Krog's Country of My Skull, *In die Skriflig.* 46(1):1-7. https://doi.org/10.4102/ids.v46i1.53

Vosloo, R.R. (2015). Difficult Forgiveness? Engaging Paul Ricoeur on Public Forgiveness within the Context of Social Change in South Africa. *International Journal of Public Theology,* 9(3):360–378. https://doi.org/10.1163/15697320-12341406

Winter, S. and Burchert, L.T. (2015). *Value change in post-apartheid South Africa.* South Africa: Konrad-Adenauer-Stiftung e.V. [Online]. Viewed from http://bit.ly/327bZBD [Accessed 22 November 2016].

# JESUS WITHIN THE GENRES OF THE HUMAN

Sylvia Wynter, African Philosophy, and Post-Colonial Conceptions of the Not Nonviolent Resistance of Jesus

*Alease Brown[1]*

## INTRODUCTION

Peace—with God, within oneself, among groups of kin and kindred, with the earth and all of creation—is the habitat in which humanity was intended to flourish. The peace which humans are designed to inhabit, however, is regularly assaulted and destroyed. This is particularly so when peace is divorced from justice and love, and married instead to legal compliance. The law, so often the hand-maiden to class-ordered divisions of society, regularly has the effect of fermenting anti-peace conditions. The law as such, often results in environmental degradation, holocausts, and alienations of affection.

In modernity, these anti-peace legal conditions are very often inseverable from racialised constructions of the human. Anti-peace laws and politics became inscribed in human flesh, rather than merely inscribed on the page, and supplanted the Human Being with the Human Looking. One's skin, hair, features, and shape, which the law recognised as either White, Black, or some degree towards one or the other—in addition to distinctions based upon sex—became determinative of one's existential rightness or wrongness within the conceptualisation of the human. Laws and politics which privileged ways of Human Looking as legitimised humanity, constituted categorical effacement of the peace of human beings in relation to other human beings on a global scale. These laws and politics did violence.

Using a postcolonial hermeneutic, this chapter will endeavour to show the ways in which a re-conceptualisation of the human renders possible a theology that uncouples humanity from political subjectivity, and from the political anti-peaceableness of Man, which then allows for the possibility of aggressive acts in furtherance of human dignity and true peace.

Drawing from Sylvia Wynter's ontology of the human, which repudiates "Man as Human" constructions and instead recognises "genres of the human," the first part

---

1    Dr. Alease A. Brown is a Post-Doctoral Fellow at the Desmond Tutu Centre for Spirituality and Society, University of the Western Cape.

of the chapter will articulate Wynter's mapping of the construction of the "Man as Human" concept, followed by Wynter's reconceptualisation of the human as genred. The chapter will then substitute the conception of Jesus as "Man," for the conception of Jesus in his kenotic, Kyriotic, and mediating human genres. The second part of the chapter will sketch the incidence of violence in the life and teachings of Jesus, and argue that, contrary to the discourse of nonviolence, there is warrant for apprehending aspects of the life and teachings of Jesus as violent. Finally, this chapter suggests that Jesus' human genres may be understood as demonstrating a necessary engagement in violence by those who would be like Jesus, and who would pursue the flourishing of creation.

## MAPPING THE EMERGENCE OF 'MAN'

In both *Sylvia Wynter: On Being Human as Praxis* (McKittrick, 2015) and 'Unsettling the Coloniality of Being/Power/Truth/Freedom: Towards the Human, After Man, Its Overrepresentation – An Argument' (Wynter, 2003), philosopher and cultural theorist Sylvia Wynter explores the roots of Western and colonial knowledge systems and furthers her sustained project of "eroding the foundation of the Western imperial (racial and patriarchal) concept of Man/Human" (Mignolo, 2015:121). Wynter begins the task of decolonising the conception of the human by undertaking the mapping of the Western conceptualisation of "Man ",[2] from the medieval to the modern.

In the medieval Western world, knowledge systems were constructed around God. The world was understood to have been created by an omnipotent God, for God's sake only, without consideration for humanity (Wynter, 2003:275). Further, humanity was deemed to be corrupt, with fallen flesh. "Sinful by nature" humanity, thus, was cognitively incapable of knowing reality. As a result, the spiritual enlightenment of the Church fixed its hegemony over all laity, including the state (2003:276).

Near the turn of the 15th century, Pico Della Mirandola ("Pico") published a treatise that provided an alternate narrative of humanity's condition. In his *Oration on the Dignity of Man* (1496) (Pico Della Mirandola, 1998), man's[3] fallenness was not

---

2    Key to Wynter's conceptualisation is the notion of "Man" as distinct from "man" or from "human" generally. As will be discussed, supra, for Wynter, "Man" represents the radical shift in thinking about humanity that occurred in medieval Europe, from God-centered existence, to human- and State-centered existence. "Man" became a political subject endowed with rights. "Man" conceptualised as such entails a referent who is situated within Western European imperialist modernity; who is descended from Europeans, raced as White, and inherently endowed with a humanity that is at the pinnacle of the hierarchy of differing humanities. "Man" who is at the pinnacle of humanity is also imagined as male. (Cf. Mignolo, for discussion of de Vinci's drawing of *Vitruvian Man*, which reflects a medieval heuristic correlating the colonisation of time and space with the geometric perfection of the male body (Mignolo, 2015:108–110)). Also, I would argue that, necessarily implied in the Wynterian concept of "Man," is the possession of, or the right to the possession of, property; modernity's *sine qua non* of realised freedom and citizenship. Capital "M" Man, will be used throughout this chapter, following Wynter's conceptualisation of the term.

3    It might be argued that Pico's re-narration intended to include women and men in his use of the term "man," since it appears that he intended to reference humans universally. However, to the

central to man's identity. Instead, man existed at the midpoint of a hierarchy in creation between beasts and the divine. Man was marked not by fallenness, but by the potential for self-actualisation. In Pico's cosmological scheme, God gave man a mandate to:

> [be] the molder and maker of thyself; thou mayest sculpt thyself into whatever shape thou dost prefer. Thou canst grow downward into the lower natures which are brutes. Thou canst again grow upward from thy soul's reason into the higher natures which are divine (1998:5).

This re-narration of man's essential human nature accomplished two things. It transformed God from uncaring and arbitrary, into "a Caring Father who had created the universe specifically for man's sake (*propter nos homines*, for our sake)" (Wynter, 2003:278) and, it unleashed Man from a fallen, cognitive incapacitation into the freedom to fully exercise human reason.

It was within this shifting space of knowledge that Copernicus offered his hypothesis[4] of an earth in motion.[5] Copernicus's theory of a moving earth made earth indistinguishable from other moving heavenly bodies.[6] Earth, he posited, was not inferior to, but of equivalent substance to other heavenly bodies. Accordingly, earth was understood to move physically, and to have moved from being a "degraded place" to being, instead, an "exalted place" (Wynter & McKittrick, 2015:14).

Copernicus consciously instigated an epistemological paradigm shift. If God created the universe for mankind's sake, it followed that the world was necessarily made "according to rational, nonarbitrary rules that could be knowable by the beings that He had made it for"[7] (Wynter, 2003:278). Thus, not only had God created man with the ability to know man's world, alá Pico, but God had created a world that could be known by man.

The evolved conception of God (as caring), of humanity (as advancing), and of the world/cosmos (as knowable), ultimately resulted in a transformation of man's relationships within the social order. Man was no longer a creature subject to God,

---

extent that Pico is regarded as a natural magician of the time (see, Alcoff, *Feminist Epistemologies* (Alcoff & Potter, 2013: 175)), it is more likely that he adhered to the less liberated outlook of the time, whereby "magnus ... [practiced magic] inside a vigorously ordered creation in which the female and passive bodies are irredeemably the male's inferiors." (Kodera, 2010: 283–284) The section will, therefore, retain his use of the term "man."

4 Copernicus' theory entailed a radical break from the Ptolemaic scientific model, which asserted earth as the unmoving center of the cosmos. Copernicus described, instead, a heliocentric solar system, in which heavenly bodies, including the earth, rotated around the sun.

5 Here, Wynter relies on *From Genesis to Genocide* (Chorover, 1980) and *The Legitimacy of the Modern Age* (Blumenberg, 1985).

6 Copernicus' idea displaced the former idea of the Scholastics that the Heavens were fundamentally divided from, and vastly greater than, the Earth; and that a static earth, fixed at the center of the universe (its dredges), was the proper abode of post-Adamic fallen man.

7 Wynter relies upon, for her citation by Copernicus, Hallyn, *The Poetic Structure of the World*, pp.53-57, as well as her own, "Columbus and the Poetics of the *Propter Nos*," pp.251-286, and Blumenberg's *The Legitimacy of the Modern Age*.

along with other created and subject beings. The potential accompanying the ability to exhibit reason freed humanity from the principal obligation of securing redemption from "enslavement to Original Sin by primarily adhering to the prohibitions of the Church" (Wynter, 2003:277).

The potential unlocked by Man's rational ability destabilised the hegemonic authority of the church. In place of spiritual leadership, came rational and political leadership. The chief aim of humanity was untethered from matters related to the Kingdom of God, and became instead occupied with constructing, and adhering to, laws governing the kingdom of Man (the natural world), and the kingdoms of Men, i.e. the State. To be human was to be one who participated in constructing and maintaining knowledge, the existence and expansion of the State, and the ownership and control of property within the State. "Man," then, fashioned as "the rational political subject of the state" (Wynter, 2003:277) supplanted "Christian," the fallen subject of the church, as the preeminent mark of being human.

Out of this "epochal rupture," as Wynter describes it, came both the advent of missions of colonial conquest and the development of the physical sciences. With respect to missions of colonial conquest, Man's[8] possession of the particular properties of rational selfhood and political subjectivity to the State, had implications for newly emerging State contexts, wherein existed a stark separation between the ruling class of landowners and the labouring class. The ruling class was invested with political rights, while the labouring class was commonly exploited and either temporarily or permanently devoid of political subjectivity (Smedley, 2007:2–3).

Colonial leaders in the newly "discovered" Americas, were generally large property owners, and "consciously contrived a social control mechanism" (Smedley, 2007:6) to protect their economic interests by impeding the unification of the racially diverse poor labouring class. "Physical features became markers of racial (social) status, to 'fix a perpetual Brand upon Free Negroes and Mulattos,'" in the words of Virginia governor William Gooch in the early 18th century (2007:6). The Brand would serve to differentiate and disunify the labouring class. Prior to the distinctions based on phenotype, none of the labouring class was included in the reigning conception of Man. Subsequently, those with European physical features were included within the concept of those who were Men, or who had the potential to become Men. Meanwhile, those with the physical features of the non-European African were explicitly excluded from the definition of Man. The African-featured were given the newly devised designation of permanently enslaved, and therefore permanent Not Man status, and ultimately ontologically categorised as not human. In this way the economic structuring of the colonial project of Western Man was responsible for the invention of racial identity (Smedley, 2007:6).

The conception of Man as rational political subject continued to adapt to the possibilities attendant to colonial expansion, possibilities that hinged upon the

8    Wynter distinguishes this particular construction of the human as Man and designates it "Man₁". Man₁ is determined by rationality and political subjectivity, without reference to his biological characteristics.

subjugation of native peoples, and the labour of African peoples. Man's advances in the physical sciences, and the development of species classification[9] during the early 18th century aided the scientific re-visioning of humanity. Man could now be known and understood according to definitive physiological characteristics.[10] Humanness came to entail differentially categorising Africans and natives in "purely biologised terms … the ostensible embodiment of the non-evolved backward Others … and, as such, the negation of the generic "normal humanness," ostensibly expressed by and embodied in the peoples of the West"[11] (Wynter, 2003:266).

By linking the colonial project to the secularising ontological construction of Man, Wynter chronicles and disrupts the conception of "Man" and of "human" being one and the same, and elucidates how the overrepresentation of Man came to be understood in relation to race and racism. She problematises "the incorporation of all forms of human being into a single homogenised descriptive statement that is based on the figure of the West's liberal monohumnist Man"[12] (Wynter & McKittrick, 2015:23).

---

9   See Gould, "The Geometer of Race," for discussion of how Linneaus revolutionised taxonomy during this time. His *Imperium Naturae* established the three kingdoms of Animal, Vegetable, and Mineral which is still in use as part of modern vernacular. His method of binomial nomenclature standardised the manner in which organisms are scientifically identified, and provided for a ranked hierarchy of organisms within the system of categorisation that he invented that includes distinctions between class, order, genus, and species. It was Linneus who developed scientific racial groupings. In his Systema Naturae of 1758 he identified four groups, Europeaus (albus), "white"; Americanus (rufescens), "red"; Asiaticus (fuscus), "dark"; and Africanus, (niger), "black" (Sauer, 2008:79). Linneaus' "scientific" categorisations of humans was based upon the straightforward mapping of people "onto the four geographic regions of conventional cartography. Linnaeus then characterised each of these groups by noting color, humor, and posture, in that order" (Gould, 1994:3).

10   Wynter regards this re-conceptualised *biologised* rational political subject as "Man$_2$."

11   Gould discusses the origins of the normitised European body. Johann Friedrich Blumenbach (1752-1840), German anatomist and naturalist, was the first to move "scientific" racial distinctions beyond customary geographic indicators, towards racial distinctions based upon hierarchical human order, in his *De Generis Humani Varietate Nativa* (On the Natural Variety of Mankind). Blumenbach postulated that those geographically situated near the Caucus mountain region must have been the first of humankind, and thus constituted the human ideal. He based this determination upon his judgment of the aesthetic beauty of the people of that region. From there Blumenbach devised a symmetrical ordering of all other groups "by relative degrees of departure from this archetypal standard" (Gould, 1994:6). For purposes of symmetry, Blumenbach added a fifth human subgroup, the Malay, to Linneaus' four. He identified two lines of departure from the idealised Caucasian. With White humanity at the pinnacle, one line of departure deemed Asians to be the furthest removed from White, with American Indians holding the intermediate place between Whites and Asians. The other line of departure deemed Africans to be the furthest removed from Whites, with Malay people occupying the intermediary space between Whites and Africans. In this way, hierarchical racial ordering came into being.

12   Wynter's problematisation of this conception of man includes the objection to the conceptual emptying of previously understood constitutive elements of the human. "Mortal/immortal, natural/supernatural, human/the ancestors, the gods/God" distinctions, upon which "all human groups had millennially "grounded" their descriptive statement/prescriptive statements of what it is to be human" were eliminated in the human as Man formulation (Wynter, 2003:264).

## Wyterian humanity

In place of this overrepresented figure of the Man, Wynter argues for the necessity of speaking of "genres" of being human. Our genre-specific *who* is determined, not by our being "primarily biologic subjects, born of the womb", but rather by our being "both *initiated* and *reborn* as fictively instituted inter-altruistic kin-recognising members of each symbolically re-encoded genre-specific *referent-we*." Which is to say, that our biologic life is heavily influenced, even dominated by, our storytelling and mythic life. "As such, kin-recognising member subjects…performatively enact themselves/ourselves as 'good men and women' of their kind according to a nongenetically determined, origin-mythically chartered symbolically encoded and semantically enacted set of symbolic life /death instructions. At the same time, at the level of bios/brain, the [origin-mythic symbols] are genetically (neurochemically) implemented" (Wynter & McKittrick, 2015:27). We become ourselves through symbolically encoded neurochemical transmission of our kin mythology. Our mythos becomes our bios. Or, to put it another way, our genre-specific logos, is made flesh.

Wynter posits that the genred human's knowledge-making practices "elaborate the genre-specific (and/or culture-specific) orders of truth through which we know reality, from the perspective of the no-less-genre-specific *who* that we already are" (Wynter & McKittrick, 2015:31–32). In other words, human knowing is determined by the praxis of human being. As a result, elaboration of a universal human knowledge is futile. Instead, knowledges facilitate a specific genre/culture/grouping's apprehension of reality from the perspective of that particular genre/culture/group.

## African conceptions of the human

Wynter's conceptualisation of genres of being diverges sharply from that of Western philosophy, with its central concern for the universal "I". Her view, however, is highly compatible with an African metaphysics, which understands the human as communitarian and necessarily existent as an "I/we".

Though Africans are not one but many peoples with a diversity of cultures, beliefs, and traditions (Okolo, 2005:248) it is not disputed that Black Africa "exhibits a certain cultural unity" (2005:248). This unity has been termed "'Africanity', which [Maquet] briefly defines as 'the totality of cultural features common to the hundreds of the societies of Sub-Saharan Africa'" (Okolo, 2005:248, citing Maquet, 1972:54).

Within this Africanity, metaphysics of reality and of the self both exist. The African conception of reality may be understood as dualistic, representing forces in both seen and unseen realms. "In the invisible or immaterial universe, according to African ontology, dwell God, or the highest being; the ancestors, or souls of the heads of class and of the departed relatives; and nature gods, or spirits. The material realm, on the other hand, contains human beings, animals, plants, and inanimate beings" (Okolo, 2005:248). In this view of reality, all existence is interconnected.

"[N]o single thread can be caused to vibrate without shaking the whole network" (Tempels, 1959:41, orig [29 digital]).

As a consequence of a view of reality that recognises a cosmic interconnectedness of beings, a defining characteristic of African culture is that of a communitarian social structure (Gyekye, 2005:349). This view of reality has implications for the view of the self. An African worldview of the person understands individuals as interconnected. There is no conceptualisation of an individuated self (Okolo, 2005:252). The individual is a self in intimate and personal relationship with other forces acting above and below the individual in the hierarchy of forces. "Every man, every individual forms a link in the chain of vital forces, a living link, active and passive, joined from above to the descending line of his ancestry and sustaining below him the line of his descendants" (Tempels, 1959:71, orig [51 digital]).

Gyekye qualifies this unrestricted communitarian conception of the human by clarifying that the communitarian self is not best understood as "a cramped or shackled self, acting robotically at the beck and call of the communal structure" (Gyekye, 2005:359). Rather, though the individual is fully embedded and implicated in communal life, the possibility is always present for a self to take a distanced view of communal values, to set different goals, and to participate in determining its own identity (2005:359). The self has the capacity for "self-assertion" or for self-willing, in other words. Further, apart from communal relations, the individual is understood as possessing "a divine spark," and as having an intrinsic value that makes the individual worthy of dignity and respect (2005:360). Gyekye's qualification results in a conception of the self that is dual-featured, contemplating the individual as one embedded in an interconnected and interdependent community, yet also possessing inherent value and self-assertiveness.

Ultimately, Gyekye's dual-featured humanity allows individual human self-assertiveness to enable the development of a human communal culture (Gyekye, 2005:359), and for a communal culture of the human to shape and inform an individual human self-assertiveness. Gyekye's humanity aligns with Wynter's conception of personhood as entailing the biologic person/individual engaging in a performance that perpetuates the mythic/symbolic life of a genre/group, while at the same time being acted upon, and constituted of, the genetic and neurochemical encoding of the genre/group (Wynter, 2003).

Following Wyterian and African conceptualisations, then, the human, is not defined by being an individual with rationality, political subjectivity, and particular physical attributes. Rather, humanness is defined by an individual existing in relation to a group of other individuals; creating and being created by various *genres of the human*.

With this conception of genres of the human in mind, we turn now to consideration of the humanity of Christ.

## Behold the Human not the "Man"

In light of the foregoing, it is necessary to contest the overrepresentation of the incarnate Christ as an instantiation of colonial Man (and of colonial Man's self-identification as messiah).[13] Examination of the social and political context in which he lived reveal Jesus to have been geographically Palestinian,[14] religiously Jewish,[15] economically disadvantaged,[16] demographically rural,[17] culturally deeply embedded in a sacred, not a secular, economy,[18] and politically, a colonised subject.[19] What is not in evidence in an examination of Jesus' identity and personhood, is a demonstrated privileging by Jesus of any kind of pre-modern scientific rationality, nor of Jesus' self-understanding being rooted in his subjectivity to state authority. On the contrary, Jesus existed on earth within a web of relationships that constituted Jewish community or a group of Jewish individuals. Wynter's conceptualisation of genres of the human aid the apprehension of Jesus, not as the image of universal Man, but rather as a human existing in different genres. The value of this conceptualisation is that it eliminates the "competitioning"[20] of Jesus idealisations, and it is reflective of the gospel witness of a multivalent God.

---

13  J. Kameron Carter's analysis of the connection between the theo-political project of the West and Christian religious anthropology is helpful. "The constitution of the White Masculine as imperial Man was tied to his assuming a messianic and mediatory role in the world, as he accumulated divinity for himself. As imperial Saviour, he functioned by "divine right" to establish a utopian kingdom—a kingdom of whiteness we might say—as the kingdom of God. Those who enter the kingdom can be saved. Yet to be saved is to be made "religious" in the proper way within a properly ordered secular space" (Carter, 2012:89).

14  Palestine being the modern geographic identifier of the region of Judea, the place in which the biblical record indicates Jesus was born and engaged in ministry.

15  Jesus's Jewish identity is clearly verified in biblical accounts. His Jewish ancestry is recorded in both the Matthean and Lucan gospels. His participation in Jewish ritual is noted from the time of his dedication as an infant to one of his final acts of observation of the Passover meal. Further, Jesus participated in Jewish customs, including attendance at synagogue, reading and studying Jewish law.

16  The biblical account of Jesus's parents' sacrifice of a pigeon upon the occasion of his dedication at the temple is indicative of the lack of means of his family; Jesus is also regarded as part of the peasant class of Judea/Galilee. (Horsley, 1993; Powell, 1998; Sanders, 1985).

17  See Morten Jensen (2012) for a description of the rural conditions of Galilee, the region where Nazareth was located.

18  See Boer, R., Abrams, M. and Nicholas, D. (2015). The Sacred Economy of Ancient Israel. London: Westminster John Knox Press.

19  Jesus lived as a Jewish peasant in volatile and occupied Judea, within the Roman Empire. See R.A. Horsley. (1993). Jesus and the spiral of violence : popular Jewish resistance in Roman Palestine. Minneapolis: Fortress Press, and R.A. Horsley. (2005). '"By the Finger of God": Jesus and Imperial Violence,' in Matthews, S. and Gibson, E.L. (eds.) Violence in the New Testament. USA: T & T Clark International, 51–80.

20  By "competitioning" what is meant is the regular substitution of one heuristic principle for comprehending God over another, depending upon one's social/political/economic context. E.g. John H. Yoder might identify God as a God of pacifism and nonresistance. Gustavo Gutiérrez might deem God's ultimate mission to be related to uplifting the poor. John H. Cone might identify God as primarily concerned with freedom. Delores Williams might determine that God is principally a God concerned with the survival of oppressed women.

The second chapter of Philippians features what has come to be known as the Christ Hymn.[21] In her commentary of Philippians, Lynn Cohick regards the Christ Hymn as a significant means of understanding the human. According to Cohick (2013:106), the Hymn describes "the person of Jesus Christ and in so doing, develops a vision for what it means to be fully human before God." Referencing the text of the Christ Hymn, found in Philippians 2:6-10,[22] allows us to view more clearly the ways in which Jesus' humanity is dual-featured - influenced by, as well as influencing, the community in which he was embedded - or, *genred*. The nature of Jesus' humanity is revealed in three significant genres: the kenotic, the kyriotic, and the mesolabŏic. Jesus was revealed as a self-emptying I/We, as an I/We of self-imperium, and as a mediating I/We.

## Jesus' kenotic human genre

In the Christ Hymn Jesus is presented as one who had the "form of God" but who emptied himself of this form, who yielded his Godly prerogative, and who entered into the humble existence of the human. This "emptying of self" (*ekenōsen*), or kenosis, entails Christ having the authority of God, yet choosing to become subject to authority as human.[23] When the gospel narratives depict Jesus as being birthed,[24] as acceding to the wishes of a woman,[25] as kneeling and washing the feet of his

---

21    Exegesis of Philippians 2:5-11 exceeds the scope of this chapter. See Gregory P. Fewster (2015). "The Philippians 'Christ Hymn': Trends in Critical Scholarship" for an overview of the major trends in research concerning Philippians 2:5-11; the themes of authorship and origin of the passage, its hymnic structure and form, and its function and theology within the letter itself.

22    5 Let the same mind be in you that was[a] in Christ Jesus,
6 who, though he was in the form of God,
did not regard equality with God
as something to be exploited,
7 but emptied himself,
taking the form of a slave,
being born in human likeness.
And being found in human form,
8 he humbled himself
and became obedient to the point of death—
even death on a cross.
9 Therefore God also highly exalted him
and gave him the name
that is above every name,
10 so that at the name of Jesus
every knee should bend,
in heaven and on earth and under the earth,
11 and every tongue should confess
that Jesus Christ is Lord,
to the glory of God the Father.

23    See Gorman (2009). Inhabiting the Cruciform God: Kenosis, Justification, and Theosis in Paul's Narrative Soteriology, for extensive treatment of Christ's kenotic emptying.

24    See, Matthew 1-2; Luke 1:26 – 2:7.

25    See, e.g. John 2:1-11; John 11:1-45; Mark 5:26-34.

disciples,[26] as allowing himself to be betrayed,[27] arrested,[28] and abused,[29] the gospels narrate for us Jesus' humbled existence; it discloses the human being as one who is for others.[30] We see Jesus influenced by his community of colonised, oppressed, and impoverished Jews, yet as influencing that community by living an alternative way of life. A way of service and submission to his peers, and fearlessness to his overlords, arising from his knowledge of his own power.

Where there has been a preoccupation with the human as Man, the "self-emptying" genre of humanity has been often overlooked as characteristic of the human. However, as Jesus' self-emptying exemplifies, humans who live within genres of powerfulness, have the capacity to choose to live for others and to embrace vulnerability. It is the human creature alone[31] that is able to choose to empty itself of power and to serve and submit to those with less or no power.

Jesus' existence within the kenotic genre of the human is rife with meaning for those who might claim for themselves the form of a god, in their exercise of and access to power.[32] Jesus' example is one of yielding the prerogative of power, and of entering into the human genre of the vulnerable. Remaining vulnerably placed despite the cost to oneself.

## Jesus' kyriotic genre

Later in the same passage of Philippians (2:11), another of Jesus' human genres is disclosed. In addition to the presentation of Jesus as embracing the surrender of his almighty prerogative while embodied, we are presented with Jesus who is the Christ and who is Lord (*Kyrios Iesous Christos*). This statement is not simply an ontological account of Jesus' divinity and absolute sovereignty, though it is both these things.[33] The assertion that Jesus is Lord constitutes an acknowledgement of the exaltation of lowly humanity. "Jesus is Lord" bespeaks the revelation that one who had the form

---

26  See, John 13:4-9.
27  See, e.g. Mark 14:18; John 13:21.
28  See, Matthew 26:46-56; Mark 14:43-50; Luke 22:47-54; John 18:21.
29  See, e.g. Mark 14:65; 15:5, 19.
30  This coheres with the saying of Jesus, "but whoever wishes to be great among you must be your servant, 27 and whoever wishes to be first among you must be your slave; 28 just as the Son of Man came not to be served but to serve, and to give his life a ransom for many" (Matt 20:26-28). See also, Mark 10:43-45.
31  It is interesting that even the angelic host, who are identified as ministering spirits, are not revealed in scripture as beings who are able to enter into a genre of being that is inferior to the genre to which they originally belong.
32  For Karl Barth godlikeness was a feature of Western Man's conception of himself. "We are not concerned with God but with our own requirements, to which God must adjust Himself ... And, so when we set God upon the throne of the world, we mean by God ourselves. In 'believing' on Him we justify, enjoy, and adore ourselves ... God Himself is not acknowledged as 'God' and what is called God is in fact Man (Barth, 1933:44).
33  "When kyrios is used in this sense, it conveys the idea of "one who is absolutely sovereign." It is a majestic title, conveying God's sovereignty and divine power, and it is a remarkable proof of Jesus' divinity when it is applied to Him in this manner" ("Ligonier Ministries", 2017).

of a slave is he who possesses ultimate value, dignity, and power. Jesus' lordship did not arise following, or because of his death on the cross.[34] He was simply revealed at that time to the world to be that which he truly was, that which the world had not apprehended.[35]

The kyriotic genre of humanity entails the revelation to onlookers of the authority, agency, and exaltation of the humble, while the humble remains shrouded in vulnerability. Thus, following the Annunciation, unmarried and pregnant Mary could be revealed as the prophet who sang a Song of Praise acknowledging that God had already brought down the powerful and exalted the lowly.[36] During the baptism of Jesus, an anonymous carpenter from Nazareth, a hovering dove and divine pronouncement could identify him as the beloved Son in whom God was well pleased.[37] Jesus could enter a synagogue and teach with an authority that learned scribes did not possess.[38] Upon ascending a mountain with his disciples, Jesus could be seen as inhabiting a body transfigured into magnificence.[39]

Where there has been a preoccupation with Man, there has been a tendency to overlook the kyriotic genre of humanity. Certainly Man has embraced the notion of the *imago Dei*, that he alone in creation has been graced with the image, and special favour, of God, which is the basis of his exalted position in the earth. This is not, however, kyriotic. The significance of kyrios embodied in Jesus' humanity, is that

---

34    We often view Christ's humiliation as the basis of his subsequent exaltation; his having been humbled so that he could be exalted. (See, e.g. 2 Cor 13: 3-4, Heb 2:9, 14-18). Yet Christ's humiliation might be viewed another way, namely at a means of displaying an exalted way of being human. Cohick articulates the reminder of redeemed humanity's participation in Christ. Accordingly, Christ's humility in the Hymn is a demonstration of "the posture of service that characterises the child of God" (Cohick, 2013:131). See also, Barth's Philippians, wherein he posits that God found glory in, "prepar[ing] his kingdom in incomprehensible condescension. And that is the right and the glory that now count also for those who are his...the right and the glory of tapeinophrosynē (humility)" (Barth, 2002:68).

35    The notion of a concealed or misperceived identity correlates with another principle emphasised by Wynter in her conceptualisation of humanity, a concept previously gestured toward by Frantz Fanon as sociogeny ("besides phylogeny and ontogeny there stands sociogeny") (Fanon, 2008:11). The same concept was articulated earlier by W.E.B. Dubois (1868-1963) as "double consciousness." Wynter's sociogenic principle identifies that phenomenon whereby racialisation results in the construction of the Black person as doubled. One experiences oneself as one is, while at the same time experiencing oneself through the lens of the subjective circumscribed disabilities imposed by a referent-we populace. So that one is at the same time both the normal and abnormal/Othered/ marginalised human. The Black person is both the normative "we" and the lesser-than "they" (Wynter & McKittrick, 2015:54-56); (Wynter, 2001). "The concept of sociogenesis underlines that: I am who I am in relation to the other who sees me as such; and, in a society structured upon racial hierarchies, becoming black is bound up with being perceived as black by a white person...This process of being seen and seeing oneself is sociogenesis or DuBoisian double consciousness" (Mignolo, 2015:116). My suggestion is that Christ's kyriotic human genre is, effectively, the true self of Jesus overwhelming the imposed selfness of Jesus.

36    See, Luke 1:46-55.

37    See, Matthew 3: 13-17, Mark 1:9-11; Luke 3:21, 22; John 1:32-34.

38    See, Matthew 7:27-29, 13:54; Mark 1:22; 6:2; Luke 4:32.

39    See, Matthew 17:1-3; Mark 9:2-4; Luke 9:28-30.

the acclaim of Kyrios is attached to Jesus, the lowly, and not to Caesar, the mighty. A kyriotic human genre acknowledges in the humiliated human the impartation of agency, glory, and the special attentiveness of the Divine. "Jesus is Lord, and always has been, even if no one recognises it," his Kyriotic genre asserts. "The lowly have power, authority, and the agency to exercise both," the kyriotic asserts, "even if no one recognises it."[40] This power, authority, and agency, revealed in the kyriotic genre, does not require permission to be or to do, but is proactive and self-directing in accordance with its self-knowledge.

## Jesus' mesolabóic human genre

The final human genre that might be contemplated via the passage in Philippians 2 is that of the mesolabóic, Jesus' mediating selfhood. Mediation is conveyed in the acknowledgement that "at the name of Jesus every knee will bow—of those who are in heaven and on earth and under the earth—and every tongue confess" Jesus' Lordship. By this statement, Jesus' life is placed in connection to all other beings in creation. The human, incarnate Jesus, thus, has a mediating function not merely between the Creator and humanity, but between the Creator and all of existence. Jesus, stands between the natural and the divine, as well as between the various objects of creation within the natural created world.[41]

The mesolabóic genre of humanity entails the human standing as mediator, following the example of Jesus standing as mediator. Jesus mediated between God and humanity, in his incarnation, ministry, death and resurrection. He mediated between God and non-human life, such as in his expressed concern for lilies and sparrows.[42] He also demonstrated a mediating humanity in relation to animals. He acknowledged that human help should be immediately given when an animal falls

---

40   Stovell helpfully problematises the classic understanding of kenosis as the complete emptying of the divine attributes of God:
     The classical kenoticists, led by Gottfried Thomasius, stretched the concept of kenosis so that it meant "emptied himself of the divine attributes not compatible with human nature." This created for them a novel way to resolve the incarnational paradox: instead of attenuating either Christ's humanity or his unity of person...they would preserve both by attenuating his divinity. But this is...a slip back from Chalcedon's hypostatic union to a natural union. It allows only God's character to be compatible with creaturely existence, and not his power. By insisting on a metaphysic that opposes divine and creaturely, heavenly and earthly, antithetically against one another, such "kenotic Christology" ultimately denies the possibility that the heavenly order can be fully realised in the created world... See various relevant essays in Evans, ed. Exploring Kenotic Christology (Stovell, 2014).

41   Gregersen's account of "deep incarnation" conceptualises the creation's comprehensive connectivity through Jesus's humanity, thus:
     God's own Logos (Wisdom and Word) was made flesh in Jesus the Christ in such a comprehensive manner that God, by assuming the particular life-story of Jesus the Jew from Nazareth, also conjoined the material conditions of creaturely existence ("all flesh"), shared and ennobled the fate of all biological life-forms ('grass' and 'lilies'), and experienced the pains of sensitive creatures ('sparrows' and 'foxes'). Deep incarnation thus presupposes a radical embodiment which reaches into the roots (radices) of material and biological existence... (Gregersen, 2013:253).

42   See, Luke 12:6, 24.

into a ditch,[43] and that pathos is evoked by a herd of shepherdless sheep or the concern for a lost sheep.[44] Jesus also mediated between humans, as seen during his interventions between those with power and those who were powerless, such as the woman caught in the act of adultery,[45] and the man who was born blind,[46] or those whom he healed of various conditions.[47] Jesus also intervened between those with authority and those with greater authority, such as when he offered a determination on paying taxes to the emperor[48]. Finally, Jesus might even be understood as one who mediated between humans and the inanimate created world, through his speaking to winds and water,[49] and his assertion that rocks might somehow cry out in worship.[50]

Where there has been a preoccupation with the human as Man, the genre of humanity as mediating being has been obliterated. Humanity, instead, fetishises the human. Jesus' incarnate identity demonstrates that one who is human, formed and influenced by one's particular community, can influence that community by serving as a mediating force between the seen and unseen, between humans, between the human and the nonhuman, and between the elements of earth and the rest of creation.

Ultimately, in Jesus' incarnation, three genres of the human are disclosed. The kenotic genre reveals that humanity is ordered in a way that affords the emptying of one's self, and one's power. The kyriotic genre of the human, on the other hand, reveals humanity's latent power can be brought to the fore. Finally, the mesolabóic genre reveals humanity's privileged place of being as a mediating force within the cosmos.

## Exemplar of nonviolent "Man"?

The movement we have seen has shifted away from Jesus as Man-as-Human, the rational political subject of the state. The way has been opened for apprehension of Jesus as habituated to different genres of the human, genres which do not necessitate conforming Jesus' actions to those that equate to good citizenship. Now begins the task of reckoning with the historical reality of the actions of Jesus which could

---

43  See, Matthew 12:11.
44  See, Matthew 9:36, 18:12.
45  See, 8:1-11.
46  See, John 9.
47  See, e.g. Matthew 4:23, 9:35; Luke 9:6, 11, 14:1-6, John 5:2-9. See also, Crossan generally for a discussion on a medical anthropological distinction between disease and illness; disease being the objective physical condition, and illness the social and communal meaning attributed to the condition. He makes a distinction between curing, which is physiological, and "healing," which encompasses community/relational aspects of making the sick well (Crossan, 2007).
48  See, Matthew 22:17-23; Mark 12:13-17; Luke 20:19-26.
49  See, Matthew 8:23-27; Luke 8:22-25; Mark 4:35-41.
50  See, Luke 19:40.

not be regarded as good citizenship, which may, in fact, be deemed constitutive of violence.[51]

The limited notion of Jesus as an agent of a strictly non-violent strategy for change is discursive. As Jeremy Punt establishes, contrary to pervasive teaching of Christian nonviolence, the New Testament does not univocally espouse this teaching.

> The position that the New Testament...unequivocally eschews violence and opts for peace...can only be maintained within what can be described as a prior conceived biblical-theological hermeneutical template...Such templates serve as filters, which too easily permit unqualified claims and disallow complexities such as the ambiguity of a verse like Romans 16:20 ("The God of peace will soon crush Satan under your feet")... " (Punt, 2012: 29, n.21).

Specifically, with respect to Jesus' life, the biblical text is replete with explicit depictions of Jesus engaging in what may be understood as physical violence, verbal violence, and ideological/eschatological violence. In Matthew alone, Jesus is shown as engaging in violent rhetoric, making references to future temporal and eschatological violence, and engaging in physical acts of violence against the temple complex and against demons and Satan.

> [Jesus'] claim in 10:34 not to bring peace but a sword is usually understood metaphorically...But as Davies and Allison observe, the sword is also associated with eschatological judgment (for example, Isa 66:16) [footnote omitted]. That judgment is under way in Jesus' ministry manifested in people's responses, and will

---

51 Though a comprehensive treatment goes beyond the scope of this chapter, a distinction is warranted between the argument that I am here advancing, and the arguments that are raised in Walter Wink's extensive body of work on domination and nonviolent resistance. (See, e.g. Engaging the Powers wherein many of Wink's arguments relating to domination and nonviolence are set forth (Wink, 1992). Wink and I both argue that Jesus advocated resistance to oppression and injustice. However, our positions otherwise differ in numerous ways. Three of which I will note here. First, we have differing views on the fundamental nature of power and domination as it relates to the Christian God and God's action in the world. Wink traces the "system of domination" and violence to ancient non-Judeo-Christian societies. He argues against all dominating violence. This seems to me to poorly account for the ways in which the Hebrew Bible characterises some acts of God's judgment. Second, Wink argues that a "third way" exists, as an alternative to either passive acceptance or violent reaction. He offers examples of resistance from Jesus's Sermon on the Mount of love-based and respectful resistance, including the example of turning the other cheek. The back-handed slap on the face was meant to humiliate, but by turning the other cheek, the victimised regained their dignity by determining their own response to being unjustly slapped. I think that Wink is naïve in his belief that turning the other cheek will effectively rob the oppressor of the will to oppress and result in transformation. An example from South Africa will suffice. Steve Biko's adhered to a non-cooperation policy when detained by state security forces. His creative resistance, and refusal to cooperate, was intended to either coerce the police to stop beating him, or force them escalate their abuse beyond what was intended or at all reasonable, thus again leading to an end to the abuse. His tactic was much the same as offering the other cheek to be slapped, in hope that it might end the humiliation or escalate it. Steve Biko was beaten to death while in the custody of state security forces. Finally, Wink proposes "nonviolent" militant resistance, yet fails to recognise the "violence" that is interpreted by the state through the mere assembly of Black bodies. When "standing your ground" while Black is sufficiently threatening to result in state-sanctioned murder of those standing, notions of what constitutes nonviolence must be re-examined.

be completed at Jesus' return. Jesus' physically violent disruption of the temple in 21:12-17 foreshadows the destruction and punishment of the elite's center of power (Jerusalem and the temple) at Rome's hands in 70 CE (22:7), and anticipates the final violent judgment effected in the cosmic war that marks Jesus' return (24:27-31) [footnote omitted]. So too do his rhetorically violent assertion that the Jerusalem elite have no place in God's purposes (15:13), his description of them as "evil" like Satan (cf. 12:34; 16:1-4 and 6:13; also tempters in 16:1 and 4:1-3), and his scathing series of condemnatory woes against them (chapter 23). His exorcisms, his "throwing out" of demons (8:16; 9:33, 38 and more) and of the temple officials (21:12), evidence the struggle with Satan and victory of God's empire (12:24-28) (Carter, 2005:99).

Many of the passages described by Carter in the above quote have parallels in the other gospels, or can be supplemented by incidents of a violent character in other gospels that are not accounted for in Matthew's gospel. When the anachronistic divisions between political, religious, relational, physical, and ideological violence that are often imposed on the biblical text are removed, there can be no question that Jesus did engage in conduct that worked damage towards family structures, religious authority, and political institutions; conduct that is constitutive of violence.

Resistance to the notion of Jesus' engagement with violence within his social/political context is often present in direct correlation to the acceptance of the conceptualisation of Jesus as Man. When Jesus is conceived as Man, the possibility of Jesus acting against the (imperial) power of the State and her agents is foreclosed, since Man, the ideal, exists by and through his being a rational political subject of the State. New Testament Scholar Richard Horsley's analysis is precisely to the point in making the connection between constructions of Jesus as nonviolent Man and constructions of Jesus as Man citizen-subject of the imperial state. Thus, I quote him at length:

The vehemence with which leading scholars insisted that Jesus was a teacher of nonviolence and even apolitical nonresistance, however, cannot be explained simply as the response to a few maverick interpreters of Jesus as politically engaged, perhaps even a sympathiser with "the Zealots" [footnote omitted]. The 1960s and 1970s, of course, were times of national liberation movements against European and American imperial rule in the "third world," and of widespread protests against the U.S. war in Vietnam and other counterinsurgency wars. Again in retrospect, it seems like no mere coincidence that European scholars constructed an elaborate synthetic picture of "the Zealots" as a longstanding and widespread movement of violent revolt against Roman rule, as a kind of ancient Jewish "National Liberation Front" [footnote omitted]. As practitioners of anti-imperial violence, "the Zealots" provided a useful foil over against which Jesus could be portrayed as a sober teacher of pacifist nonresistance. It seems no mere coincidence, moreover, that New Testament scholars thus focused the issue of violence on resistance to foreign imperial rule rather than on imperial rule itself. Like many other academic fields, New Testament studies originated in late nineteenth- and early twentieth-century Germany and England during the heyday of imperialism. That Western nations were ruling and exploiting subject peoples was simply assumed as the standard order of things [footnote omitted]. It was also assumed that the Gospels belonged to European Christians, whose responsibility it was to take them as authoritative

Scriptures to those subject peoples. The portrayal of Jesus as a sober advocate of nonresistance in opposition to the revolutionary violence of "the Zealots" thus perpetuated the Western Christian appeal to Jesus' teaching of "love your enemy" as a device to suppress resistance to Western domination, including repressive imperial violence (Horsley, 2005:52).

Just as conceptions of Man arise concurrently with a Western imperialist agenda, according to Horsley, it appears that the Western scholarly project of constructing a nonviolent Jesus, is likewise directly related to the project of Western imperialism.

Instead of reckoning with Jesus as he is presented in the pages of scripture, Western man adapted Jesus to suit his drive to conquer and to amass power and wealth. For the imperial subject, Jesus is Man. He represents Man's power to rise in stature to become like God. Jesus is the exemplar of Man's authority and imparts Man with the destiny of exploring, discovering, plundering, subduing, and exerting dominion by physical, psychological, and technological force, if necessary, in order that the world might be sculpted into the shape that Man deems best, alá Pico. For those who are objects of the imperialist agenda, however, Jesus must not be recognised as Man, with limitless agency and power. The attributes of self-actualisation, so prized by Western Man, must be withheld from the colonised, lest the colonised exercise their agency to disallow their subjugation. The colonised must engage a Jesus who is the nonviolent Saviour from sin, and not the Jesus who is Man.

That there could be two Jesuses simultaneously legitimated in the mind of Western Man, affirms the concept of Jesus occupying more than one genre. This seeming consistency with genres of humanity is only partial, however. The Western construct of Jesus as Man and of Jesus as nonviolent Saviour both corrupt and invert the concept of the genred human, and of genred Jesus. Instead of either of Western Man's genres moving humanity toward peace, flourishing, and unity of life, both move, instead, toward injustice and dehumanisation, and an "I/we" that takes the creation being *prompter nos homines* ("for our own sake") to always further extremes. None of which, ultimately, is faithful to honour the person and work of Jesus.

The Christ Hymn, alternatively, provides guidance as to what genres might be more faithful reflections of who Jesus is. If Jesus is understood within the genre of the kenotic, we might, perhaps, regard him as exemplar of a humanity which properly enters into the social realm of the marginalised. Who engages in a violent ideological resistance that rejects existing hierarchies of power; or as a provocateur whose life could not be considered one that promoted "peace (law) and order".

In regions where there are staggering levels of inequality, such as South Africa,[52] there are implications for a kenotic humanity. Such a humanity would task those

---

52  Twenty-eight years after the end of apartheid, the effects of apartheid continue. Separation largely remains. Over 7 million people, nearly all Black South Africans, live in informal dwellings, which consist, primarily, of shacks. (Statistics South Africa, 2016:59). Over 60% of the population do not have piped water inside their dwellings (2016:64) Economic disparities also endure. A study in 2013 revealed dire inequality, not merely in income, but of wealth. "[T]en percent of the population own more than 90 percent of all wealth while 80 percent have no wealth to speak of" (REDI & Orthofer, 2016:4).

with wealth to pursue transformation of the heart, so that meaning in life might be reimagined as tied to the work of justice for the violated, and to securing the basic needs of the poor. A kenotic culture might censure concern by the wealthy for increasing their wealth and possessions, and encourage instead the disregard of the wealthy's own loss of money, prestige, and security.

If Jesus is understood within the genre of the kyriotic, we might, perhaps, regard him as exemplar of a humanity that allows the spark of the Divine to blaze into a renunciation of the imposed identity of colonised-subjugated Lesser-Being. A renunciation that does not eschew the performance of acts of verbal and/or physical violence. Renunciation that might encompass, like Jesus, vociferous public condemnation of those wielding oppressive authority, and the disruption of the operation of oppressive, exploitative, or destructive institutions, without regard for harm to property.

If Jesus is understood within the genre of the mesolabŏic, we might, perhaps, regard Jesus as exemplar of a humanity whose interest lies in fostering a harmonious creation, inclusive of the earth, animals, and humanity, and whose life and actions reflect a radical concern for the flourishing of all, as opposed to a preoccupation with the mere absence of physical violence between humans. This might involve restructuring communities to honour communal, multi-family, living. It might involve providing radical care for and treatment for victims and perpetrators of gender-based violence. It might involve the stringent imposition of consequences on unethical poachers, and affirmative steps to restore balance to the habitat of the poached. It might involve rigorous reform to humanity's relationship with water.

Reimagining the human in accordance with different genres is a seed that bears much fruit in its application to our lives.

## Conclusion

Wynter has mapped the development of the ideology of "Man" in place of human. She then offered a corrective by conceptualising genres of the human. Examples of Jesus' incarnate identity within different human genres was shown as a counter-production to the image of Jesus as Man. Finally, the notion of Jesus as nonviolent Saviour was deconstructed, and a suggestion for the possibility of alternative views of Jesus' humanity within the kenotic, kyriotic, and mesolabŏic genres of the human suggested.

The "we" who have been culturally molded in the image of Jesus as Man face an urgent 21st century task of reimagining Jesus' humanity. "[We] have to replace

---

Educational disparities reflect similar inequalities. A 2007 study showed 41% of rural Grade 6 children, largely Black South Africans, were functionally illiterate; a 2011 study showed that 50% of children who whose home language is not English or Afrikaans, could not read by Grade 4; other data shows that only 44% of Black and Coloured youth graduated high school, while 88% of Whites graduated. (See, Spaull (2014), "Education in SA – Still separate and unequal". Added to these are the staggering instances of gun violence, as well as gender based violence, including rape.

the ends of the referent-we of liberal monohumanist Man with the ecumenically human ends of the *referent-we on the horizon of humanity*. We have no choice" (Wynter & McKittrick, 2015:24).

# REFERENCES

Alcoff, L. and Potter, E. (2013). *Feminist Epistemologies.* New York: Routledge.
https://doi.org/10.4324/9780203760093

Barth, K. (1933). *The Epistle to the Romans* (trans. Edwyn C. Hoskyns) (Reprint ed.).
Oxford: Oxford University Press.

Barth, K. (2002). *The Epistle to the Philippians: 40th Anniversary Edition.*
Louisville, KY: Westminster John Knox Press.

Blumenberg, H. (1985). *The Legitimacy of the Modern Age.* Cambridge, MA: MIT Press.

Boer, R., Abrams, M. and Nicholas, D. (2015). *The Sacred Economy of Ancient Israel.*
London: Westminster John Knox Press.

Carter, J.K. (2012). 'Between W.E.B. DuBois and Karl Barth: The Problem of Modern Political
Theology', in Lloyd, V.W. (ed.) *Race and Political Theology.*
Stanford: Stanford University Press, pp.83–111.

Carter, W. 2005. 'Constructions of Violence and Identities in Matthew's Gospel,' in Matthews, S.
and Gibson, E.L. (eds.) *Violence in the New Testament.* USA: T & T Clark International.

Chorover, S.L. (1980). *From Genesis to Genocide: The Meaning of Human Nature and the Power
of Behavior Control.* Cambridge, MA: MIT Press.

Cohick, L.H. (2013). *Philippians.* Grand Rapids, MI: Zondervan.

Crossan, J.D. (2007). *God and empire: Jesus against Rome, then and now.* San Francisco: Harper.

Fanon, F. (2008). *Black Skin, White Masks.* (Trans. Charles Lam Markmann) (Revised ed.). London:
Pluto Press.

Fewster, G.P. (2015). The Philippians 'Christ Hymn': Trends in Critical Scholarship. *Currents in
Biblical Research,* 13(2):191–206. https://doi.org/10.1177/1476993X13504167

Gorman, M.J. (2009). *Inhabiting the Cruciform God: Kenosis, Justification, and Theosis in Paul's
Narrative Soteriology.* Grand Rapids: William B. Eerdmans.

Gould, S.J. (1994). The Geometer of Race. *Discover,* 15(11):64–69.

Gregersen, N.H. (2013). Deep Incarnation and Kenosis: In, With, Under, and As: A Response to
Ted Peters. *Dialog: A Journal of Theology,* 52(3):251–262. https://doi.org/10.1111/dial.12050

Gyekye, K. (2005). 'Person and Community in African Thought', in P.H. Coetzee and Roux, A.P.J.
(eds.) *The African Philosophy Reader* (2nd edition). London: Routledge. pp.348–366.

Horsley, R.A. (1993). *Jesus and the spiral of violence: popular Jewish resistance in Roman
Palestine.* Minneapolis: Fortress Press.

Horsley, R.A. (2005). '"By the Finger of God": Jesus and Imperial Violence,' in Matthews, S. and
Gibson, E.L. (eds.) *Violence in the New Testament.* USA: T & T Clark International, pp.51–80.

Jensen, M.H. (2012). Climate, Droughts, Wars, and Famines in Galilee as a Background for Understanding the Historical Jesus. *Journal of Biblical Literature*, 131(2):307–324. https://doi.org/10.2307/23488227

Kodera, S. (2010). *Disreputable bodies: magic, medicine and gender in Renaissance natural philosophy*. (Centre for Reformation and Renaissance Studies no. 23). Toronto: CRRS Publications [Online]. Viewed from https://www.itergateway.org/resource_samples/19.pdf [Accessed 3 February 2018].

Ligonier Ministries. (2017) *Jesus Is Lord* [Online]. Viewed from https://www.ligonier.org/learn/devotionals/jesus-lord/ [Accessed 5 February 2018].

Maquet, J.J.P. (1972). *Africanity: The cultural unity of Black Africa* (Translated from French by Joan R. Rayfield). New York: Oxford University Press.

McKittrick, K. (ed.). (2015). *Sylvia Wynter: On Being Human as Praxis*. Durham: Duke University Press. https://doi.org/10.1215/9780822375852

Mignolo, W. (2015). 'Sylvia Wynter: What Does It Mean to be Human?' in K. McKittrick (ed.) *Sylvia Wynter: On Being Human as Praxis*. Durham: Duke University Press, pp.106–123. https://doi.org/10.1215/9780822375852-004

Okolo, C.B. (2005). 'Person and Community in African Thought,' in Coetzee, P.H. and Roux, A.P.J. (eds.) *African Philosophy Reader* (Digital 2d ed.). London: Routledge, pp.247–258.

Pico Della Mirandola, G. (1998). *Oration on the Dignity of Man* (trans. by Wallis, C.G., Miller, P.J.W. and Carmichael, D.) (Reprint ed.). Indianapolis, IN: Hackett Publishing.

Powell, M.A. (1998). J*esus as a Figure in History: How Modern Historians View the Man From Galilee*. London: Westminster John Knox Press.

Punt, J. (2012). 'Violence in the New Testament and the Roman Empire: Ambivalence, Othering, Agency,' in de Villiers, P.G.R. and van Henten, J.W. (eds.). *Coping With Violence in the New Testament*. Leiden, The Netherlands: Brill, p.310. https://doi.org/10.1163/9789004221055_003

REDI and Orthofer, A. (2016). *Wealth Inequality in South Africa: Insights from Survey and Tax Data*. (Working Paper 15). SALDRU, Univ. of Cape Town: Research Project on Employment, Income Distribution & Inclusive Growth [Online]. Viewed from http://bit.ly/2vU2DwQ [Accessed 5 February 2018].

Sanders, E.P. (1985). *Jesus and Judaism*. London: SCM.

Sauer, N.J. (2008). Applied Anthropology and the Concept of Race: A Legacy of Linnaeus. *NAPA Bulletin*, 13(1):79–84. https://doi.org/10.1525/napa.1993.13.1.79

Smedley, A. (2007). 'The History of the Idea of Race ... and Why It Matters,' Paper presented at the conference Race, Human Variation and Disease: Consensus and Frontiers, Warrenton, Virginia, 14-17 March.

Spaull, N. (2014). Education in SA – Still separate and unequal (Extended version of CityPress article) [Online]. Viewed from http://bit.ly/2SMr9ZP [Accessed 30 September 2017].

Statistics South Africa. (2016). Community Survey 2016 Statistical Release. Pretoria.

Stovell, J. (2014). *Kenosis and the Kingdom of God: On Suffering, Obedience, Trust and Surrender as the vessels of Eschatological Glory* [Online]. Viewed from https://go.aws/2vROEHY [Accessed 5 February 2018].

Tempels, P. (1959). *Bantu Philosophy*. Preśence africaine [Online]. Viewed from http://bit.ly/2vVmQmg [Accessed 1 May 2017].

Wink, W. (1992). *Engaging the Powers: Discernment and Resistance in a World of Domination*. Minneapolis: Fortress Press.

Wynter, S. (2001). 'Towards Sociogenic Principle,' in Duran-Cogan, M.F. and Gomez-Moriana, A. (eds.). *National Identities and Sociopolitical Changes in Latin America*, New York: Routledge, pp.31–61.

Wynter, S. (2003). Unsettling the Coloniality of Being/ Power/ Truth/ Freedom. CR: *The New Centennial Review*, 3(3):257–336. https://doi.org/10.1353/ncr.2004.0015

Wynter, S. and McKittrick, K. (2015). 'Unparalleled Catastrophe for Our Species?: Or, To Give Humanness a Different Future: Conversations,' in McKittrick, K. (ed.) *Sylvia Wynter: On Being Human as Praxis*. Durham, NC: Duke University Press, pp.9–75. https://doi.org/10.1215/9780822375852-002

Empire, Structural Violence and the *Missio Dei*

*Jaco Botha[1]*

## Introduction: Dead body walking

On the 16th of August 2012, 34 mineworkers were killed by police in a conflict between Lonmin's Marikana[2] mine management and their workforce (Botha & Forster, 2017). The leader of the striking miners, Mgecineni Noki,[3] died that day after advocating for basic increases and a more dignified life. This event has been likened to the Sharpeville[4] of the new South Africa.[5] The situation was a boiling pot consisting of a multinational company seeking best financial return at the expense of the dignity of mine workers, radicalised unions, militarised police and the misuse of political power, which resulted in violent and blatant murder as uncovered by the Farlam Commission[6] (Botha & Forster, 2017). What preceded this event is a clear example of structural violence,[7] and the subsequent strike was a reaction to

---

1    Revd. Jaco Botha is a Minister of the Dutch Reformed Church and PhD candidate at Stellenbosch University.

2    For more details on the whole Marikana tragedy, see Rehad Desai's (2014) documentary *Miners Shot Down* (86 min, color) South Africa. Viewed from http://www.minersshotdown.co.za. [Accessed 12 May 2018]

3    Although this chapter largely uses the story of Mr. Noki, he is an icon to point to all those who died during the Marikana tragedy.

4    For more information on this, please see Mia Swart and Ylva Rodny. Rodny-Gumede (2015). Introduction: Considering the aftermath of Marikana. *Social Dynamics*, 41(2):323-326. Viewed from https://www.academia.edu/19802896/Introduction_considering_the_aftermath_of_Marikana [Accessed 12 May 2018].

5    For a more nuanced perspective of different political role players and their reactions towards the Marikana massacre, see 'Marikana shooting "like Sharpeville"', News24, 17 August 2012, viewed from http://www.news24.com/SouthAfrica/News/Marikana-shooting-like-Sharpeville-20120817 [Accessed 13 May 2018].

6    It is officially named the Marikana Commission. Please see https://www.sahrc.org.za/home/21/files/marikana-report-1.pdf for the full report titled: Marikana Commission of Inquiry: Report on Matters Of Public, National And International Concern Arising out of the Tragic Incidents at The Lonmin Mine in Marikana, in The North West Province. The report was compiled by the Farlam Commission under judge Ian Farlam. [Accessed 19 August 2019].

7    The term "structural violence" in this chapter relies heavily on the work done by John Galtung, but should be understood as distinct from "cultural violence", also defined by Galtung in his later work.

this manifestation of violence. Mgecineni Noki's life of struggle and his inhumane death have come to serve as a symbol for all those who have lost their lives in such conflicts, as well as those who are still held captive by an unjust social, political and economic system. This chapter does not aim to go into detail about Mr. Noki's life, but use his social location as a lens to critique church[8] engagement in issues of violence that undermine the dignity of the most vulnerable peoples.

## Structural violence

It is not Mr. Noki's death that is the guiding factor of this chapter, but his life. In the months prior to the Marikana incident, workers of Lonmin were participating in a strike for better living conditions and improved salaries. At the centre of this strike was a call for dignity, a life of enough food, job security and liberation from inhumane living conditions. This is evident in the pleas for a raise in income as pursued by the workforce of Lonmin. Investigations into the life of Mr. Noki and his colleagues reveal that miners had to make due with a salary of about R4000 per month sending most the income home to family. This was often not enough to support a whole family forcing individuals to lend money from short term lenders, sometimes with an interest rate of 50% per month (Davies, 2015).

At the core of this is what social theorists call structural violence. In Johan Galtung's 1969 article[9] 'Violence, Peace and Peace Research', Galtung creates a distinction between personal or physical violence and what he calls structural violence.[10] This notion of structural violence, which precedes the physical violence endured by Mr. Noki and his fellow workers, is argued here to be distinct but connected. Furthermore, Gultung names structural violence not as 'exploitation' but explicitly as a form of violence and a profound injustice (1969:171). This injustice is rooted in a lived experience of being denied certain rights such as a dignified living quarters and a just wage, but also denial of access to fair representation and, in the case of Marikana, access to dignity. Galtung's argument rests on his definition of violence being the difference between actual outcome and potential outcome. He goes further to explain that violence is contextual and time bound. Using an example of a child dying from tuberculosis, Galtung (1969:168) explains that this would never be understood as violent in the 18th century. Yet, when the same event occurs in a 21st century context where the prevention and cure of certain strands of tuberculosis is possible, the event of a child's death is considered violent. Therefore, when the potential to avoid personal or societal pain or bodily harm is present, but the outcome is not the realisation of this avoidance, violence is present (Galtung, 1969:169). Galtung takes this understanding of violence even further and distinguishes between violence directly caused by a person and violence indirectly

---

8   "Church" in this chapter refers to the ecclesial structures in South Africa. The term is therefore used in a theological way and not linked to specific denominations or congregations unless otherwise specified.

9   See J. Galtung. (1969). Violence, peace, and peace research. *Journal of Peace Research*, 6(3):167-191.

10   Important to note is that this chapter refers to 'structural violence'. Other writers such as Gutiérrez use the term 'institutional violence,' which is indistinguishable from the term structural violence.

caused by a person or persons as part of a structure[11] (1969:171). Here the face of violence is expressed not necessarily with instantaneous bodily effect on the human, but is absorbed into the structure which then is presented as, for example, the just distribution of resources. Most importantly, Galtung (1969:171) defines this form of structural violence as the power to influence the distribution of life-giving resources resulting in it being unequally distributed. Within this understanding, the situation at Marikana was violent before the first shots were fired. The power dynamic present at the Lonmin mine, which equated to a small number of privileged employees having the power[12] to exclude workers from certain resources to advance dignity, is in this argument considered structural violence. Noting the above, any form of reactionary violence from the workforce against this structural violence, is just that – reactionary and not primary violence, as one might believe.

Crucial to this understanding of violence is its unseen nature. This form of violence is largely invisible and therefore difficult to expose and report on. What is easier, is to expose and report on is physical violence, thus inadvertently labelling the victims of structural violence as the primary violent oppressors to which the 'structures' must react. One can therefore discern between a primary and silent lingering forms of violence perpetuated by institutions, cultures or people groups, which then is reacted upon with visible protest, which sometimes result in physical violence to people or infrastructure. This one might call reactionary violence. The argument by Galtung does not condone reactionary violence but merely tries to define more pervasive and silent forms of violence not experienced by the powerful or privileged in society. This reactionary violence seen in protests must therefore be understood as a means of communicating 'last resort' rather than destruction for the sake of destruction.

Theologically this takes form in the denial of a person being made in the *imago Dei* (Wolterstorff, 1983:78-79). A person or group of people on the receiving end of unseen (structural violence) might still live a physically healthy life, but with deep wounds carved in the image of God residing in them. Liberation theologian Gustavo Gutiérrez approaches the problem of structural violence from a theological perspective, stating that this form of violence is violent because it is violent to the truth of the Peace of the Lord (2014:64). This understanding frames structural violence not only as violence against the *imago Dei*, but against the body of Christ and its Mission of Peace. Walter Wink (1992:13-31) argues that the notion of 'redemptive violence' is a myth embodied in postmodern society, which underscores violence as an act of liberation or even national pride. Violence, therefore, not only chains the most vulnerable to suffering, but also chains the powerful to oppression. Albert Nolan

---

11    Gil Bailie (1995:55-57) notes an important trajectory in the conversation regarding violence. Bailie argues that (at least in the United States) there is a tendency for the political right to focus on physical violence whilst the political left tends to focus on structural violence. This contribution does not aim to underline structural violence above Physical Violence, but rather to help understand the causes of unseen violence precisely because it is unseen. Furthermore, this contribution in heavily influenced by Walter Wink's work which condemns any form of violence whether seen or unseen.

12    Rodney Tshaka (in Welker et al. 2017:197-200) does well to problematise colonial influence, power dynamics and black theology within the context of the events at Marikana.

(1988:83), writing on the South African context of violence in the 1980's, notes how a culture of violence has made violence a virtue, for example, being a soldier or part of the security force was culturally understood as honourable. This then also scars the *imago Dei* and forms humanity into something that believes violent dominion over humanity is not only needed, but virtuous. The notion of a sacred image of God is clear in the work of Beverly Mitchel (2009:27) writing on the experiences of Jews in Nazi concentration camps where victims were denied adequate latrines:

> The human body, originally designed by the Divine, to convey sublime beauty, was now the source of stench and visible filth that assaulted the senses.

The idea of a living being denied a right is for Galtung (1969:175) directly linked to dynamics of power. This unequal access and rights is upheld by notions of power, which are entrenched in society on a cultural, economic and political level (Roberts, 1987:85). Juliana Claassens (2016:103), in an important work of feminism and dignity, shows how poverty[13] can be understood as a direct effect of structural violence and embedded in power. Claassens (2016:103) is influenced by the work of Paul Farmer (in Saussy, 2010:344) who argues that the effects of structural violence on vulnerable peoples are that these people are more likely to suffer because of structural violence, and their suffering is more likely not to be heard. According to Claassens, "systematic reasons" can be given to why so many in this world suffer, and that reason is a systemic and violent system working only to advance the needs of a selected social group, i.e. those with access to power.

In the life of Mr Noki, this is underlined by the truth of his life narrative. His father had died before his birth as a result of Tuberculosis which he contracted at Impala Platinum Mine just 50km from Marikana (Davies, 2015). Both men, father and son, were on the receiving end of structural violence and might explain Mr Noki's drive to advocate for more just wages and living conditions. Access to dignified living escaped both father and son and their inability to access power, hampered access to dignity. This notion of power and its influence on human beings is what Beverly Mitchell (2009:11) understands as the root cause of violence to human dignity.

> The absence of empathetic imagination, the inability to see members of the "paraiah" group as being like one's self is the psychological foundation for participating in dehumanising a fellow human being.

Social science, as in the work of Galtung, have contributed enormously to the understanding and deconstruction of social power dynamics. The notion of power embedded in social structures for the benefit of a few is not new in theology. What follows is an attempt to relate some of the work done by the social sciences, to specific strands of theological thinking in order to frame a theological understanding of structural violence and the church's challenge to such dehumanising actions.

---

13    When using the notion of poverty to explain 'structural violence', I do not want to negate the other forms of structural violence experienced by, for example, woman or persons with LBGTIQA+ identities. These individuals are equally victims of structural violence and therefore the term should not be understood as only relevant to notions of financial exclusion.

Following the Accra sitting of the General Council of the World Alliance of Reformed Churches in 2004, work was done by a group of theologians to unpack the challenge of the Accra confession for church communities. In this work, titled *Dreaming of a Different World*, a statement is made to clarify the theological understanding of empire (Boesak, Weusmann and Amjad-Ali (eds.) 2010:2).

> We speak of empire, because we discern a coming together of economical, cultural, political and military power in our world today. This is constituted by a reality and a spirit of lordless domination, created by humankind. An all-encompassing global reality serving, protecting and defending the interests of powerful corporations, nations, elites and privileged people, while exploiting creation, imperiously excludes, enslaves, and even sacrifices humanity. It is a pervasive spirit of destructive self-interest, even greed – the worship of money, goods and possessions; the gospel of consumerism, proclaimed through powerful propaganda and religiously justified, believed and followed. It is the colonisation of consciousness, values and notions of human life by the imperial logic; a spirit lacking compassionate justice and showing contemptuous disregard for the gifts of creation and the household of life.

It is important that while the notion of empire[14] is contextual[15] and contested, it is a crucial part of the forming narrative of Christianity (Rieger, 2007:1). Although disputed, there are some historical marks that show the start of systematic economic, militarised and political domination of one society over others (Wink, 1992:39-46). I use the above definition, as it is a well-articulated definition considering some of the other work done in defining empire. A Western perspective can be found in the work of Brueggemann (2014:129-131), who places empire as a metanarrative in opposition to what he calls 'neighbourly love' (in the context of Marikana, neighbourly love might entail a company CEO seeking just living conditions for employees and not primarily the needs of shareholders). Brueggemann (2014:131) frames empire in three broad social power structures working for the amalgamation of aggressive predation. Brueggemann (2014:132) argues that empire is made of 1) an economy structured to resemble a pyramid which channels the flow of money to the centre of

---

14   The term 'empire' here is used as a theological term. It must be noted that within various contexts, other vocabularies have been used to give expression to the same notion. One example of this is in South Africa where Albert Nolan notes the use of the term 'system' (1988:69). Another term used is 'domination system' as presented by Walter Wink, specifically in his book *Engaging the Powers* (1992:13-107).

15   It is important to note Rieger's critique of contextual theology in which he argues that this form of theology aims to be relevant, but tends to "miss the gaps and silences in culture where the actual pain is" (2007:6-7). This chapter aims not to focus on the event of Marikana, but rather use this event as a lens to try and articulate deeper truths about church community. Moreover, this chapter tries to place focus not so much on the context of Marikana, but rather emphasise the social location of Mr. Noki and his colleagues to elicit critique of dominating power structures both within and outside of the ecclesial realm.

the empire;[16] 2) Political monologue that silences all voices from below by co-opting social structures like media in order to sell its metanarrative; and 3) the existence of a religious society one dimensional in nature with no critical edge. Similarly, Joerg Rieger (2007:271-278) traces his understanding of empire also to economic power, but also includes cultural and political power as a means to gain influence over the other.[17] Another example of framing empire is in the work done by Vuyani Vellem, who argues from the perspective of the Global South. Vellem contends that modernity is a project that stands in strong correlation with imperialism and colonialism and is therefore inherently anti-black. Vellem (2015) has a much more basic, but striking understanding of empire as an opaque life denying power that is built on racism and power which is a threat to life. Both arguments above as presented by Wink and Vellem are to some extent present in the above definition of empire as presented by the Accra working group. Thus, we can conclude that although there is no strict understanding of empire, we can ascertain that empire is a social power structure co-opting various structures in society such as economy, politics, race and even religion. The aim of empire is a structure existing solely for the gain of itself (and by implication the powerful elites in society) to the detriment of life and creation. The first to experience empire is therefore those exposed to its wrath, i.e. those without power. One can therefore argue that because of its aims of adding power to the powerful, empire creates structures that are violent to the dignity of those in which it preys.

Evaluating both the notions of structural violence and empire, I want to propose a framework for understanding the existence of the former as a direct result of the latter. Structural violence is the direct result of empire manifesting in different forms. Empire uses various forms of power to institutionalise the gathering of power. One of these powers are direct military power as used by colonial empires throughout the ages (Rieger, 2007:5). Most of these various power dynamics exist in significantly subtler and even invisible expressions of violence. One example of this kind of violence is, as Vellem notes, racism. It must be noted that these expressions of empire do not revolve around individuals or even modern forms of nation states. As Rieger (2007:1-2) points out, empire can no longer be equated to a nation state (although the United States might well qualify) but finds its roots in the vast global economy created by globalisation (Howard-Brook & Gwyther, 1999:236-242). This death-dealing reality is so saturated in the daily spheres of life that it is impossible for one human being to stop it (Rieger, 2007:2). This being said, care must be taken not to assign imperial power structures to an individual or a society; it must rather be understood as a tapestry of interwoven relationships existing between political, economic and societal structures. This tapestry is fuelled by the goal of gathering power and influence, to gather yet more power and influence.

---

16    For more on the economic side of empire and its connection with globalisation, see Sampie Terreblanche's (2009) chapter, 'The American Empire and the Entrenchment of Global Inequality,' in A.A. Boesak and L.D. Hansen (eds.) Globalisation Vol 1: The politics of empire, justice and the life of faith. African Sun Media, pp.31-47.

17    Rieger (2007:278) frames this in another way using the work of Meikens Wood (2005:47). Here Rieger explains the mechanism of empire is to economic hegemony without direct political domination.

Boesak (2009:59-63) argues that the time for avoiding imperial terminology is over, because of the rise of the American Empire and its military industrial complex. Boesak argues that the United States is becoming the first borderless nation with no limits to its political, economic and military power. This is a danger to life on earth, as for the first time in history, humanity has the ability to end all life as we know it. This is propelled, Boesak (2009:60) argues, by an unrestricted pursuit of consumerism, economic growth and political power, where human relations are secondary to economic prosperity. This seems evident in the example of Marikana where the profit motive seemed to silence the pleas of the workers. I want to contend that although the United States might be the head and heart of this new global empire, this empire is vastly more complex and far-reaching than most would admit. As mentioned above, the existence of multinational companies with more value than entire countries[18] are one of these reasons. For example, in 2012, the financial institution and culprit in the global financial meltdown of 2008, Fannie Mae's revenue was more than the GDP of Peru. Serious study with regards to multinationals and their connection to structural violence is necessary, however this is not the place to do so. What should be evident is that the notion of empire in a modern world is argued here to be more than just the one-headed dragon of the American Empire and more a seven-headed dragon made up of complex political, economic and military relations of which the church is a part[19] (Compier et al. 2007:1-3).

Because empire is a complex sociological phenomenon with vastly different contextual faces all revolving around the accumulation of power, another approach is necessary in order to understand and confront the structural violence in its wake. One such approach is to look at the consequences of structural violence through the eyes of those with the most intimate knowledge of its devastation.

Outlining his proposal of a theology of restitution, Tinyiko Maluleke (2008) argues for an approach to theology that always takes seriously the lived realities of those most vulnerable in society. He calls them the "un-people", those on who's back the powerful build the empire and who are in the first line of fire of structural violence. People who are unbanked, unemployed, unmedical-aided, unskilled, uneducated, unreached: the homeless, the illegal immigrants and the refugees or in the case of Marikana, the workers. Confronting the very nature of domesticated Western Christianity, he points to those around whom a theology of restitution (and by implication a theology of counter-empire) should be formed:

> These people stand out like 'ugly warts and blots' in the 'enchanting' and 'smooth' narrative landscapes of 'glorious' stories of 'progress', 'reconciliation' and 'development' not only in our country but in many countries as well. They are the squatter camp dwellers who spoil the 'beauty' of the Cape Town landscape and its serene suburbia by installing their dirty, toilet-less, electricity-less and road-less ugly dwellings. These people remain disenchanted and dissatisfied despite living in

---

18    For a list, see Vincent Trivett. (2011). '25 US Mega corporations: Where they rank if they were countries'. Business Insider (online). Viewed from: http://bit.ly/37OtTtU [Accessed 15 May 2018].

19    For a more in-depth discussion of the relationship between Christianity and Empire, see Rieger's work in Compier et al. (2007:1-13).

the 'greatest economic boom' South Africa has experienced ever. Discourses like they are the 'thankless' people who, primarily because of 'their own fault', have 'failed to grasp the opportunities' of our times are abundant. These are the people we would rather not see. Such people should hide themselves, or else we will find ways and means to keep them hidden[20] (Maluleke, 2008:689-690).

Nicholas Wolterstorff is another contemporary theologian who advocates for a theology from the perspective and placement of the marginalised in society. Wolterstorff's theory of justice starts not from the traditional philosophical frameworks, such as presented by John Rawls, who argues from an existential viewpoint (Botha & Forster, 2017). Rather, Wolterstorff (2013:7) starts with those on the under-side of history and power. Wolterstorff challenges the contemporary view of rights being bestowed onto people by law. Rather, he argues that humans are given fundamental rights at creation deriving from the reality of the *imago Dei*.

The resulting implications for a study on violence, at least from a theological perspective, are significant. From this perspective, humans cannot be given rights, but rather rights can only be acknowledged. Humanity and its structures therefore have no dominion over any human and attempts to do so, is violent to the very nature of what Christianity believes to be human. Wolterstorff (2013:22-32) therefore argues for understanding justice from the perspective of the marginalised[21] to promote rights for those who cannot 'earn' rights as easily as those with social, political or economic power.

The belief of 'earned rights' as bestowed upon people by institutions or law has had devastating effects on people and society, specifically when combined with empire. The imperial power of the German Reich in the 1930's sought to bestow more rights on Aryan Germans than on Jews. This is a clear example of how empire translates power into structural violence, which disavows the very nature of human identity to which only God has sovereignty over. Dietrich Bonhoeffer, contesting the German Reich's publication of the *Law for the Restoration of the Professional Service of April 7 1933*, is deeply critical about this perspective (Green & Dejonge (eds.) 2013:370-378).

What one can draw from this perspective is that if the existence of empire is such that power and its manifestations in political, economic and military forms, are gathered for the sake of power. A just society in contrast, is vastly different. Wolterstorff's notion of a just society is one reliant on the dignity of another and therefore beyond self-gain. Empire is to dominate the other as well as creation whereas a just society is to be in just relation to other. In a context of structural violence, what then might the contours be of ecclesial counter-narrative be when the church itself struggles with detachment from empire?

---

20  One might even add that we drive by these human beings with such detachment that we do not even acknowledge their existence.

21  Elsewhere Wolterstorff traces the theological orientation of justice starting from the marginalised back to the Old Testament. Here marginalised is understood as the most vulnerable in society and named as the 'widow, the fatherless and the stranger' (2013:69-78). It is of interest to note that Mgecineni Noki was an orphan. His father died at the Impala mine before his birth and his mother was murdered whilst he was a young boy ("Under the green blanket", 2013).

When discussing the *missio Dei* the reality to which the church is called, is the reality of the emerging Kingdom of God (Bosch, 2011:71-74). As discussed above, this notion of God's reign or Kingdom is inherently in contrast to the notion of empire.[22] Mission therefore chooses sides by standing against all powers that aim to dominate humanity which is not from God. Botha (2015:19-21) argues that this implies mission being done by a church standing in solidarity with 'the other' rather than those with access to power and privilege.[23] Emmanuel Katongole, however, argues that the church is also not immune to the pursuit of power. He argues that Christian social ethics in Africa demand that the church (which is also in pursuit of power, domination and invincibility) take a very different view of power in order to guard against the further entrenchment of violence (2011:131).

The church's public missional calling to combat empire is in its identity to harbour vulnerability and neighbourliness (Brueggemann, 2014:143-156). As was shown, the existence of both empire and structural violence is dependent on power. Arguing for a completely powerless society would be naïve and unwise; however, the form of power and, more importantly, its influence on relations, particularly toward the most vulnerable, are questioned. Brueggemann (2010:62-63) argues for a subversion of imperial power in the Old Testament by way of three theological concepts: steadfast love,[24] justice,[25] and righteousness. [26] These concepts, it seems, are inherently anti-empire because they aim to distribute access and power, rather than to hoard access and power. Furthermore, these active verbs ask of any citizen to pursue a life of meaning beyond the self and for the goodness of God's creation. Therefore, the notion of neighbourliness does not negate power, nor does it abandon power, but sees power merely as a tool to establish just harmony within community. One such power that the church has used in order to gain power rather than to establish a peaceable and harmonious world, is the mission of the church, which must be acknowledged. However, the obvious connection between colonialism and Christian mission[27] shows that even the Gospel can be manipulated to serve the

---

22    See also Brueggemann. (2010), *Journey to the Common Good*, pp.1-35

23    Botha's argument is based on the work of David Bosch in *Transforming Mission* (2011:463-464) where Bosch argues for mission being 'convivencia' or 'life together'.

24    The term *hesed* is defined by Brueggemann as "to stand in solidarity, to honor commitments, and to be reliable towards all partners" (2010:62).

25    The term *mišpat* is defined by Brueggemann as "distribution in order to make sure that all members of the community have access to resources and goods for the sake of a viable life of dignity" (2010:62).

26    The term *sedaqah* is defined by Brueggemann as "active intervention in social affairs, taking an initiative to intervene effectively in order to rehabilitate society and to correct every humanity-diminishing activity" (2010:63).

27    Willie Jennings illuminates the connections between Christianity, colonialism and power when he points out the effects of power on colonial Christians. Jennings points out that the notion of Christian hospitality (or neighbourliness) was inverted by colonial Christians when these missionaries claimed the identity of host within foreign land and then imprinting foreign cultural and ethical paradigms upon native peoples (2010:8-9).

interests of empire. Brueggemann (2014:15-23) traces phenomena of Judeo-Christian religion and its relationship with power seeking ideology right back to the prophetic traditions of the seventh century B.CE Brueggemann argues that during this time period, religious tradition was transported to the urban centres in order to serve the goals of elites.

The issue here is not to promote the *missio Dei*[28] as a direct action against empire therefore placing the sole mandate of the church likened to some resistance movement. The truth is far more confronting. The mission of the church is understood to partake in the *missio Dei*, therefore being in relational co-creation of the emerging resurrected reality in which we believe and confess. This places the focus on God and not empire, on God and not the acts of humans. Missional theology acting out of worship of God (and therefore not of human enterprise) it is argued, is much more dangerous to empire than reaction against structures of violence. This is not because church should react in times of crises, but because reaction implies waiting for human lives or creation to be violated. Whereas missional theology acting out of worship of Christ as *Kyrios* and not Empire, is inherently connected to the marginalised and rooted in justice[29] (Bosch, 2011:76). Mission, therefore, is not only an evangelising action where 'those out there' are helped out of oppression and converted. Mission is also a spiritually rooted counter-narrative exposing Empire and its structural violence by living an emergent reality of resurrection.[30] Yet as mentioned, this can only be done when in relational proximity to those experiencing structural violence.

Considering that the church operates within empire and that the church is susceptible to the lure of imperial theology (Rieger, 2007:5-9), careful reflection needs to be taken to ask how to faithfully, ethically and prophetically be part of the *missio Dei*. Some contours to guide the discernment of the church might be caught up in the following clues:

## a) Relational solidarity

Brueggemann (2014:142-150) gives some guidance to the identity of the ecclesial community within a world of imperial violence. One striking argument Brueggemann makes, where he argues that resistance to the meta-narrative of empire starts from 'below', resonates with the work of Joerg Rieger and Wolterstorff:

> This alternative narrative is characteristically told and enacted 'from below'. It arises form a bodily reality of suffering and exploitation. It is manifested in nonconformist conduct, and it is geared to specific human reality on the ground among those who have found the large universalising claims of the imperial narrative false, toxic and lethal (Brueggemann, 2014:143).

---

28  One must also acknowledge that the *missio Dei* itself was and still is coerced into forming part of the power of the church which aims to dominate. Thus, one might be wise to consider Katongole's statement above as a warning to the church not to claim its mission mandate so easily as has been the case in many Western churches.

29  Here one can add steadfast love and righteousness, as argued by Brueggemann above.

30  See also L. Newbigin. (2015). *The Open Secret: An Introduction to the Theology of Mission*. Revised Edition. Grand Rapids: Eerdmans, pp.92-95.

Brueggemann argues the essence of Christian action amid imperial reality and structural violence starts with those experiencing the violence of this empire. Crucially, Brueggemann notes the core of what Wolterstorff also argues to be the starting point of a just society: being in relational proximity to those suffering. This results in a challenge to the church first and foremost to be aware of the nature of structural violence, its mechanics and the names of those it violates. Mission against structural violence then implies experiencing the effects thereof in the lived realities of the black and poor bodies that are systemic targets of empire and having the lived reality inform missiology. Koopman (in Smith, Ackah, Reddie & Tshaka, 2015:217-223) argues for a theology of hybridity which aims to challenge certainties and essentialisms regarding human identity. This, according to Koopman, requires the acknowledgement of complexity and ambiguity within proximity, with the aim to acknowledge fragments of 'the other' in the self.

Furthermore, it is the relational solidarity with the marginalised that enables prophetic action. As Brueggemann notes, the prophetic counterculture of the seventh century was rooted in reality. By reality Brueggemann means the reality of the kingship of YHWH as well as the reality of the poor working class, and not the imperial reality as perpetuated by those seeking to increase their social, political or economic stance (even if on paper the wealthy belong to the Jewish same religion). This act of relational solidarity from the bottom up does not have the inherent intent of dismantling self-serving power structures. Relational solidarity is rather in itself the ethical confession of a Christianity which understands the *missio Dei* as an act, not because of the socio-political context of the world, but of who the triune God is. Newbigin (1995:59) notes a different but related angle on mission. He states that this mission that the church is called to participate in, not only convicts the world, but also brings the church to conversion. This conversion then, for the church, is one turning ever more toward God and then inherently toward the least of these.

Tracing this argument to the Marikana context, many are aware of the religious devotion of South Africa's political elite, which has been well documented. Yet if the abovementioned is to be taken seriously, critical questions must be asked of the spheres of politics, private business and church and what truly lies in the spirit of these communities. These questions in the context of Marikana are born therefore, not primarily out of moral ideology, but rather out of lived reality.

To summarise: the challenge put forth by the prophetic traditions throughout history is whether society has a relational posture living out of solidarity with the widow, the orphan and the foreigner. These challenges are at the core of a missiology which operates not to colonise the other for the expansion of Christian religion, but rather to saturate humanity with real reality as the peaceable Kingdom of God. This is important because relational solidarity with the most vulnerable exposes the eschatological truth to which the church holds.

## b) Confession

A second tool for guidance in the church as mission operating in a reality of empire and violence is the notion of Christian confession.

When writing about structural violence because of empire, care must be taken not to view the church as an entity functioning in a vacuum, not implicated by imperial theology.[31] This is evident in how theology and the church have been co-opted by empire to form colonial narratives with enormous structural violence, where the distinction between Mission and colonialism was, at various times, vague to say the least (Bosch, 2011:309-310). Some notion of this can be found in Hannah Arendt's (1963:298) idea of "the banality of evil". Care must be taken not to create a false equivalency between different historical events, yet Arendt's contribution shines a light on a deep human truth. It is mostly ordinary people who are coerced into evil structures that deny life even without being able to recognise their participation. Mission and the ecclesial calling to be sent has been, and still is, susceptible to the lure of imperial power. Rieger (1998:21) argues what he calls 'Liberal Theology' is a strand of theology which tends to promote and support the politically and socially powerful. This has made the church an entity also guilty of structural violence (Rieger, 2007:10-13). This is evident in the South African narrative where the state and church[32] promoted imperial theology for the benefit of a few white people (De Gruchy, 1982:69-85). Life of this facade of empire has the tendency to isolate persons from those who suffer precisely because of the effects of power.

Roberts (1989:90) correctly points out the difficulty in dismantling structural and cultural violence, as groups with power do not voluntarily relinquish their power, especially when they are co-opted. This is even more challenging when taking note of the realities of consumerism in the modern world. James Smith (2009:93-101) gives an insightful and challenging contribution by showing how consumerism is a sociological phenomenon creating a desire within humanity which is destructive to life. Therefore, care must be taken as phenomena such as consumerism are violent to this identity of the church and a means to be co-opted into imperial theology that can easily evolve into structural violence.

Theologically speaking, the church is understood as the entity with the calling of participation in the eschatological imminence of reality with a clear focus on the *missio Dei*, and not the *missio hominis*. Sociologically however, the church, just as any

---

31    Willie Jennings does well in his book *The Christian Imagination: Theology and the origins of race* to describe the complexities of white missionaries and their role in supporting Western white supremacy among Africans, specifically in South Africa. Jennings describes these events as having something to do with a lack of 'theological vision' thereby being caught up in the narrative of colonial powers (2010:199-132).

32    As argued, this imperial ethics of power is present in structures such as those present at the Marikana tragedy. Forster (2016:68-69) has even warned that some of South Africa's past experiences with church and state might be returning. He notes the current political complexities within the Methodist Church in Southern Africa and its relationship with the ANC particularly noting the actions of reverend Vukile Mehana as being very dangerous in the context of the powers linking church and state.

other structure, is very susceptible to the lure of the empire. This is especially true in a world where consumerism can easily be linked to imperial ideologies violent toward life in an unseen manner. Metzger (2007:45-48) does well to link the existence of consumerism to a narrative which divides and destroys human dignity by selling a message of worth as needing to be bestowed and not as inherent.

Therefore, confession firstly is of our complicacy in empire and structural violence, even if it is not active participation. The global reality of empire, as mentioned above, makes life without empire extremely difficult and the denial of this adds to structural violence.

Secondly, confession is also centred around Christ as Lord. The notion of a confessing church is picked up by Hauerwas and Williamson (1989:44-46) who makes a distinction between an 'activist church' (which is mentioned above as a church reacting to context) and a confessing church. Confessing church firstly calls people to conversion linking to the above understanding of confession of being culpable. Thirdly, to be a visible church, meaning being present in body and spirit, for example at the events of Marikana, which is also linked to notions of Public Theology. Hauerwas and Williamson (1989:46-47) notes that church "has no interest in withdrawing from the world, but it is also not surprised when its witness evokes hostility from the world." Confessing church, lastly, is a cross-centred society, which does not allow for compromise, but continually pursues to enact the peaceful victory of Christ over the powers of empire (1989:46-47).

The lesson from the confessing church is that confession of culpability is necessary in the journey of healing and liberation from partaking in structural violence. This is a journey and one which does not come without sacrifice. Yet in the process of healing and liberation, action which speaks of Christ as Lord is possible. One such example is given by Botha and Forster (2017) which speaks of the 'public confession' given by Beyers Naudé against a company very active in structural violence. Although we do not know what words were spoken, this can be interpreted as an embodied confession of Christ as Lord. Naudé in a prophetic act confronted Dutch Royal Shell and told the company to remove itself from South Africa as it was supporting state sponsored apartheid. Another example is Union Theological Seminary, which in 2014 divested all its endowment from fossil fuels therefore acting against structural violence impacting creation.[33] This divestment is a prophetic action in a reality of globalisation where return on investment trumps justice. The challenge to post-1994 church communities is not only socio-political in nature, but also personal. What is the stance of the church in a country which seems to be on its way to elect a president who himself was directly involved in the death of Mr. Noki? How do we deal with our own compliancy in empire? How do we account not only for our actions within a reality of empire, but our inactions in times of violence especially violence towards the widows, foreigners and the fatherless? These are questions of confession.

---

33   The full statement on the divestment can be found here: Time. (2014). 'Union becomes the world's first seminary to divest from fossil fuels,' June 10, Time [Online]. Viewed from http://time.com/2853203/union-fossil-fuels/ [Accessed 12 May 2018]

## Conclusion

The industrialised era has given rise to vast improvements in human life and complemented the pursuit of dignity for all life. Yet realities of structural violence remain present because of empire. The *missio Dei* challenges the church as custodians and participants in a new reality to act out of this missional calling to become aware and confront life denying structures which are violent to creation in unseen ways. This chapter argued that violence is a consequence of empire and that the church has an active mission to resist this reality. One way to do so is by acting out of relational solidarity with those such as Mr. Noki. This, however, can only be done with integrity when our own shortcomings are confessed together with the hopeful confession of Christ as true Lord.

In some way, it is telling to know that after the Marikana massacre, Mr. Noki's widow received a house with a flush toilet and a septic tank. Plans are also in place to build houses for each of the 34 mineworkers' families who died at Marikana. These houses are not built by Lonmin who are guilty of primary violence, nor by the police who pulled the triggers, nor by the church which has the mission toward protecting widows. It was built by a trust set up by the workers union AMCU (Sunday Times, 26 June 2017). Although Lonmin did not supply the housing, the events of Marikana did change circumstances for workers. Minimum salary per worker is as of 2017, R10 000 p.m., excluding benefits, and the company pledged to build adequate housing for workers over a period of time. A memorial park is also in progress to be built (Omarjee, 2017). This seemingly hopeful ending asks whether a just and peaceable dignified world can emerge without tragedy. It might seem that change comes more quickly through trauma than through human conversion towards justice. This, however, is as Wink (1992:13-17) puts it, "the myth of redemptive violence". The more confronting and challenging truth is that this change is precisely the eschatological mission to which the church is called.

# REFERENCES

Bailie, G. (1995). *Violence Unveiled: Humanity at a Crossroads*. New York. Crossroads Publishing Company.

Boesak, A. and Hansen, L. (eds.) (2009). *Globalisation: The Politics of Empire, Justice and the Life of Faith*. Stellenbosch: African Sun Media.

Boesak, A., Weusmann, J. and Amjad-Ali, C. (eds.). (2010.) *Dreaming of a Different World: Globalization and Justice for Humanity and the Earth the Challenge of the Accra Confession for the Churches*. [eBook] Germany: Evangelisch-reformatierte Kirche/ Uniting Reformed Church of South Africa. Viewed from http://bit.ly/2Pdylw9 [Accessed 10 May 2017].

Arendt, H. (1963). *Eichmann in Jerusalem: A Report on the Banality of Evil*. New York: Viking Press.

Bosch, D. J. (2011) *Transforming Mission: Paradigm Shifts in Theology of Mission*. New York: Orbis Books.

Botha, J. (2015). 'Presencing Hope: Exploring the Rubicon of Public Theology in the Dutch Reformed Church in Relation to the Framework Document on the Missional Nature and Calling of the Dutch Reformed Church.' Masters thesis (unpublished), Stellenbosch University.

Botha, J. and Forster, D. (2017). Justice and the Missional Framework Document of the Dutch Reformed Church. *Verbum et Ecclesia*, 38(1):1-9. https://doi.org/10.4102/ve.v38i1.1665

Brueggemann, W. (2010). *Journey to the Common Good*. Louisville: Westminster John Knox Press.

Brueggemann, W. (2014). *Reality, grief, hope: Three Urgent Prophetic Tasks*. Grand Rapids: Eerdmans.

City Press. (2013). *Under the green blanket* [Online]. Viewed from http://bit.ly/3alOlid [Accessed 15 January 2018].

Claassens, J.M. (2016). *Claiming Her Dignity: Female Resistance in the Old Testament*. Minnesota: Liturgical Press.

Compier, D., Kwok, P. and Rieger, J. (eds.) (2007). *Empire and the Christian tradition: New readings of classical theologians*. Minneapolis, MN: Fortress Press.

Davies, N. (2015). 'Marikana massacre: the untold story of the strike leader who died for workers' rights.' *The Guardian*. 19 May [Online], Viewed from http://bit.ly/2uhSGJg [Accessed 8 January 2018].

De Gruchy, J. (1982). *The church struggle in South Africa*. 2nd ed. Grand Rapids: Eerdmans.

Desai, R. (2014.) *Miners Shot Down* (86 min, colour) South Africa. Viewed from http://www.minersshotdown.co.za. [Accessed 12 May 2018]

Forster, D. 2016. A state church? A consideration of the Methodist Church of Southern Africa in the light of Dietrich Bonhoeffer's 'Theological position paper on state and church'. *STJ/Stellenbosch Theological Journal*, 2(1):61-88. https://doi.org/10.17570/stj.2016.v2n1.a04

Galtung, J. (1969.) Violence, Peace, and Peace Research. *Journal of Peace Research*, 6(3), 167-191. https://doi.org/10.1177/002234336900600301

Green, C.J. and Dejonge, M.P. (eds.). (2013). *The Bonhoeffer Reader*. Minneapolis: Fortress Press. https://doi.org/10.2307/j.ctt22nm627

Gutiérrez, G. (2014). *A Theology of Liberation*. (25th Edition). New York: Orbis.

Hauerwas, S. and Willimon, W.H. (1989). *Resident Aliens: Life in the Christian Colony*. Nashville: Abingdon Press.

Howard-Brook, W. and Gwyther, A. (1999). *Unveiling empire: Reading Revelation then and now*. New York: Orbis.

Jennings, W. (2010). *The Christian imagination: Theology and the Origins of Race*. New Haven: Yale University Press.

Katongole, E. (2011). *The Sacrifice of Africa: A Political Theology for Africa*. Grand Rapids: Eerdmans.

Maluleke, T.S. (2008). Justice in post-apartheid South Africa: Towards a Theology of Restitution. *Verbum et Ecclesia*, 29(3). https://doi.org/10.4102/ve.v29i3.36

Metzger (2007). *Consuming Jesus: Beyond Race and Class Divisions in a Consumer Church*. Grand Rapids: Eerdmans.

Mitchell, B.E. (2009). *Plantations and Death Camps Religion, Ideology, and Human Dignity*. Minneapolis: Fortress Press.

Newbigin, L. (2015). *The Open Secret: An Introduction to the Theology of Mission*. Revised Edition. Grand Rapids: Eerdmans.

News24. (2012). 'Marikana shooting "like Sharpeville"', News24, 17 August (Online), Viewed from http://bit.ly/2TdCXEQ [Accessed 13 May 2018]

Nolan, A. (1988). *God in South Africa*. Cape Town: David Philip.

Omarjee, L. (2017). 'Lonmin: Five years after Marikana,' Fin24, 16 August (Online). Viewed from http://bit.ly/2TglhqU [15 January 2018].

Rieger, J. (1998). *Remember the poor: The challenge to theology in the twenty-first century*. Bloomsbury T & T-Clark: London.

Rieger, J. (2007). *Christ & empire: From Paul to Colonial Times*. Minneapolis: Fortress Press.

Roberts, J.D. (1987). *Black Theology in Dialogue*. Philadelphia: Westminster Press.

Saussy, H. ed. (2010). *Partner to the Poor: A Paul Farmer Reader.* Los Angeles: University of California Press.

Smith, D.R., Ackah, W., Reddie, A.G. and Tshaka, R.S. (2015). *Contesting Post-Racialism: Conflicted Churches in the United States and South Africa.* Jackson: University Press of Mississippi. https://doi.org/10.14325/mississippi/9781628462005.001.0001

Smith, J. (2009). *Desiring the kingdom: Worship, Worldview and Cultural Formation.* Grand Rapids: Baker Academic.

Swart, M. and Rodny-Gumede, Y. 2015. Introduction: considering the aftermath of Marikana, *Social Dynamics,* 41(2):323-326. https://doi.org/10.1080/02533952.2015.1060684

Sunday Times. (2017). 'Amcu hands over house for family of "man in green blanket" killed at Marikana' (Online). Viewed from http://bit.ly/2VcKvsK [Accessed 15 January 2018].

Terreblanche, S. (2009). 'The American Empire and the Entrenchment of Global Inequality,' in A.A. Boesak and L.D. Hansen (eds.) Globalisation Vol 1: The politics of empire, justice and the life of faith. Stellenbosch: African Sun Media, pp.31-47.

Time. (2014). 'Union becomes the world's first seminary to divest from fossil fuels,' June 10 (Online). Time. Viewed from http://time.com/2853203/union-fossil-fuels/ [Accessed 12 May 2018]

Trivett, V. (2011). '25 US Mega corporations: Where they rank if they were countries'. Business Insider, 27 June (Online). Viewed from: http://bit.ly/37OtTtU [Accessed 15 May 2018].

Welker, M., Koopman, N. and Vorster, J.M. (2017). *Church and Civil Society: German and South African Perspectives.* Stellenbosch: African Sun Media. https://doi.org/10.18820/9781928355137

Wood, E.M. (2007). *Empire and Capital.* London: Verso.

Vellem, V. (2015). Black Theology of liberation: A theology of life in the context of Empire. *Verbum et Ecclesia,* 36(3):1-6. https://doi.org/10.4102/ve.v36i3.1470

Wink, W. (1998). *When the powers fall: Reconciliation in the Healing of the Nations.* Minneapolis: Fortress Press.

Wink, W. (1992). *Engaging the Powers: Discernment and Resistance in a World of Domination.* Minneapolis: Fortress Press.

Wolterstorff, N.P. (1983). *Until Justice & Peace Embrace.* Grand Rapids: Eerdmans.

Wolterstorff, N.P. (2011). *Justice in Love.* Grand Rapids: Eerdmans.

Wolterstorff, N.P. (2013). *Journey Towards Justice: Personal Encounters in the Global South.* Grand Rapids: Baker Academic.

## In Search of a Contextual Pastoral Approach[1]

*C.H. Thesnaar*[2]

## INTRODUCTION

In general, the Truth and Reconciliation Commission (TRC) was a salient process with a firm mandate to set a process in place to face and deal with the apartheid past of South Africa. However, the lack of implementing the TRCs recommendations[3] as well as the reluctance of government, civil society and the religious[4] groupings to lobby, network and facilitate this commitment is evident. As time elapsed since the onset of transition in South Africa to the current situation new insight has come to the fore regarding how the transition was managed and the impact of the TRC on current and future generations. Subsequently, there has been an escalation of resistance to transformation and justice on many levels of our society. What is also evident is that the intensity of the resistance, more often violent than not, has increased. In addition, the language has shifted from a focus on reconciliation to having a strong emphasis on justice, reparation and restitution. Meanwhile, in South Africa, the majority of people are disillusioned, as the promises made to them during the transitional process as well as subsequent election campaigns by the government has not materialised. Political freedom is largely in place but economic justice is still an ever-increasing challenge. The resultant disillusionment and desperation is causing more and more people from different sectors of society to turn to violence in their search for justice, as they literally have nothing to lose.

According to the power transition theory, as indicated by Kegley and Wittkopf (1997), hegemonic periods, in general, last approximately sixty to ninety years, and conflicts, which result in a period stabilisation of power distribution last

---

1   The research and writing of this contribution was made possible by the fellowship I received from the Protestant Theological University (PThU) in Amsterdam, Netherlands, from 7 April to 7 June 2017.

2   Christo Thesnaar is currently a professor of Practical Theology at the Department of Practical Theology and Missiology at Stellenbosch University, South Africa. He is also Head of the Unit for Reconciliation and Justice, Beyers Naudé Centre for Public Theology, Stellenbosch University.

3   See the Truth and Reconciliation Commission. (1998). *Truth and Reconciliation Commission of South Africa Report.* Volume 6. Cape Town: Juta and Co Ltd, p.589.

4   Cf. C.H. Thesnaar. (2015). 'Report on the re-enactment of the Truth and Reconciliation Commission's faith hearing consultation'. Unpublished report. Stellenbosch University, Stellenbosch, 8–9 October 2014.

approximately 20 years.[5] War-weariness and the tendency (although this was broken in the first half of the twentieth century) for nations not to engage themselves in another conflict after being involved in a traumatic transition are reasons for this lack of engagement.[6] This argument by Kegley and Wittkopf highlights an aspect of temporarily that has to do with the period of time that has elapsed since the conflict ended, and in particular, what has developed, changed and transformed within the timeframe of 20 to 25 years after the transition. Although this contribution will only focus on South Africa, there are numerous examples of reports from other countries in relation to the significant timeframe of 20 to 25 years after the culmination of their conflict, the beginning of the transition process to a new democracy, and the period following the transition. However, for brevity's sake, I will only mention the following examples of reports: The 20 year anniversary of the Dayton Peace Agreement that ended the civil war in Bosnia and Herzegovina published in 2015.[7] The study by Treisman (2009) on the dramatic changes in the mid-1980s in Central Eastern Europe, and Russia called "20 years of political transition."[8] The IMF published a report regarding the transitions in Eastern Europe 25 years later.[9] The Red House also started a series of debates that reflected on the previous 25 years of Bulgarian development post-1989 under the theme: "25 years after 1989: What has happened to the idea of social equality?"[10] There were also some reports that looked at the first 20 years of democracy in South Africa.[11] The Conversation Africa's politics and society editor, Thabo Leshilo asked academics to review how well Namibia and Zimbabwe, the other two most recently independent countries on the continent, had performed 22 years into their independence journey.[12]

Based on the above-mentioned transition theory and examples, it is clear that 20 to 25 years following a transition, countries go through a critical time, as serious questions are often raised regarding transformation and change. It is particularly

---

5    Cf. Kegley, C.W and Wittkopf, E.R. (1943/1997). *World politics: Trend and transformation* (6th ed). New York: St. Martin's Press.

6    See the definition of "war-weariness". (n.d.) In *Wikipedia: The Free Encyclopedia* [Online]. Viewed from https://en.m.wikipedia.org/wiki/War-wearines. [Accessed: 16 February 2017]

7    Cf. Srebrenica Massacre, After 20 Years, Still Casts a Long Shadow in Bosnia https://nyti.ms/2HRKwud [Accessed: 18 February 2017]
     Also see: Srebrenica Massacre. (2015). After 20 Years, Still Casts a Long Shadow in Bosnia [Online]. Viewed from http://bit.ly/2TAjfSy [Accessed 15 February 2017].

8    Treisman, D. (2009). 20 years of transition in rap Eastern Europe and the Soviet Union [Online]. Viewed from http://bit.ly/38S3Qne [Accessed 15 February 2017]

9    Cf. Roaf, J., Atoyan, R., Joshi, B., Krogulski, K. and an IMF Staff Team. (2014). 25 Years of Transition Post-Communist Europe and the IMF Regional Economic Issues [Online]. Viewed from http://bit.ly/2SSrb2i [Accessed 16 February 2017].

10   Cf. Red House debate. (2014). 25 years after 1989. What has happened to the idea of social equality? [Online]. Viewed from http://bit.ly/2vWoq7g [Accessed 16 February 2017].

11   Cf. Newman, K.S. and De Lannoy, A. (2014), *After Freedom: The Rise of the Post-Apartheid Generation in Democratic South Africa.* Boston: Beacon Press; The twenty-year review 1994 – 2014. Document of the office of the Precedency [Online]. Viewed from http://bit.ly/39k94IA [Accessed: 13 January 2018].

12   Cf. T. Leshilo. (2016). What Africa's most newly independent states did with 22 years of freedom. In The Conversation. (Online). Viewed from http://bit.ly/2SQOQAm [Accessed: 13 January 2018]

the next generation who raises these questions as they engage with existential issues on a daily basis. In this regard, the time that has elapsed since the transition to the current reality within South Africa epitomises the fact that theologians will need to think carefully about the way they currently speak and write about the concepts of "reconciliation" and "healing," as the whole playing field has changed. There is a need for theologians to become less arrogant in this regard. For this reason, this chapter seeks to explore whether the theory of contextual pastoral care based on the "dialogical perspective" of Boszormenyi-Nagy,[13] and further developed theologically by the Dutch scholars Hanneke Meulink-Korf and Aat van Rhijn, if integrated within the African cultural context, will help break through the frozen conflict. It will begin with a brief discussion of the term "frozen conflict" and argue for a broader understanding of the term. Following this, this chapter will reflect further on relevant concepts from the theory of contextual pastoral care. Lastly, the chapter will conclude with a few final remarks.

## WHAT DEFINES FROZEN CONFLICT?

Clancy and Nagle (2009:14), referring to the work of Nodia (2004), define "frozen conflicts" as "those in which violent ethno-political conflict over secession has led to the establishment of a *de facto* regime that is recognised by neither the international community nor the rump state from which the secession occurred."[14] This term is commonly used for post-Soviet conflicts and other perennial territorial disputes, as well as conflicts in the Balkans, Cyprus, and on the Korean peninsula, to name a few. As Peet (2008:1) explains, these conflicts are "frozen" because "a string of nasty small wars have been settled not through peace deals but simply by freezing each side's positions."[15]

As the violence surrounding the secession has largely abated, the conflict remains "frozen". Although the armed conflict has been terminated, there are, in most cases, no official peace treaties in place, nor any other political framework with the goal to resolve the conflict between the opposing parties. Nor is there any process in

13  Cf. Boszormenyi-Nagy, I. and Framo, J. (eds.) (1985). Intensive family therapy: *Theoretical and practical aspects.* New York: Brunner/Mazel; Boszormenyi-Nagy, I. and Spark, G. (1984). *Invisible loyalties: Reciprocity in intergenerational family therapy.* New York: Brunner/Mazel; Boszormenyi-Nagy, I. and Krasner, B. (1986). *Between give and take: A clinical guide to contextual therapy.* New York: Brunner/Mazel; Boszormenyi-Nagy, I. (1987). *Foundations of contextual therapy: Collected papers of Ivan Boszormenyi-Nagy, MD.* New York: Brunner/Mazel; Boszormenyi-Nagy, I., Grunebaum, J. and Ulrich, D. (1991). 'Contextual Therapy', in Gurman, A. and Kniskern, D. (eds.) *Handbook of Family Therapy, Vol 2.* New York: Brunner/Mazel; Krasner, B.R. and Joyce, A.J. (1995). *Truth, Trust, and Relationships: Healing Interventions in Contextual Therapy.* New York: Brunner & Mazel.

14  Cf. Clancy, M.A.C. and Nagle, J. (2009). 'Frozen Conflicts, Minority Self-Governance, Asymmetrical Autonomies – In search of a framework for conflict management and conflict resolution'. Paper presented at the Sixth Asia-Europe Roundtable, University of Ulster, Republic of Ireland, 10-12 June [Online]. Viewed from www.incore.ulster.ac.uk [Accessed 17 January 2017].

15  Cf. Peet, J. (2008). 'Frozen conflicts: Europe's unfinished business'. The Economist. [Online]. Viewed from http://www.economist.com/node/12494503 [Accessed 13 September 2015].

place to seek reconciliation. Therefore, the threat of conflict is always imminent and can erupt unpredictably at any moment. Traumatic contexts such as these create an insecure and unstable environment for citizens.

In an attempt to broaden the understanding of the term "frozen conflict," it is necessary to reflect briefly on the Northern Irish situation. The armed conflict in Northern Ireland largely ended in 1998 with the signing of the Good Friday Agreement, also known as the Belfast Agreement.[16] To this day, this agreement has largely succeeded in keeping the two opposing sides separate in their own neighbourhoods, although they engage well in public spaces. Almost 20 years later, Northern Ireland continues to remain in a situation that could be described as a "frozen conflict." Despite several lengthy public consultations on how to deal with the past, no systematic, state-supported process has been implemented. In this regard, Clancy and Nagle (2009:14) argue that there is always an interplay between endogenous and exogenous factors that obviates conflict transformation and/or conflict resolution, and this is what separates "frozen conflicts" from other minority disputes. In their explanation they refer to the conflict in Northern Ireland and indicate that this conflict "could be considered to be 'frozen' as its integrity has not been altered; Nationalists and Unionists retain their discordant political preferences. However, the way in which this conflict manifests itself endogenously (through power-sharing, as opposed to violence), and the relationships between the key external actors to the conflict (i.e. the UK and Irish governments) have been transformed" (Clancy & Nagle, 2009:14).

To further broaden and deepen the understanding of frozen conflict, van der Merwe and Gobodo-Madikizela (2007:26) indicate that when people continue to be overwhelmed by a traumatic experience, there is a silence of the senses, which they describe as a state of being frozen.[17] To them, silence after an ongoing traumatic experience is more than the lack of words; it actually shows that victims of trauma have a lack of understanding of what has happened to them. They argue that trauma overwhelms the psyche, as it contains no reference point in terms of one's former experiences (van der Merwe & Gobodo-Madikizela, 2007:26). Silence and a lack of understanding of what has happened to an individual, family, community, or even a nation, normally manifests in denial, as there are limited safe spaces where people can voice there trauma.

Where peace and reconciliation processes have not managed to constructively address the past, the opposing sides in the conflict will continue to be haunted by it and their destructive understanding will then be transmitted to subsequent generations.[18] Unhealed traumas from the past have the potential to capture the future and, in the extreme, destroy the next generation(s) by reinforcing the identity of particular ethnic, racial, or religious groups. The implication of unhealed trauma is that it creates narratives that lead to destructive memory. Destructive memory is

---

16   Democratic Progress Institute. (2013). The Good Friday Agreement: An Overview [Online]. Viewed from http://bit.ly/2v9WRHz [Accessed 19 February 2017].

17   van der Merwe, C.N. and Gobodo-Madikizela, P. (2007). *Narrating our Healing. Perspectives on Working through Trauma.* Newcastle: Cambridge Scholars Publishing.

18   Cf. van der Merwe and Gobodo-Madikizela, (2007). *Narrating our healing,* p.33

in turn kept alive as it is transmitted to the next generation by the different actors of the conflict generation. In this way, the conflict becomes "frozen" with the potential to feed into trans-generational trauma that can erupt at any moment. The opposing sides in the colonial and apartheid conflict within South Africa is an example of trans-generational trauma that was passed on from the one generation to the next, following particular frozen conflicts in the past.

Based on this argument, the understanding of frozen conflict should not only be limited to the traditional definition of frozen conflict that is based on ending the conflict at all cost without any process of peace or reconciliation in place. The current violence, frustration, anger, and intolerance that we find in our society reemphasises that frozen conflict should always be understood in a temporal way, as it could erupt at any moment if the endogenous factors have not managed to transform (on all levels—politically, socially, economically and spiritually) and reconcile the nation. What is significant from this scenario is that conflict can be "frozen" for a length of time even after a successful transition that was followed by specific provisions, such as the TRC process, to mention but one example. In relation to the argument by Clancy and Nagle (2009:14) who emphasise exogenous factors, as well as the argument by Van der Merwe and Gobodo-Madikizela (2007), I am of the opinion that South Africa still finds itself in a "frozen conflict" situation. This is over and above the fact that it went through endogenous transformation (political change and new constitution) and a healing process (facilitated by the TRC) more than 20 years ago. Given the discussion above, it is probably better to use the term "intergenerational frozen conflict."

## CONTEXTUAL PASTORAL CARE APPROACH

Pragmatically, and based on the argument thus far, it is clear that there is not one specific prescribed method or strategy that will break through intergenerational frozen conflict in today's societies. For a contextual pastoral care approach to make a contribution towards this goal it will need to be trans-disciplinary, hermeneutical and intercultural with a key focus on the African cultural context. As Mkhize (2016:1) indicates, one cannot pretend that the notion of "African" is in any sense imaginable, monolithic, and has not been influenced by what has happened over time, with massive forces at work such as slavery, colonialism and socio-political systems such as imperialism, capitalism, Christianity, western education and apartheid.[19] Therefore, any approach on the African continent cannot afford not to take the vast indigenous knowledge systems of Africa seriously.

After the conclusion of a workshop[20] on contextual pastoral theory, it became clear that its emphasis of the contextual pastoral approach on relations and how we as

---

19  See Mkhize, V.V.O. (2016). 'Umsamo – The quest for an African-centred approach in pastoral care. Learning from the African traditions, culture, values, ancestral wisdom and African healing'. Paper presented at the trans-disciplinary workshop on contextual pastoral care in Africa, Stellenbosch University, Stellenbosch, 19 July.

20  A three-day workshop was held to discuss the relevance of contextual pastoral care for the African context with African scholars at the Faculty of theology at the Stellenbosch University from

human beings are connected to one another and previous generations resonates well with popular African cosmology. Mkhize (2016:8) states that contextual theory "resonates pretty well with how in our culture, as is the case in so many African cultures now in Southern Africa, with the idea of living a life that is interlinked to that of others through various chains of loyalties based on direct and indirect kinships." In this regard, Africans are not only connected to one another but they are also multi-connected to their ancestors. Mkhize (2016:9) concludes: "There is a plethora of examples I could give, to show that what Boszormenyi-Nagy are articulating, shares so much with the philosophical ethos espoused at the Umsamo Institute. Now that we have found one another, the opportunities before us, are enormous. At the heart of it is the possibility of investing research resources on the theorisation of Umsamo, which I have begun doing. Also, as a way of indigenising pastoral care, the Umsamo African Institute has laid a foundation, and what remains, is for kindred minds and souls to come together and, as we say in my language, slaughter the beast."[21] The journey to develop an approach that continuously represents the African context is of the utmost importance for a contextual pastoral care approach to be able to contribute to breaking through the intergenerational frozen conflict.

Another pertinent question is whether it is possible and appropriate to apply a therapeutic approach developed for a family context within a collective socio-political environment. This is indeed a very relevant question because in a therapeutic context, the focus is more on individuals and small groups, whereas in a socio-political context the focus is more on groups and communities, and therefore, the collective. Van den Berg-Seiffert (2015:165) indicates that Boszormenyi-Nagy himself refers to loyalties within families and the broader society, as well as within religious groups in the same manner.[22] Boszormenyi-Nagy (2000:167) grapples with the impact of criminality and political terrorism on a society, as it always has a devastating impact on innocent victims.[23] However, in no uncertain way, he states that there can be no justification, excuse or acceptance for the suppression of persecuted and innocent people (Boszormenyi-Nagy, 2000:171). With this in mind, he then focuses on the collective and socio-political context and realises that people become terrorists. For example, they develop destructive behaviours because there are limited spaces of trust where people with different loyalties can voice themselves. He bemoans that there are no peaceful channels through which exposed and suppressed groups, in terms of self-determination, are able to present their claims. There is no platform where ethnic, religious and radical groups can discuss their claims in a decent and legitimate way (Boszormenyi-Nagy, 2000:169). He correctly states that throughout history it was always clear that the supporters of governments continually rejected and distrusted groups that had a different loyalty obligation (Boszormenyi-Nagy, 2000:170).

11-13 October 2016.

21   The Umsamo Institute hosts a centre for contextual family healing and therapy. For more information on the work done by the Umsamo Institute, please refer to their website: http://umsamo.org.za/wpp/

22   van den Berg-Seiffert, C.C.L.H. (2015): "Ik sta erbuiten – maar ik sta wel te kijken" ("I'm on the outside - but I'm watching"). Zoetemeer: boekencentrum.

23   See Boszormenyi-Nagy, I. (2000). *Grondbeginselen van de contextuele benadering.* (Fundamentals of the contextual approach). Haarlem: De Toorts.

Because there is no safe space for groups to communicate their claims, they have no choice but to resort to violence or conceal their loyalty. In this regard, we do not realise the impact of suppressed loyalty obligations on people's behaviour (Boszormenyi-Nagy, 2000:172). It is only then, when we are able to focus on distinguishing between real differences and mutual conflicting interests in a communal way that we can find a way to construct alternatives to replace the notion of endless hatred that acts as a chain reaction (Boszormenyi-Nagy, 2000:172). The key issue at stake here is the conflict created in societies, caused by exclusion because the loyalty of the other is different from that of those in power. As indicated earlier, the critical problem is that there is a lack of understanding and an inability to deal with the conflict in a constructive and life-giving way.

Rein Brouwer (2004:290) has done research within faith communities to explore whether the contextual pastoral approach is applicable in this context.[24] His research indicates that conflict is more dramatic in local faith communities, and that there is an inability to address these conflicts in a unified way. Furthermore, he is of the opinion that these conflicts bear witness to destructive justice, and assumes that these faith communities are in dire need of trust and acknowledgement (Brouwer, 2004:291). In this regard, he has, to my mind, illustrated that this approach is indeed applicable to the broader religious community.

Based on the discussion thus far, I want to highlight a few key concepts in the contextual pastoral care approach in relation to the theme of this chapter. The term "context" in the theory of the contextual pastoral care approach is not merely situational. Instead, the focus is to understand a person within the network of relationships (context) they find themselves in. This is particularly relevant for intergenerational relations. Nobody exists alone by him/herself. As humans, we are always connected to a significant "other," and in Africa, to even more significant "others." As the family is seen as the first relational network people are part of, the contextual pastoral care approach works with the assumption that every person has a father and mother no matter whether they can take care of the person or not. Beginning early in one's life, there is a movement of, what the contextual pastoral care approach calls, ethics (a deep value for justice and fairness) within relationships.[25] This entails mutual giving and receiving between parents and children, grandparents and children, and between significant others and children, and given the context of South Africa, between the perpetrators and victims of colonialism, and more recently, the apartheid policy (intergenerational). Thus, where these relationships are balanced and trustworthy it

---

24  Brouwer, R. (2004). 'Leiderschap in systemisch-contextueel perspectief. Friedman en Nagy over leiderschap (Leadership in systemic-contextual perspective. Friedman and Nagy on leadership)', in van Ark, J. and de Roest, H.P. (eds.) *De weg van de groep. Leidinggeven in gemeente en parochie* (The way of the group. Leadership in the congregation and parish). Zoetermeer: Meinema, 283-291.

25  Boszormenyi-Nagy and Krasner, *Between give and take, p.58 and p.147.* Also see Boszormenyi-Nagy and Krasner's (1986:420) description of the notion of ethics: "The notion of ethics is rooted in the ontology of the fundamental nature of living creatures, i.e. life is received from forbears and conveyed to posterity. Life is a chain of interlocking consequences linked to the interdependence of the parent and child generations. In human beings, relational ethics require people to assume responsibility for consequences. But consequence per se constitutes unavoidable, existential reality".

will influence the manner in which a person is able to give to the "other" (Meulink-Korf & van Rijn, 2016:14).[26] This is also why the contextual theory of Boszormenyi-Nagy referred to it as a trust-based theory (Meulink-Korf & van Rijn, 2016:7). The aim of this approach endeavours to restore trust in human relations, damaged by hurt and separation caused by conflict.[27] South Africans affected by the past need to seek ways to deal with the past trauma and restore the balance[28] (trust) in relations.

In order to transform and reverse a conflict within a relationship, Boszormenyi-Nagy and Krasner's (1986:176) relational ethic emphasises the core aspects of trustworthiness and justice. This is based on the assumption that all involved in the relationship have agreed to take responsibility to break the shackles of the intergenerational frozen conflict and to engage in a process of reconciliation and transformation. Trustworthiness is not necessarily present in a relationship; therefore, from the outset, those involved in the relationship should engage in a process that develops a balance between give and take. In this process, a person develops trust through giving and receiving, and by adhering to this principle a person is able to acknowledge the trustworthiness of the other. That is why Boszormenyi-Nagy and Krasner (1986:422) defines trustworthiness as follows: "Trustworthiness accrues on the side of the reliable, responsible, duly considerate partner in a relationship and is a characteristic of realistic, deserved trust" and "from an ethical perspective, trustworthiness is always earned over the long-term by balancing the consequences of give and take between two relatively reliable partners." In this sense, then, those on all sides of the conflict are born within a context in which at times they are justified in receiving and at other times they are obliged to give. Thus, to develop trustworthiness in a relationship is an on-going process that demands commitment to that relationship.

In this approach, Boszormenyi-Nagy and Krasner (1986:420) uses the concept of "rejunction" to assist both victims and perpetrators to engage in a process of connecting with and restoring relations with those whom they are in conflict. The intention of this concept is to enter into responsible dialogue[29] with the other, so that each person will experience the dialogue as beneficial to themselves and the other. According to Boszormenyi-Nagy and Krasner (1986:420), rejunction characterises relationships in which family members choose to earn entitlement through self-

---

26  Meulink-Korf, H. and van Rijn. A. (2016). *The unexpected third Contextual pastoral, counselling and ministry: An introduction and reflection* (transl. Noeme Visser) Wellington: Christian Literature Fund Publishers.

27  According to Boszormenyi-Nagy and Krasner (1986:413), "Some conflicts of interests, needs and entitlements are inevitable between relating partners and are to be viewed as natural rather than pathological. Other interpersonal conflicts of interests are avoidable, however, and attempts to resolve all interpersonal conflicts of interests are unrealistic. A realistic therapeutic attitude is linked to working on inevitable conflicts (e.g. a capacity to tolerate real attitudinal differences-political, religious, social-that do not require joint decision-making. In any case, an effort to work on a foundation of underlying trust resources is always a more realistic therapeutic goal than designing an attack on symptoms."

28  According to Boszormenyi-Nagy and Krasner (1986:420), the ultimate destination of people is to search for a balance.

29  Boszormenyi-Nagy and Krasner, *Between give and take*, p.415.

validation. As indicated earlier, the contextual pastoral care approach puts an emphasis on the ethical dimension and seeks to restore the balance within relations. This dimension should, however, not be confused with morals or dogma that is manipulated and forced from the outside (for example, a religious moral forced upon others). Rather, it should be understood as intrinsic justice that is determined by a dynamic balance of give and take within important existential relationships. The focus of the engagement between those in conflict is not merely for the sake of dialogue. Instead, the intention should be to take responsibility to seek transformative justice in the balance between give and take in order to restore existential relations.[30]

Therapeutically, Boszormenyi-Nagy and Krasner (1986:418) indicate that the way to go about restoring the relationship is to listen carefully to the victim(s) and the perpetrator, and acknowledge their suffering and pain. In order to listen and assist in building a bridge within the intergenerational frozen conflict, it is particularly important to note that everyone who is part of this network of relationships is a subject, and is given the opportunity to speak. According to Botha (2014:41), the language required in this process is connecting language. This relational language does not reject or break down, but expresses the courage to touch fragile and painful situations. The aim is not just to confirm the negative, but also to look for positives aspects in the relationship and to name these too. Botha (2014:41)[31] indicates that Boszormenyi-Nagy looks for a gap that will open up the future. Language that connects thus strives to enable those involved to see each other — to acknowledge each other's humanity and even their fragility and what, in spite of this, they have been able to give and receive from each other. Mkize (2016:1) quotes Ngugi wa Thiong' o's words on the primacy of language and culture: "Language is what most helps in the movement of a community from *the state of being in itself to state of being for itself* and this self-awareness is what gives the community its spiritual strength to keep on reproducing its being as it continually renews itself in culture, in its power relations, and in its negotiations with its entire environment. It is its culture which enables a community to imagine and re-imagine itself in history" (italics in original).

Boszormenyi-Nagy and Krasner (1986:418) calls the method that will assist caregivers to listen and not to take sides "multidirected partiality," and defines it as follows: "Multidirected partiality is contextual therapy's chief therapeutic attitude and method... Methodologically, multidirected partiality takes the form of sequential siding with (and eventually *against*) member after family member. The therapist tries to emphasise with and credit everyone on a basis that actually merits crediting." According to Botha (2014:39), Boszormenyi-Nagy's aim is that in

---

30   Meulink-Korf, J.N. (2009). Verbindend waarnemen en werken: kerkelijke conflicten in contextueel perspectief. (Connecting observing and working: Ecclesiastical conflicts in a contextual perspective). *Tijdschrift Conflicthantering*, 4(6):12-17.

31   Botha, T.J. (2014). 'Ons sal mekaar nie los nie' 'n Kwalitatiewe ondersoek na die aard van die onderlinge verbondenheid van leraars binne die Verenigende Ring van Stellenbosch'. ('We will not leave each other' A qualitative inquiry into the nature of the interdependence of pastors within the Uniting Circuit of Stellenbosch'.) Unpublished master's thesis. Stellenbosch University [Online]. Viewed from *https://scholar.sun.ac.za/bitstream/handle/.../botha_ons_2014.pdf?* [Accessed 18 February 2017].

therapy there should always be an encounter together with dialogue: this is what "trust based therapy" requires for healing to take place. Multidirected partiality is very helpful when we create platforms for people from different loyalties to meet in dialogue, face the conflict, and work towards breaking the intergenerational frozen conflict. Multidirected partiality entails that we pay equal attention to the pain (destructive justice) as to the longing for trust, and through acknowledgement of merits in a space where the conflicting parties can talk and develop to regain their trust. Forgiveness and reconciliation that is forced by outsiders, or by the victim or perpetrator, or is presented in a simplistic way, does not restore the trust that is required to build a bridge between those in conflict in the relationship.

It is always important to understand that where conflict within a relation is a reality there is always an invisible ledger, kept intact by those within the conflict. According to Boszormenyi-Nagy and Krasner (1986:417), "The ledger is a calculus concerned with the balance between the accumulating merits and debts of the two sides of any relationship. Just how much entitlement or indebtedness each party has at a given time depends on the fairness of give-and-take that exists between them." In this sense, numerous constructive and destructive narratives based on the relations human beings have with one another compile the ledger. We, as human beings, then communicate these narratives from one generation to the next. Botha (2014:32) indicates that Boszormenyi-Nagy describes a number of factors (excluding race and gender) that can either contribute to the transmission of constructive change and transformation to the next generation or can have a destructive effect that will limit the next generation and lead to stagnation. These factors are:

- Biological and blood relationships;
- A divided family history, which brings both acquired assets and liabilities from a previous generation;
- Traditions, faith traditions, norms and values, beliefs around justice, the arrangements and rules of the family system, and roles, etc., that have been passed down from previous generations; and
- The conservation and continuation of life (procreation).

Although these factors focus on destructive family narratives that are transferred from one generation to the next, they are equally applicable to the transference of constructive and destructive historical, social and religious narratives passed down to subsequent generations. Destructive narratives normally have deep-seated roots in the history of a generation. In his own life and in working with families, Boszormenyi-Nagy discovered that loyalty is an irrevocable bond between family members.[32] Meulink-Korf and van Rijn (2016:79) quotes Boszormenyi-Nagy to emphasise the importance of the irrevocability of relations: "My father will always remain my father, even though he is buried thousands of miles from here."[33] In essence, one should not underestimate the deep-rooted sense of family and community loyalty, which plays a key role in the transference of narratives from the one generation to the next. To me, deep-rooted loyalty is particularly relevant to the African context.

32  Boszormenyi-Nagy and Krasner, *Between give and take*, p.418.
33  Here refers to his country of birth – Hungary.

In order to understand the depth of this transference it is not possible to limit loyalty to just a psychological memory, an emotional feeling, or knowledge we have of the past. It entails much more than a particular cause and effect understanding of the past. It is about life-giving and our ability to create meaning. Its frame of reference is trust, merit, commitment and action, rather than the "psychological" functions of "feeling" and "knowing." In this sense, loyalty is always present (sometimes more visible and sometimes not) in trust and trustworthiness, in merits and credits, in actions that help us to understand what is fair and what is not. It is clear from the theory that loyalty has the ability to develop quality relationships. To explain this, Boszormenyi-Nagy and Krasner (1986:315) refer to two types of loyalties - vertical and horizontal.[34] In terms of vertical loyalty, grandparents, parents and children connect to each other by an asymmetrical vertical loyalty. Therefore, this loyalty is then intergenerational and irreversible. The concept of legacy is helpful to explain what is meant by loyalty, as it intertwines with the concept of loyalty.

Legacy is a positive concept because it is the ethical obligation to take what is inherited from previous generations, and to integrate it into the present in such a way that it can make a constructive contribution to future generations. Boszormenyi-Nagy and Krasner (1986:418) define it as follows: "Legacy is an obligation to help free posterity from crippling habits, traditions and delegations of previous generations." In addition, they call the commitment to give back and pass on to the next generation "trans-generational solidarity" (Boszormenyi-Nagy & Krasner, 1986:129-133). This, they explain with the well-known statement: "We benefit from the past; we owe to the future." The inheritance passed on is not only limited to biological relationships, but also includes a common history, political ideologies, religious beliefs, family traditions, economic privileges, as well as concepts such as justice, laws, etc. In this way, legacy functions as a bridge between the past, the present, and the future of a generation. However, legacy has the potential to become destructive when one generation transfers such narratives to the next generation. In this way, a destructive legacy actively distorts the balance and keeps the frozen conflict intact. This occurs when, based on the past, the preferences or beliefs about what is important for one generation (parents) weighs heavier than the yet uncultivated potential of the next generation (children). These are then unconsciously projected onto the next generation(s) with the expectation to be fulfilled, thereby shifting what is of importance to the next generation into the background, and bringing forth the preferences and beliefs of the past and current generation as the core narrative.

The second type of loyalty that Boszormenyi-Nagy and Krasner (1986:315) indicate is the horizontal type. They describe horizontal loyalty as the choice between individuals within the same generation (friends, partners, colleagues, etc.). To them, this loyalty is symmetrical and reflexive (Boszormenyi-Nagy & Krasner, 1986:417). Within the relationships where horizontal loyalty is present there cannot be one core ledger or narrative that exists for everyone. From the beginning, each person or community is involved in numerous relations that represent many balances on a number of different levels that may or may not directly form part of the conflict. It

---

34   Meulink-Korf and van Rijn, *The unexpected third*, p.16.

is needless to say that all these diverse balances influence each other, and therefore, are never static. It is always dynamic, and each person or community involved in the conflict is constantly placing them on the scale. In this way, the needle will oscillate a little bit more … a little bit less … first by the one person and then by the other (Botha, 2014:19).

What one needs to be aware of is the danger of when vertical and horizontal loyalty is undermined or not recognised because it has the ability to be concealed and become invisible.[35] The influence and impact of invisibility could be to postulate in ways that illustrate destructive entitlement, such as aggression, criminality, addiction, and gangs, as an extended family. The result of invisible loyalty can develop into conflicts within relations if a person is not able to openly demonstrate their loyalty to the different people they are connected to. The term "conflicting loyalties" is more appropriate in a broader context, than only within the family context. According to Boszormenyi-Nagy and Krasner (1986:418), "Loyalty and loyalty conflict are, therefore, difficult to separate. For loyalty conflict applies to a situation in which a person is caught between two explicitly competing loyalty objects." In this regard, it refers to being loyal to your religion, culture or an ideology such as apartheid. Conflicting loyalties occur when a white son (current generation), for example, is in conflict with his white parents (previous generation) regarding apartheid. Normally, the conflict is destructive, and therefore, dialogue is not possible. What the son needs to do is to develop insight into the way his parents grew up and sift the knowledge gained. Insight is about acknowledging the context of his parents, but not absorbing everything from that context. He only has to take what is relevant from that relation and not everything, as is sometimes expected. In this way, he takes responsibility for the past and decides to pass constructive narratives on to the next generation. Invisible loyalties are indeed an example of how a person or a community can be stuck in an intergenerational frozen conflict.

Due to the importance of loyalty and legacy within a generation, it forms a central part of the relational ethical dimension. The complexity or danger is in the fact that people can develop their meaning and identity from this ethical relational dimension. When a destructive narrative becomes the basis for a person and community to form their meaning and identity, it could be devastating to the current as well as subsequent generations. However, according to Boszormenyi-Nagy's theory, people immersed in relationships where intergenerational frozen conflict exists are able to transform or reverse these destructive narratives. This is possible as all sides of the conflict carry just as much responsibility to balance the relation in a fair way and deepen the trust. In this regard, Meulink-Korf (2009:17) states: "To whom will I be unfaithful or who do you fear if you are unfaithful when you work towards ending the conflict?"

This requires continual sensitivity regarding when to give and when to receive, when to focus on one's own needs, and when to notice and acknowledge the needs of others. Thus, if the process of give and take is central to relational justice, then those in the relationship will need to be aware of guilt and guilt feelings, as it has the ability to damage relationships. Martin Buber (1983:65) indicates that guilt is existential, and therefore, it cannot just be a feeling.[36] Guilty feelings involve the anxious fear of rejection thereby damaging one's sense of self-worth or self-image. In contrast, existential guilt is the honest acknowledgement and recognition that my or your actions have damaged the order of the human world.[37] This, then, entails the need to take responsibility to deal with the guilt in a way that can do justice to the relation. Boszormenyi-Nagy and Krasner (1986:420), however, indicate that when we neglect to take responsibility to deal with the guilt it will develop into what they call a "revolving slate." They define this as follows: "…It is a relational consequence in which a person's substitutive revenge against one person eventually creates a new victim. The term "slate" refers to a fixed account between people that ordinarily merits fair consideration. Instead, it gets turned against a substitute and innocent target who is treated as if he or she were the original debtor." In terms of the family, the adult child "pays back" the debt owed to him by his parents through destructive actions, either to self or to others. To me, this is also true in terms of the current generation's reaction to the debt of past generations, as the second generation always claims the injustices of the previous generation.[38] This reaction leads to destructive entitlement and can manifest itself in two ways - either to choose not to give or to choose not to receive—and both will have a stagnating effect on any relationship. Such a person neither notices his/her own destructive behaviour, nor opens up space for another to restore the balance. White guilt based on colonialism and apartheid, according to the theory of Boszormenyi-Nagy and Krasner (1986:416), asserts that it is important to settle the account of guilt. This guilt does not only rest with the person or the community, but in the transaction that has disturbed the order, namely, in the relational reality. The restoring of the balance or the settling of the account can only occur when those who have damaged the relationship take responsibility to engage in a process with those who have been harmed. This is why Boszormenyi-Nagy and Krasner (1986:182) state that the legacy of ancestral shame and guilt requires redress and exoneration insofar as they are possible.

Within the process of settling the account, the notion of punishment comes to the fore. According to Botha (2014:38), Boszormenyi-Nagy had difficulty accepting that any punishment, which did not fit the extent of the debt, would be able to restore the damaged order. Punishment had more to do with addressing the sense of injustice, but did not address the damage done: what the person had broken still remained. This is indeed very relevant to the South African context, as it raises the question whether the victim can just accept the acknowledgement of the perpetrator and offer forgiveness without any justice. As Tutu (1999:221) states in his book *No future without forgiveness*, "Confession, forgiveness and reparation, wherever feasible,

---

36  Buber, M. (1983). 'Schuld en schuldgevoelens (Guilt and guilt feelings),', in de Bruin, T. (red.), *Adam waar ben je?* (Adam where are you?). Hilversum: B. Folkertsma Stichting, pp.208-235.

37  For Buber existential guilt occurs when someone injures an order of the human world whose foundations he/she knows and recognizes, as those of his/her own existence and of all common human existence (Buber, 1998, p.117).

38  See *Between give and take* by Boszormenyi-Nagy and Krasner (1986:390) on how the survivors and their children (different generations) react to the legacy of the past.

form part of a continuum."[39] Therefore, acknowledgement of guilt requires more than mere words, such as: "I apologise for apartheid, I am sorry about our past, and now we can forgive and forget and move on." When the perpetrator expresses guilt, it should be an honest acknowledgement and recognition that he or she has damaged the order through his or her actions.[40] Acknowledging guilt entails that the perpetrator will grieve because of what is broken and will address his or her existential guilt.

The victim should not offer forgiveness to the perpetrator in a cheap or hastened manner. One should remember that Boszormenyi-Nagy did not use the word forgiveness because it is often used too cheaply and mostly does not change the ethics between victims and perpetrators, between relationships, and between generations and cultures. Forgiveness that does not deal with the core issue that has damaged the order of humanity cannot restore the damage done to humanity (Boszormenyi-Nagy & Krasner, 1996:29). In the process of restoring the relationship, one must never underestimate the potential for power play involved in this process.[41] This could accrue when the perpetrator confesses to the victim from a position of self-created power.[42] Due to the power, the one who is on the receiving end of the deed is then obliged to offer forgiveness. The person who has damaged the order of humanity is thus the one who should forgive. The person who has committed the deed is not in the position to forgive. This lies with the one who has damaged the order. Forgiveness depends on the generosity of the forgiver (Boszormenyi-Nagy & Krasner, 1986:416). Now, the power rests with him/her. Forgiveness in itself does not lead to a balance in the relationship, but rather to a reversal of power, thereby leaving the situation in the domain of guilt feelings. The tragedy is that there has been no true encounter and even less attention given to the process of making the

---

39    Tutu, D. (1999). *No future without forgiveness*. London: Rider.
40    See Kayser, U. (1998). 'Creating the past Improvising the present'. Unpublished Honours thesis, Centre for African Studies, University of Cape Town, Cape Town. For Kayser, a perpetrator is someone who actively perpetrates the violation of the human rights of others, and a bystander is someone who was present during the violation of the human rights of others, but declines to say or do anything about it. Apart from a perpetrator and a bystander, there is also a beneficiary. Also, see Thesnaar, C.H. (2001). 'Die proses van heling en versoening: 'n Pastoraal-hermeneutiese ondersoek van die dinamika tussen slagoffer en oortreder binne 'n post-WVK periode'. (The process of healing and reconciliation: A pastoral hermeneutical investigation of the dynamics between victim and offender within a post-TRC period) Unpublished DTh thesis, Stellenbosch University. He describes beneficiaries as those who were not actively or passively involved, but who benefited from the apartheid system, economically, politically, physically, either socially, or in a religious way.
41    Pollyfeyt, D. (1996). 'Het onvergeeflijke vergeven? Een etische analyse van kwaad en verzoening. (Forgive the unforgivable? An ethical analysis of evil and reconciliation)', in Burggraeve, R. and De Tavernier, J. (red) *Terugkeer van de wraak?* (Return of revenge?) Averbode: Gooi en Sticht, pp.155-178. He writes on the way perpetrators use power during reconciliation.
42    See Holtmann, B. (1998). Victim Empowerment. *Social Work Practice*, 1:8-14. He describes the United Nations definition of a victim: "... someone who, individually or collectively, has suffered harm, including physical or mental injury, emotional suffering, economic loss or substantial impairment of their fundamental rights, through acts or omissions that are in violation of criminal laws ... including those laws prescribing criminal abuse of power ... the term victim also includes, where appropriate, the immediate family or dependents of the direct victim and persons who have suffered harm in intervening to assist victims in distress or to prevent victimisation".

guilty party un-guilty. In order to restore the relationship the perpetrator will need to be set free from his or her guilt.

Although Boszormenyi-Nagy and Krasner (1986:416) do not understand the concept of guilt in a theological way, they offer a different perspective in dealing with the guilt, and that is, to spread the guilt. Their theory entails that they do not want to load the guilt onto one person and then excommunicate the guilty party from the community, as that would be detrimental to restoring the relationship. To spread the guilt would entail placing the actions done and the cause of the guilt within previous generations. The concept they use to explain this is "exoneration," which they define as the "… process of lifting the load of culpability off the shoulders of a given person whom heretofore we may have blamed. It differs from forgiveness. The act of forgiveness usually retains the assumption of guilt and extends the forgiver's generosity to the person who injures her or him. Offering forgiveness, a person now refrains from holding the culprit accountable and from demanding punishment" (Boszormenyi-Nagy & Krasner, 1986:416). Exoneration deeply concerns trust, responsibility, accountability and justice. This implies a commitment to actively engage in dialogue, and negotiate, address and transform the challenges of the current context in order to establish a shared future that is sustainable for all involved. It is about taking responsibility for the past in order to make sure that what we pass on to the next generation is constructive. In my view, this is more in line with what Tutu (1999:220) refers to when he argues that the act of forgiveness is a change for a new beginning not only for the victim but also for the perpetrator.

## CONCLUSION

After reflecting on the timeframe, the content of frozen conflict, and the theory of contextual pastoral care, I am of the opinion that it does offer an approach that can assist in breaking through the cycle of intergenerational frozen conflict within an African context. This will, however, be neither simplistic nor easy. On the contrary, it will be challenging, yet rewarding. This approach helps us to understand that victims and perpetrators exist within a network of relationships. These relationships are not relationships we can choose, as we are bound by their legacy. These relationships are connected through loyalty, whether it is visible or invisible. The victims and perpetrators are therefore products of the legacies of the South African past. Due to colonialism and apartheid, South Africans are still currently carrying the weight of relations and trust that was damaged and destroyed. These relationships buckle under the weight of the guilt and shame that arises from an experience or existence of destructive entitlements/rights. In this chapter, I presented an argument for a process of transforming relationships in order to break through the intergenerational frozen conflict that victims and perpetrators would need to take responsibility to enter into dialogue with one another and be accountable to address the destructive narratives and build new ones. Caregivers within local religious communities are obliged to create safe spaces where victims and perpetrators can engage with one another in a non-judgmental way, to embody give and take within a space of trust, and specifically, transformative justice. We need to listen to the conflicting loyalties people struggle with. This will enable the intergenerational frozen conflict to come to the surface via a narrative, and thereby identify connections and balances, which make healing possible.

The theory of contextual pastoral care reminds us that trustworthiness is the fulcrum of all vital relationships. In these spaces public theologians as caregivers should assist participants to search for the tiny jewels of mutual care, love, and experiences that lead to hope and trust. This is why the theory of contextual pastoral care emphasises that only trust and transformative justice can break the legacy, and therefore, the intergenerational frozen conflict. It is of grave importance to resolve the conflict and facilitate a greater understanding between people and cultures in general, but also between groups, clans, villages, races, as well as perpetrators and victims. If we do not contribute to restore trust in relations and transformative justice does not take place, it will take generations to change the legacy of our past in South Africa.

# REFERENCES

Bilefsky, D. and Sengupta, S. (2015). 'Srebrenica Massacre, After 20 Years, Still Casts a Long Shadow in Bosnia,' The New York Times, London, 8 July. Viewed from https://nyti.ms/2HRKwud [Accessed 18 February 2017].

Boszormenyi-Nagy, I. (1987). *Foundations of contextual therapy: Collected papers of Ivan Boszormenyi-Nagy, MD.* New York: Brunner/Mazel.

Boszormenyi-Nagy, I. (2000). *Grondbeginselen van de contextuele benadering.* (Fundamentals of the contextual approach). Haarlem: De Toorts.

Boszormenyi-Nagy, I. and Framo, J. (eds.) (1985). *Intensive family therapy: Theoretical and practical aspects.* New York: Brunner/Mazel.

Boszormenyi-Nagy, I. and Krasner, B. (1986). *Between give and take: A clinical guide to contextual therapy.* New York: Brunner/Mazel. https://doi.org/10.2307/583562

Boszormenyi-Nagy, I. and Spark, G. (1984). *Invisible loyalties: Reciprocity in intergenerational family therapy.* New York: Brunner/Mazel.

Boszormenyi-Nagy, I., Grunebaum, J. and Ulrich, D. (1991). 'Contextual Therapy', in A. Gurman and D. Kniskern (eds.) *Handbook of Family Therapy, Vol 2.* New York: Brunner/Mazel.

Botha, T. J. (2014). 'Ons sal mekaar nie los nie' 'n Kwalitatiewe ondersoek na die aard van die onderlinge verbondenheid van leraars binne die Verenigende Ring van Stellenbosch'. ('We will not leave each other' A qualitative inquiry into the nature of the interdependence of pastors within the Uniting Circuit of Stellenbosch.') Unpublished master's thesis. Stellenbosch University [Online]. Viewed from http://bit.ly/3ahJaoO [Accessed 18 February 2017].

Brouwer, R. (2004). 'Leiderschap in systemisch-contextueel perspectief. Friedman en Nagy over leiderschap (Leadership in systemic-contextual perspective. Friedman and Nagy on leadership)', in van Ark, J. and de Roest, H.P. (eds.) *De weg van de groep. Leidinggeven in gemeente en parochie (The way of the group. Leadership in the congregation and parish).* Zoetermeer: Meinema, pp.283-291.

Buber, M. (1983). 'Schuld en schuldgevoelens (Guilt and guilt feelings)', in T. de Bruin (red.), *Adam waar ben je?* (Adam where are you?). Hilversum: B. Folkertsma Stichting, pp.208-235.

Clancy, M.A.C. and Nagle, J. (2009). 'Frozen Conflicts, Minority Self-Governance, Asymmetrical Autonomies – In search of a framework for conflict management and conflict resolution'. Paper presented at the Sixth Asia-Europe Roundtable, University of Ulster, Republic of Ireland, 10-12 June [Online]. Viewed from www.incore.ulster.ac.uk [Accessed 17 January 2017].

Democratic Progress Institute. (2013). The Good Friday Agreement: An Overview [Online]. Viewed from http://bit.ly/2v9WRHz [Accessed 19 February 2017].

Holtmann, B. (1998). Victim Empowerment. *Social Work Practice,* 1:8-14.

Kayser, U. (1998). 'Creating the past Improvising the present'. Unpublished Honours thesis, Centre for African Studies, University of Cape Town, Cape Town.

Kegley, C.W. and Wittkopf, E.R. (1943/1997). *World politics: Trend and transformation* (6th edition). New York: St. Martin's Press.

Krasner, B.R. and Joyce, A.J. (1995). *Truth, Trust, and Relationships: Healing Interventions in Contextual Therapy.* New York: Brunner & Mazel.

Leshilo, T. (2016). What Africa's most newly independent states did with 22 years of freedom. In The Conversation. [Online]. Viewed from http://bit.ly/2SQOQAm [Accessed: 13 January 2018]

Meulink-Korf, J.N. (2009). Verbindend waarnemen en werken: kerkelijke conflicten in contextueel perspectief. (Connecting observing and working: Ecclesiastical conflicts in a contextual perspective). *Tijdschrift Conflicthantering*, 4(6):12-17.

Meulink-Korf, H. and van Rijn. A. (2016). *The unexpected third Contextual pastoral, counselling and ministry: An introduction and reflection*, transl. Noeme Visser, Wellington: Christian Literature Fund Publishers.

Mkhize, V.V.O. (2016). 'Umsamo – The quest for an African-centred approach in pastoral care. Learning from the African traditions, culture, values, ancestral wisdom and African healing'. Paper presented at the trans-disciplinary workshop on contextual pastoral care in Africa, Stellenbosch University, Stellenbosch, 19 July.

Newman, K.S. and De Lannoy, A. (2014). *After Freedom: The Rise of the Post-Apartheid Generation in Democratic South Africa.* Boston: Beacon Press; The twenty-year review 1994–2014. Document of the office of the Precedency [Online]. Viewed from http://bit.ly/2VEXgN1 [Accessed: 13 January 2018].

Peet, J. (2008). 'Frozen conflicts: Europe's unfinished business'. The Economist. [Online]. Viewed from http://www.economist.com/node/12494503 [Accessed 13 September 2015].

Pollyfeyt, D. (1996). 'Het onvergeeflijke vergeven? Een etische analyse van kwaad en verzoening. (Forgive the unforgivable? An ethical analysis of evil and reconciliation)', in Burggraeve, R. and De Tavernier, J. (red) *Terugkeer van de wraak?* (Return of revenge?) Averbode: Gooi en Sticht, pp.155-178.

Red House debate. (2014). 25 years after 1989. What has happened to the idea of social equality? [Online]. Viewed from http://bit.ly/2vWoq7g [Accessed 16 February 2017].

Roaf, J., Atoyan, R., Joshi, B., Krogulski, K. and an IMF Staff Team. (2014). 25 Years of Transition Post-Communist Europe and the IMF Regional Economic Issues [Online]. Viewed from http://bit.ly/2SSrb2i [Accessed 16 February 2017].

Srebrenica Massacre. (2015). After 20 Years, Still Casts a Long Shadow in Bosnia [Online]. Viewed from http://bit.ly/38VQiHb [Accessed 15 February 2017].

Thesnaar, C.H. (2001). 'Die proses van heling en versoening: 'n Pastoraal-hermeneutiese ondersoek van die dinamika tussen slagoffer en oortreder binne 'n post-WVK periode'. (The process of healing and reconciliation: A pastoral hermeneutical investigation of the dynamics between victim and offender within a post-TRC period) Unpublished DTh thesis, Stellenbosch University.

Thesnaar, C.H. (2015). 'Report on the re-enactment of the Truth and Reconciliation Commission's faith hearing consultation'. Unpublished report. Stellenbosch University, Stellenbosch, 8–9 October 2014.

Treisman, D. (2009). 20 years of transition in rap Eastern Europe and the Soviet Union [Online]. Viewed from http://bit.ly/38S3Qne [Accessed 15 February 2017].

Truth and Reconciliation Commission. 1998. *Truth and Reconciliation Commission of South Africa Report.* Volume 6. Cape Town: Juta and Co Ltd, p.589.

Tutu, D. (1999). *No future without forgiveness.* London: Rider. https://doi.org/10.1111/j.1540-5842.1999.tb00012.x

Van der Merwe, C.N. and Gobodo-Madikizela, P. (2007). *Narrating our Healing. Perspectives on Working through Trauma.* Newcastle: Cambridge Scholars Publishing.

A Practical Theological Approach

*Benaya Niyukuri*[1]

## INTRODUCTION

Situated in east-central Africa, Burundi is a small landlocked country of 10,750 square miles (27,830km$^2$) that accommodates a population of around 10 million people belonging to three ethnic groups, namely: Hutus (85%), Tutsis (14%), and Twas (1%) (Lemarchand, 1995). Its neighbouring countries are Rwanda, Tanzania, and the Democratic Republic of the Congo. Although these three ethnic groups share the same culture and mother tongue, Burundi has experienced a sequence of ethnic conflicts (Lemarchand, 1995). Various attempts to deal with the ethnic conflicts have been put in place but these have failed to achieve sustainable peace. The current situation has raised concern. This chapter looks at the history of conflicts in Burundi and suggests the role of practical theology in bringing about reconciliation to the nation.

## THE SOURCE OF CONFLICT IN BURUNDI

Long before independence, the Burundian community was united and peaceful. This is emphasised by the fact that during the pre-colonial period, all the ethnic groups living in Burundi were under one king (*Umwami*), believing in the same god (*Imana*), sharing the same culture, and speaking the same language (*Kirundi*), as they lived together in the same territory (Hatungimana, 2011). In addition, people in Burundi recognised themselves as *Barundi* despite the fact that the different ethnic groups had settled in Burundi at different times (Ntahombaye & Nduwayo, 2007). There were no known severe ethnic conflicts during the pre-colonial period. In the case of minor conflicts, there existed an institution of *Bashingantahe*, the council of the elders coming from among the *Baganwa*, the *Bahutu* and the *Batutsi* who were judges and advisors at all levels of power in order to settle the conflicts in the community.[2] Therefore, the question that arises is, where did the ethnic conflicts in Burundi come from?

---

1   Benaya Niyukuri is currently a PhD candidate in Practical Theology at the Stellenbosch University and Director of Paraclete Counselling Mission.

2   Arusha Peace and Reconciliation Agreement for Burundi. (2000). Viewed from http://bit.ly/2HN9b3a [Accessed 20 May 2017]. (Hereafter, Arusha Agreement).

Until its independence in 1962, Burundi was firstly part of a German colony (1897-1916) and, after Germany's defeat in the First World War it was placed under Belgian trusteeship (1916-1962) (Daley, 2000). During the colonial period, the colonial administration played a pivotal role in exacerbating the ethnic divisions by putting in place a strategy based on morphology in terms of physical characteristics and character traits to help them execute a divide and rule plan that resulted in tensions between the ethnic groups (Vandeginste, 2014; Arusha Agreement, 2000). In this way, the Tutsi minority, being considered by the colonisers as higher in status than the Hutu majority, were given the privilege of education and administration, which frustrated the Hutus. The colonisers established the demarcations by defining Tutsis as tall, thin, and with a sharp straight nose, while Hutus are known to be short, big, and with a big flat nose; even though there are Tutsis with the same characteristics as Hutus, and vice versa (Hatungimana, 2011). To make matters worse, the colonisers introduced an identity card pointing out ethnic origin, allowing them to treat each ethnic group differently, thereby destroying cultural values that promoted national unity and cohesion (Arusha, 2000). In 1934, a census by the Belgian colonisers complicated the social boundaries even more. Furthermore, cows had acquired more value than other Burundian products. Persons owing more than ten cows were arbitrary classified as Tutsi. As a result, relatively wealthy Hutu suddenly became Tutsi, and some poorer Tutsi became Hutu. Ethnic identity cards were issued freezing Hutu, Tutsi, and Twa social identities into law and ethnic groups. Already identified with relative deprivation, Hutu and Twa became strongly associated with poverty and powerlessness. The census classified 85% of the population as Hutu, 14% as Tutsi, and 1% as Twa (Ndayizigiye, 2005). These percentages of the population provided by the Belgian colonial government have been almost universally accepted although the percentages and ethnic distinctions are themselves only approximations (Krueger & Krueger, 2007).

As a result, the Belgian colonisers favoured the Tutsi whom they regarded as 'born to rule', while the Hutu were 'born to farm' (Walters, 2008), so that the Tutsi minority took control and oppressed the Hutu majority, a situation that caused severe ethnic tensions after the independence of Burundi on the 1st of July 1962 (Lemarchand, 1995).

As a matter of fact, when Burundi gained independence from the Belgian government in 1962, the Tutsis took control of the government with Louis Rwagasore, the hero of independence, becoming the first Prime Minister. After a few weeks, Rwagasore was assassinated by his own people (Tutsis) and was then replaced by Andre Muhirwa, his brother-in-law. The rule of Tutsis never gave any regard to the Hutus. During an election in 1964, Pierre Ngendandumwe, a Hutu, won and became Prime Minister. The Tutsis did not accept to be ruled by a Hutu Prime Minister, and therefore assassinated him in 1965. Ngendandumwe's assassination sparked anger among the Hutus who then started a rebellion which was immediately violently put down. In 1966 Michel Micombero, a Tutsi army chief, launched a coup that replaced the monarchy with military rule. His party, UPRONA, was declared the only legal party in the country and this resulted in more Hutu deaths (Lemarchand, 1995). Furthermore, a civil war in 1972 resulted in the mass killing of about 300,000 Hutus while many others fled to the neighbouring countries. In 1992, the United Nations enticed President Pierre Buyoya to introduce a multi-party democracy. In this way, the first democratic elections saw President Melchior Ndadaye elected as the first Hutu president in 1993. Three months after his inception as president, Ndadaye was assassinated by the army which was still controlled by Tutsis. The death of Ndadaye angered the Hutus who then decided to take up arms against the Tutsi army. This led to a severe civil war that resulted in a lot of deaths and refugees (Lemarchand, 1995). The civil war continued until the Arusha Peace Agreement in which all political actors in Burundi were invited to take part in order to find lasting solutions through negotiations that started in 1998 and led to the agreement that was signed on 28 August 2000 (Hatungimana, 2011).

The Arusha Peace Agreement made provision for a democratic power sharing among the ethnic groups in the army and government in order to achieve ethnic balance and to prevent acts of genocide and coups d'état (military coups) by providing for civilian supremacy over military matters and for the ongoing adjustment of imbalances in the composition of the defense and security forces (Vandeginste, 2015; Hatungimana, 2011; Arusha Agreement, 2000:39). This was put in place in order "to reconcile and unite Burundians and lay the foundations for a democratic and united Burundi, inter alia by promoting a broad programme of education in peace, democracy and ethnic tolerance" (Arusha Agreement, 2000). Eventually, the Arusha Agreement enabled Burundians to achieve a conflict resolution geared towards politico-ethnic reconciliation and pacification in which ethnicity is no longer a tool to justify violence (Vandeginste, 2015). This was achieved by crafting a constitution that favours the majority, while at the same time protecting the minority groups, so that the 2005 and 2010 elections were no longer primarily a matter of ethnic competition. This was quite an achievement in a country torn apart by politico-ethnic strife for decades (Vandeginste, 2015). In this way, the problem of ethnic conflicts in Burundi was solved by recognising and naming each person by his/her ethnicity and giving them the dignity that is due to them. The Burundi power-sharing agreement was instrumental in playing a dual role in leading to the termination of war and creating a more inclusive political governance. It has been considered as the best peace-building achievement on the African continent (IRIS, 2016; Vandeginste, 2015).

As a result, a coalition government was set up after the 2005 elections which saw the CNDD-FDD, a former Hutu rebel movement led by President Pierre Nkurunziza, to ascend to power. According to the new constitution, the President was only allowed two terms in office. In 2010, after the first term, the transition to peace suffered a significant blow as most of the opposition parties boycotted the presidential elections after alleging that the ruling party had rigged the first round of elections, a situation that gave an opportunity for President Pierre Nkurunziza to run unopposed and gain an overwhelming victory with 91% of the votes cast (Vandeginste, 2015).

After the 2010 elections, the political situation in Burundi started deteriorating. In November 2013, the Burundian government initiated a constitutional amendment process which was perceived and feared by the public as an attempt to do away with the Arusha Agreement in order to scrap presidential term limits (Omondi, 2015; Vandeginste, 2015). Eventually the parliament, by a single vote in 2014, rejected the government's proposal to amend the constitution (IRIS, 2016; International Crisis Group, 2016). Still, President Pierre Nkurunziza decided to campaign for a third term of office, thereby sparking massive protests against his decision in April 2015 which was followed by violence, fear, socio-economic decline and deepening social fractures; with urban guerrilla-like warfare and a failed coup attempt on 13 May 2015, resulting in a rise of targeted assassinations, torture and disappearances. More than 250,000 became refugees including most of the opposition leaders (Impunity Watch, 2016; International Crisis Group, 2016).

The decision taken by President Pierre Nkurunziza to campaign for a third term was criticised by many stakeholders including the opposition, the international community, and even some from his own government and party (International Crisis Group, 2016). Consequently, the exiled opposition joined hands and formed a coalition known as the National Council for the Restoration of the Arusha Accord and the Rule of Law (*Conseil National pour le Respect de l'Accord d'Arusha pour la Paix et la Réconciliation au Burundi et de l'Etat de Droit*) (CNARED) in order to oppose the third term of President Pierre Nkurunziza (International Crisis Group, 2016). President Nkurunziza's third term caused a lot of concern both locally and internationally, making it unclear as to why he had decided to breach the term limit set by the Arusha Agreement. There can be different answers given for his conduct. For example, it is asserted that "in Burundi, just like in some other African countries, politics is likened to a milking cow, an appointment to a political position is likened to the securing of something to eat or a place where one can stay forever" (Ntahombaye & Nduwayo, 2007:246). In this way, some African leaders are "known for their reluctance to leave office and one way they ensure to stay on is by amending the constitution. Thus, when constitutions have been amended 'presidents for life' are again installed, with a bad reputation of eliminating of opposition, narrowing of the political field, establishing personal armies, often looting national wealth and using the constitution to consolidate personal power" (Botha, 2012:30). In fact, while remaining in power has been the practice of most African presidents over the years, it is noted that between 2000 and 2015 alone, fifteen African leaders attempted to adjust the constitutions by doing away with term limits (Le Bas, 2016).

Taking the example of the Great Lakes region where Burundi is located, President Yoweri Museveni came to power in 1986 and is among the longest serving presidents in Africa. He ended up tabling a motion to change the constitution and remove term limits in 2005, thereby being allowed to continue campaigning for presidency and winning his fifth term in the 2016 elections, with a desire to remain in power at least until 2035 (Dulani, 2011).[3] On the other side, President Paul Kagame of Rwanda tabled a constitutional change by a referendum in 2015, which allowed him not only to be re-elected for a third term in 2017, but also to continue campaigning for presidency until 2034, and, after that, remain excepted from prosecution for any

---

3   See also The Electoral Commission of Uganda. (2016). 2015/2016 General Elections Report. Submitted to Parliament through the Ministry of Justice and Constitutional Affairs in accordance with the provisions of Section 12 (1) (o) of the Electoral Commission Act, Cap 140 (as amended). Viewed from http://bit.ly/2w36K9S [Accessed 18 June 2017].

serious crimes (Bardall & Arieff, 2017). This move that created fear among many people who thought it would create havoc and endanger the development already achieved in that country (Mbaku, 2017; IRIS, 2016). Eventually, President Kagame won his third term with 99% of the votes in the 2017 elections in which he was not contested after the Rwandan Electoral Commission disqualified three of the opposition candidates (Bardall & Arieff, 2017). Also in the Democratic Republic of Congo (DRC), President Joseph Kabila's refusal to step down after his two terms in 2016 caused havoc in the country and resulted in the negotiations that added a year to his term in office to allow a smoother transition of power (IRIS, 2016:10; Mbiatem, 2015). An agreement to extend President Kabila's term in office until the end of 2017 was mediated by the Catholic Church and signed between him and the opposition groups. However, the elections have been postponed to 23 December 2018, a decision that has caused deadly protests.[4] Looking at all these examples, President Nkurunziza of Burundi did not hesitate to sacrifice the hard earned peace by going ahead with the 2015 elections that allowed him to run unopposed and be re-elected for a third term amidst opposition boycotts and protests (IRIS, 2016; Lebas, 2016). Furthermore, President Nkurunziza has been campaigning for a constitution referendum to be held in May 2018. The new constitution to be rectified provides for a seven year term instead of five, and President Nkurunziza is allowed to vie for the 2020 elections.[5] The situation in Burundi has thereby become so unbearable that it requires urgent attention.

## THE WORK OF THE CHURCH IN THE CRISIS IN BURUNDI

The church in Burundi has been instrumental in holding the government accountable, especially in condemning the massacres and other evils threatening the society. For example, the Catholic Church leaders quickly condemned ethnic massacres in the 1970s and spoke out for the population (Riedl, 2015). During the reign of President Bagaza, when the political space was tight, the church became the only stronghold defending freedom of speech; even though this bravery brought a lot of consequences such as threats and attacks directed towards the Bishops and catechists as well as their relatives, resulting in the nationalisation of seminaries and banning of charismatic community meetings in 1986 (Prunier, 1994). At the same time, the state took over the civil society organisations to reinforce state ideology. As Krueger and Krueger (2007:29) assert, "To Bagaza, all Christian churches represented challenges to his dictatorial authority and were therefore enemies of the state. Consequently, he confiscated church properties, banished most missionaries, and directly controlled all religious practices." As a result, youth and women associations as well as labour unions became the property of the single party government and were used as instruments of propaganda to brainwash the citizens in order to privilege the state. As the Catholic Church provided education to the people, it was

---

4    Cf. 'UN Urges DR Congo Leader to Keep Promise to Step Down', *Gulf Times*, 1 January 2018. Viewed from http://bit.ly/37Vt6aN [Accessed 25 January 2018].

5    'Burundi to hold referendum of constitution in May 2018: electoral commission', *Xinhua*, 6 December 2017. Viewed from http://bit.ly/2Tj3vo1 [Accessed 25 January 2018].

viewed as a threat and a potential vehicle for alternative beliefs. This influence of the church was challenged by the fact that some clergy often served as the agents of the state (Ndikumana, 2005).

Nevertheless, the church did not stop its involvement in the resolution of conflicts, supporting the war victims, street kids, orphans and demobilised child soldiers to find safe place and rehabilitation. In this way, the church has offered significant support to the government in terms of caring for the poor, providing free education for all, as well as free medical care for children under five years as well as maternity fees for mothers.[6] In the same way, Ubuntu Centre, a Burundian NGO has been created by the Catholic Church to collaborate with UNICEF in order to work on peacebuilding and to deal with violence among youth, discrimination, as well as promoting dialogue between the conflicting ethnic groups (Haro, 2016). Another organisation put in place by the Quaker Church and supported by the Mennonite and Church of Friends is called The Ministry of Peace and Reconciliation under the Cross (MI-PAREC). This organisation started in 1998 and deals with training in conflict management and peacebuilding, especially targeting the youth who, being easily manipulated by adults and political leaders, are known as the most active in violence. The organisation contributes to the management of the post-conflict through socio-economic reintegration and rehabilitation (Musser, 2015; Niyonkuru, 2012).

Furthermore the Catholic Church has established Radio Maria, a radio station and Ndongozi, a newspaper in order to influence the situation by acting as a herald for the population.[7]

Even when President Pierre Nkurunziza wanted to campaign for a third term the Catholic Church did not hesitate to stand up and speak against the President's violation of the constitution. The Catholic Church leaders issued a statement in a pastoral letter that was circulated and read in the congregations across the country (Riedl, 2015). Their standpoint did not please President Nkurunziza, a "born-again" charismatic preacher and pastor who believes that God has appointed him to run for the third term so that "anyone opposed to his third term is opposing the will of God."[8] The decision by the leaders of the Catholic Church in Burundi to challenge the President's bid for a third term became dangerous for the Catholic Bishops, with several of them receiving death threats or being detained for opposing the president's decision to run for the third term.[9] Consequently, the Catholic Church

---

6    Anglican Peace and Justice Network. (2007). *Community Transformation: Violence and the Church's Response*. Anglican Peace and Justice Network in Rwanda and Burundi. Viewed from http://bit.ly/2vZnX4I [Accessed 26 August 2017].

7    Media Support. (2015). *Burundi's Media During the 2015 Election Crisis*. Viewed from http://bit.ly/2HSdqdT [Accessed 26 August 2017].

8    *Catholic Herald*. (2015). 'Violence Increases as Burundi's President Announces He Will Run Again.' Catholic News Service, April 28, 2015. Viewed from http://bit.ly/2SROnzF [Accessed 26 August 2017].

9    International Religious Freedom. (2015). Burundi 2015 International Religious Freedom Report. Viewed from https://www.state.gov/documents/organization/256211.pdf. [Accessed 15 August 2017].

decided to withdraw its priests appointed to assist in organising the elections which are seen to be full of shortcomings (Niyungeko, 2015).

On the other hand, ethnic differences are not absent in the church. For example, The Catholic Church during and after the colonial period was closely aligned with Belgium, and its hierarchical structure reflected values and practices similar to those of the ruling colonial power. Thus, just as Tutsis were identified in Brussels as those deserving education and positions of leadership in secular society, so, in Rome, Tutsis had been similarly identified as the natural leaders of the church in Burundi. Tutsis therefore composed most of the priesthood, especially its highest positions. Even so, by the 1990s the times were a-changing in the church as they were elsewhere, and the Vatican began naming Hutus as bishops. To some Tutsis, naming a Hutu bishop was seen as a direct and intentional insult (Krueger & Krueger, 2007).

This reality was also a contributing factor during the war, especially in 1972 during the massacres of educated Hutus. Missionaries from Europe witnessed the killings even in confessional schools (both Catholic and Protestants) as well as in churches, with twelve Hutu priests reported to be killed, along with thousands of Protestant pastors, school directors and teachers (Lemarchand, 2008).

This situation has also been observed during the war that followed the assassination of President Melchior Ndadaye in 1993. As Kopwe (2013:187) posits, the church was very polarised, with the majority of church leaders being Tutsi with most of the Hutu church leaders being in exile. The problem became worse when the church leaders in the country worked with the army and politicians while the church leaders in exile worked with the rebels (Kopwe, 2013).[10] It was only during the reconciliation period that this situation was alleviated; as Kopwe (2013) further relates, "In the process of dealing with the pain of the people, a number of actors were involved. On the local scene, individual church denominations which co-operated within the Christian Council of Burundi (CNEB) and their foreign partners were very active in spite of the deep mire of pain and division; local organisations like Trauma Healing and Reconciliation Services (THARS) and World Outreach Initiatives (WOI) were in the forefront of seeking the healing of the nation. Many organisations from outside Burundi joined hands with local entities in search for solutions. One of these organisations was African Evangelistic Enterprise (AEE), working in partnership with the above-mentioned local entities." Thus, it is fair to say that the church was instrumental in dealing with the conflicts in Burundi. However, there is also a negative side to be dealt with in order for the church to make a significant contribution in alleviating the ethnic tensions the country is facing.

---

10   The author witnessed the division in the church, whereby church leaders betrayed each other in conspiracies that even cost the lives of others in the opposite ethnic group. For example, in Nyanza-Lac, a town along Lake Tanganyika in the Province of Makamba, a Senior Pastor in the Pentecost was seen celebrating the death of President Melchior Ndadaye. As a result, members of the church were angry with him and decided not to sit in the church service with him. On a Sunday service, the people complained and made a revolt that was meant to chase the Senior Pastor from the church but because of the connection he had with the army, many people were arrested and executed. As a result, another church, the EUSEBU, was born.

## THE POLITICAL ATTEMPT TO DEAL WITH THE CURRENT CRISIS IN BURUNDI

The escalation of violence in Burundi calls for diplomatic efforts and political solutions to ensure that the crisis does not turn into another long war as Burundians increasingly face pressure in the current climate of fear, militarisation and violence (IRIS, 2016; Impunity Watch, 2016). In this regard, the polarised African Union (AU) decided to authorise the deployment of an African Prevention and Protection Mission in Burundi (MAPROBU), a decision that was virulently rejected by the President and government of Burundi (Bouka & Nyabola, 2016; Impunity Watch, 2016). In addition, the AU has requested a dialogue between the Burundi government and opposition, but such a dialogue has so far not yielded any fruit since the government has been refusing to sit at the negotiating table with CNARED whom it accuses of being the perpetrators of the failed coup of 13 May 2015 (Impunity Watch, 2016; IRIS, 2016).

In spite of the President and government's refusal to engage in a dialogue with the opposition, it is widely believed that dialogue is the most important strategy to bring an end to conflict and violence prevailing in Burundi (Impunity Watch, 2016). As a matter of fact, peace negotiations have been underway, while some have lost trust in the mediation process as neither the government nor the heavily fragmented opposition are making honest overtures towards its resolution (IRIS, 2016).

## A PRACTICAL THEOLOGICAL PERSPECTIVE ON THE CRISIS IN BURUNDI

Louw (2008:71) describes the nature and the task of Practical Theology as follows: "Practical theology is the science of the theological, critical and hermeneutical reflection on the intention and meaning of human actions as expressed in the practice of ministry and the heart of faithful daily living. It is related to life skills within the realm of spirituality. In this regard Practical Theology is connected to the praxis and will of God within the encounter of God and human beings." Reflecting on Louw's understanding, it is fair to say that Practical Theology has to do with the relationship between God and man; God appears to His people and communicates to them His Word which must be contextually interpreted and understood in order to be applied to the people's context, and must then be communicated to them so that it influences their lives.

Furthermore, Practical Theology can be interpreted as being instrumental in making the Word of God relevant to people's lives, which calls for a hermeneutical approach. With regard to the relationship between Practical Theology and a hermeneutical approach, Hendriks (2004) and Polling (2010) see Practical Theology as a continuing hermeneutical concern that discerns how the Word of God should be proclaimed in word and deed to the world by means of moving from theory (word) to practice (deeds). In this view, it is important to highlight the concept of discernment which is significant in the sense that the interpretation of God's Word requires careful thought and reliance on the Holy Spirit through prayer and the study of God's Word to avoid making wrong interpretations that go against God's will. This agrees with the idea of inhabitational theology, which has to do with an interpretation of Scripture that goes beyond moralistic thought to determine appropriate God-images in times of specific existential issues such as illness and stigma (Louw, 2008; Polling, 2010).

In other words, practical theology has to do with the adequate interpretation of the gospel that must foster transformation in the lives of people in order to change their present practices and encourage them to adopt a new way of living inspired by the Word of God after a careful interpretation (Fowler, 1985). This is what Dingemans (1996) means when he refers to the shift from the application of biblical data and statements of faith to the primary task of the investigation of Christian practice which leads to practical theology being understood as a science of action.

In this way, the solution to the Burundian crisis requires an accurate interpretation and application of God's Word, since it is the task of practical theology to challenge and "unmask the systematic distortions in the person, social, cultural, historical and religious models of human transformation" (Fowler, 1985:52). Thus, it is fair to refer to Practical Theology as an application of theology to life and ministry.

Regarding the role of practical theology in terms of finding a solution to the Burundian crisis, it will be helpful to look at Scripture and apply its interpretation to the situation in order to come up with a workable plan to deal with the prevailing conflict in Burundi. First of all, practical theology has to draw from the spirituality of Burundians in order to establish a plan of action on resolving the crisis in Burundi. Regarding the spirituality of Burundians, it is helpful to notice that, while the constitution establishes a secular state, it makes provision for freedom of religion, thereby respecting all religions and prohibiting religious discrimination. For that reason, Burundian citizens can be converted to a religion of their choice. In addition, all religions have the right to evangelise, work in schools, hospitals, and media; with freedom to build places of worship and do fundraising.[11] In Burundi, approximately 75% of the population is Christian (60% Roman Catholic and 15% Protestants), 20% Traditional Religions, 3% Muslim, with other religions occupying 2%.[12] From this analysis, Christianity is considered as the main religion, with the Catholic Church being powerful and dominant in its influence on all levels of Burundian society. During the civil war, Evangelical Churches have however mushroomed all over the country. President Pierre Nkurunziza is a born-again Christian with him and his wife being pastors in an evangelical church (Bouka & Nyabola, 2016; Wallis, 2015; Jones, 2014).

Amidst conflict and violence in Burundi, the church can make use of the Bible message to bring about reconciliation. In fact, since the majority of Burundians are Christian, the church can take the opportunity to emphasise the message of Christ in order to promote peace and reconciliation. In the course of conflicts, believers are admonished, "Do not seek revenge or bear a grudge against one of your people, but love your neighbour as yourself" (Lev 19:18). This attitude depicts the holiness between human beings that must be shown in the social, economic, and political areas

---

11 International Crisis Group. (2016). *Burundi: A Dangerous Third Term.* Africa Report N°235. Translated from French. Viewed from http://bit.ly/2HMw9HN [Accessed 22 June 2017].

12 International Religious Freedom. (2015). *Burundi 2015 International Religious Freedom Report,* p.3.

of life and be expressed in public life (Chingota, 2006). In the same way, believers are told, "Do not do anything that endangers your neighbour's life" (Lev 19:16). The love of the neighbour involves taking care of them and avoiding anything that may be harmful to others. In order to achieve this love of their neighbour, believers have to strive to "live in peace with everyone" (Rom 12:18). When believers live in peace with everyone, striving to live in harmony with one another instead of being responsible for any lack of peace in their communities or in their relationships with unbelievers (Kasali, 2006; Witmer, 2000). Peace is an integral part of Burundian culture. In their greetings, for example, Burundians use a basic greeting, "Amahoro!" which means, "Peace!" (Jacques, 2009). The use of such a greeting means that they wish each other peace on a daily basis. Christians in Burundi can therefore use that cultural dynamic to promote peace.

Furthermore, Christians are called to be salt and light in the world (Matt 5:13-16). Like salt which purifies, preserves and enhances the flavour of food; Christians are expected to influence society and make the earth a better and more wholesome place (Kapolyo, 2006). Just as the light shines to illumine the world and remove darkness (Kapolyo, 2006), Christians are to live by example and promote peace in a war torn country like Burundi. In this way, Christians will be known as "peacemakers" (Matt 5:9). According to Kapolyo (2006:1119), "Africa desperately needs men and women of peace, sons and daughters of God who make peacemaking a priority so that the continent may live in peace. The peacemakers are rightly called the sons of God because they demonstrate in reality not just their relationship with God but their participation in his most characteristic work. In so doing they establish realms where the kingdom of heaven is indeed effective." In Burundian tradition, peacemaking is not a strange concept. Conflict resolution has always been part of Burundian culture. Whenever disputes occurred in the community, the *Bashingantahe*[13] were there to intervene in order to restore peace by bringing together the disputing parties for reconciliation (Babatunde, 2014). Christians in Burundi can learn from this practice in order to effectively play the role of peacemaking and bring harmony in the country that is affected by conflicts.

Another aspect of reconciliation is telling the truth, which involves the Truth and Reconciliation (TRC) in order rewrite history by correcting the distortions of the events that occurred during the interethnic conflicts in Burundi (Ntamahungiro, 2014). In a parliamentary session of 03 December 2014, the TRC was adopted in a vote that was boycotted by the Tutsi members of Parliament who thought the commission was dominated by the Hutu majority, even though Bishop Jean-Louis Nahimana (Hutu) of the Catholic Church was voted as the president of the commission, while Archbishop Bernard Ntahoturi (Tutsi) of the Anglican Church was put in the position of the vice-president.[14] The adopted Burundi TRC was given a mandate "to uncover

---

13  Bashingantahe is an institution that dates back to the 1600s and is comprised of an inter-ethnic council made up of elder tribesmen who have a 'highly developed sense of justice and fairness and whose focus is primarily on reconciliation, peacekeeping, social cohesion, and harmony.

14  'Burundi: Adoption d'une Commission Vérité et Réconciliation' *Arib News*, 3 December 2014. Viewed from http://bit.ly/2TvUiHW [Accessed 20 January 2018].

the truth about the events that the country experienced between 1962 and 2008, and to start a process of transitional justice and collective forgiveness."[15] However, the TRC faced major challenges to accomplish its mandate due to the political crisis that followed shortly after the TRC was adopted.[16]

## THEOLOGICAL REFLECTION ON RECONCILIATION IN THE BURUNDI CRISIS

In order to understand the notion of reconciliation, it is useful to consider the origin of reconciliation. In fact, reconciliation starts with God Himself who is called the God of reconciliation (Ndlovu, 1999). After the fall of man, the relationship between God and man was broken, and God sought man for reconciliation. In Genesis 3:9-10, "But the Lord God called to the man, "where are you?" He answered, "I heard you in the garden and I was afraid because I was naked; so I hid." Because of sin, man was overwhelmed by fear and guilt so that God took the first step towards saving man, seeking the person confused by shame (Asohoto, & Ngewa, 2006). As a result, God acknowledged the shame, fear, and guilt that Adam and Eve felt because of their nakedness and provided them with garments of skin (Gen 3:21). God's provision of garments of skin involved the shedding of blood, which foreshadows God's removal of sin, with the final fulfilment in the shedding of Christ's blood on the cross (Asohoto, & Ngewa, 2006).

Concerning the sacrifice offered by God to reconcile sinners to Himself, Paul writes, "For if, when we were God's enemies, we were reconciled to him through the death of his Son, how much more, having been reconciled, shall we be saved through his life! Not only is this so, but we also rejoice in God through our Lord Jesus Christ, through whom we have now received reconciliation." (Rom 5:10-11). In this way, the sinner can enjoy a restored relationship with God so as to receive the right to become His ambassador after being entrusted the ministry of reconciliation in the world (2 Cor 5:18-20). Christ's death on the cross makes possible human reconciliation to God. Reconciliation involves removing rebellious and sinful man's enmity toward God. This is one of the many marvellous accomplishments of the Godhead on behalf of a person the moment he believes in Christ for salvation from sin (Lowery, 2000). Schreiter (2013) refers to this type of reconciliation as *vertical reconciliation*. According to Merdassa (2014), it is the way of reconciliation that depends on man's repentance and forgiveness in order to heal the broken relationship between God and human beings, whereby God opens the closed door and reveals Himself for His people in Christ.

After the vertical reconciliation has taken place between God and human beings, there follows another type of reconciliation called *horizontal reconciliation* that takes place between human beings, either in individuals or in groups (Schreiter, 2013). In this sense, "reconciliation in a biblical sense means to restore the relationships between

15  Human Rights Council. (2016). Report of the United Nations Independent Investigation on Burundi (UNIIB) established pursuant to Human Rights. Council resolution S-24/1. Viewed from http://bit.ly/39jdO1d. [Accessed 15 January 2018]
16  Human Rights Council. (2016), Report of the United Nations, pp.16-17.

people and God vertically, and among people horizontally through the redemptive work of Christ" (Merdassa, 2014:47). The horizontal reconciliation is best defined as the social level of reconciliation whereby God heals the victims whose perpetrators do not repent for their offences. For that reason, God operates through Christians to effect reconciliation in the lives of those who struggle to embrace reconciliation (Robinson, 2011). This kind of horizontal reconciliation is the one Jesus advocates for when He says, "Therefore, if you are offering your gift at the altar and there remember that your brother has something against you, leave your gift there in front of the altar. First go and be reconciled to your brother, then come and offer your gift" (Matt 5:23-24). In these verses, it is clear that the two types of reconciliation, namely vertical and horizontal, go hand in hand, so that "without reconciliation, gifts presented at the altar mean nothing" (Barbieri, 2000:30). In other words, "the teaching implies that even offering thanks to God is inappropriate for a person who had wronged another human being, suggesting once more that religion and ethics cannot be separated" (Robinson, 2011:24). Furthermore, as Merdassa (2014:12) relates, in order to make an acceptable offering to God, the one who goes to the altar to present an offering to God needs to first repent and forgive fellow brothers and sisters so that the horizontal reconciliation heals unhealthy relationships in the community. In that way, the relationship between God and man is healed vertically, making it possible for the horizontal relationship to be restored as well.

In the teaching about prayer, Jesus instructs His disciples to "Forgive us our sins, for we also forgive everyone who sins against us" (Luke 11:4). While prayer is directed to "Our Father in heaven" (Matt 6:9) which is a *vertical relationship*, it must also take into consideration the horizontal relationship between the worshiper and other people. In fact, the phrase "as we also have forgiven our debtors" is a reminder that we should be eager to forgive others as we seek from God (Kapolyo, 2006). Thus, while forgiveness brings into picture the generous, compassionate forgiveness of God to a pleading sinner who owes Him an unpayable debt, no one can claim to walk in fellowship with God and refuse to forgive others (Barbieri, 2000; Turaki, 2006). Hence, anyone who believes to have been forgiven by God should be ready to forgive small offenses against them by others. In the same way, in the situation of ethnic conflicts in Burundi, the church needs to facilitate reconciliation both vertically and horizontally by bringing a message of reconciliation to the community.

## Conclusion

In the effort to bring reconciliation in the Burundian crisis, practical theology has a big role to play. This chapter has established that practical theology has to do with taking the Word of God from theory to practice through the correct interpretation. In this endeavour, the church is so instrumental in ensuring that the Word of God is put in practice. In Burundi where ethnic conflicts have been persisting for a long time, the church has already played a role toward reconciliation through speaking out against violence and creating programs aiming at bringing about reconciliation among the conflicting parties. Burundi is a country that is predominantly Christian. Thus, the majority of people in Burundi can follow the teaching of Christ in order to practice reconciliation and forgiveness in the effort to live in peace with each other regardless the ethnic, political, religious, and regional identity. In order to achieve that, the church needs to help people understand the correct interpretation of God's word based on historical, cultural, religious, and social aspects of Burundian society. Furthermore, the church needs to avoid any implication into the conflicts. It is only by being neutral that the church will be able to preach peace, justice, unity, forgiveness, in order to promote lasting reconciliation for a healthy society. ʼ

# References

Anglican Peace and Justice Network. (2007). *Community Transformation: Violence and the Church's Response*. Anglican Peace and Justice Network in Rwanda and Burundi. Viewed from http://bit.ly/2vZnX4l [Accessed 26 August 2017].

*Arib News* (2014). 'Burundi: Adoption d'une Commission Vérité et Réconciliation,' *Arib News*, 3 December 2014. Viewed from http://bit.ly/3a1JHei [Accessed 20 January 2018].

Arusha Peace and Reconciliation Agreement for Burundi (2000). Viewed from http://bit.ly/2HN9b3a [Accessed 20 May 2017].

Asohoto, B. and Ngewa, S. (2006). 'Genesis,' in Adeyemo, T. (ed.). *Africa Bible Commentary. A One-Volume Commentary Written by 70 African Scholars*. Nairobi: Word Alive Publishers, pp.9-84.

Babatunde, A.O. (2014). 'Harnessing Traditional Practices for Use in the Reintegration of Child Soldiers in Africa: Examples from Liberia and Burundi.' *Intervention*, 12(3):379-392. https://doi.org/10.1097/WTF.0000000000000057

Barbieri, Jr. L.A. (2000). *Matthew*. The Bible Knowledge Commentary: An Exposition of the Scriptures by Dallas Seminary Faculty. [New Testament Edition]. Walvoord, J.F. and Zuck, R.B. (eds.). Colorado: Cook Communications Ministries.

Bardall, S.G. and Arieff, A. (2017). *Rwanda's August 4 Presidential Election*. CRS INSIGHT. Viewed from https://fas.org/sgp/crs/row/IN10743.pdf. [Accessed 28 June 2017].

Bertelsmann Stiftung. (2016). Burundi Country Report. Gütersloh: Bertelsmann Stiftung. Viewed from http://bit.ly/2SSPL39 [Accessed 24 June 2017].

Botha, M. (2012). 'African leadership and the Role of the Presidency in African Conflicts: A Case Study of Uganda's President Yoweri Museveni.' Thesis presented in partial fulfillment of the requirements for the degree of Master of Arts (International Studies), Stellenbosch University.

Bouka, Y. and Nyabola, N. (2016). *The Crisis in Burundi and the Apathy of International Politics*. Viewed from http://bit.ly/38WFSHI [Accessed 28 June 2017].

Catholic Herald. (2015). *Violence Increases as Burundi's President Announces He Will Run Again*. Catholic News Service. Viewed from http://bit.ly/2SR0nzF [Accessed 26 August 2017].

Chingota, F. (2006). 'Leviticus,' In Adeyemo, T. (ed.) *Africa Bible Commentary. A One-Volume Commentary Written by 70 African Scholars*. Nairobi: Word Alive Publishers, pp.129-168

Daley, P. (2000). 'Ethnicity and Political Violence in Africa: The Challenge to the Burundi State,' *Political Geography*, 25(6):657- 679. https://doi.org/10.1016/j.polgeo.2006.05.007

Dingemans, G.D.J. (1996). 'Practical Theology in the Academy: A Contemporary Overview,' *The Journal of Religion*, 76(1):82-96. https://doi.org/10.1086/489737

Dulani, B.M. (2011). 'Personal Rule and Presidential Term Limits in Africa.' Unpublished doctoral dissertation for the degree of Doctor of Philosophy in Political Science, Michigan State University.

Fowler, J.W. (1985). 'Questions Practical Theology and Theological Education: Some Models and Questions,' *Theology Today*, 42(1):43-58. https://doi.org/10.1177/004057368504200106

Haro, J. (2016). *Youth are Key Actors for Peace in Burundi*. Viewed from http://www.centre-ubuntu.bi/fr/node/220. [Accessed 20 August 2017].

Hatungimana, J. (2011). *The Cause of Conflict in Burundi. International Relations II. Research Paper*. Viewed from http://bit.ly/2TAtNB8 [Accessed 25 August 2017].

Hendriks, H.J. (2004). *Studying Congregations in Africa*. Wellington: Lux Verbi.

Impunity Watch. (2016). *Crisis in Burundi: African solutions...?* Great Lakes Dispatches. Issue 3, January 2016. Peace Beyond Borders Programme. Viewed from http://bit.ly/2T5WQwe [Accessed 3 June 2017].

International Crisis Group. (2016). *Burundi: A Dangerous Third Term*. Africa Report N°235. [Translated from French]. Viewed from http://bit.ly/2HMw9HN [Accessed 22 June 2017].

International Religious Freedom. (2015). *Burundi 2015 International Religious Freedom Report*. Viewed from https://www.state.gov/documents/organization/256211.pdf. [Accessed 15 August 2017].

IRIS. (2016). *Crisis in Burundi: A Three-Year Outlook for the Region 2016-2019*. Humanitarian Foresight Think Tank. A think tank of the: Humanitarian and Development Programme. Viewed from http://bit.ly/2HNpZqD [Accessed 28 May 2017].

Jacques, B. (2009). *'Greetings' in Burundian Culture*. Viewed from http://afjn.org/greetings-in-burundian-culture/. [Accessed 25 June 2017].

Jones, C.E. (2014). Why Jogging or Going to Church Can Get You Arrested (in Burundi). *The Washington Post*, 23 July 2014. Viewed from https://wwrn.org/articles/43043/. [Accessed 29 June 2017].

Kapolyo, J. (2006). 'Matthew,' in T. Adeyemo, (ed.) *Africa Bible Commentary. A One-Volume Commentary Written by 70 African Scholars*. Nairobi: Word Alive Publishers, pp.1105-1170.

Kasali, D.M. (2006). 'Romans,' in Adeyemo, T. (ed.) *Africa Bible Commentary. A One-Volume Commentary Written by 70 African Scholars*. Nairobi: Word Alive Publishers, pp.1349-1376.

Kopwe, E.Z. (2013). 'Mediation Between Ethnic Groups: The Rwanda and Burundi Experience,' in Schreiter, R. and Jørgensen, K. (eds.). *Mission as Ministry of Reconciliation*. Edinburgh: Regnum, pp.184-190.

Krueger, R. and Krueger, K.T. (2007). *From bloodshed to hope in Burundi: Our Embassy Years during Genocide*. Viewed from http://bit.ly/32nr5TF [Accessed 28 August 2017].

LeBas, A. (2016). *Term Limits and Beyond: Africa's Democratic Hurdles. Current History* (May 2016), pp.169-174. Viewed from http://www.currenthistory.com/CurrentHistory_ LeBas.pdf. [Accessed 29 July 2017].

Lemarchand, R. (1995). *Burundi: Ethnic Conflict and Genocide.* Cambridge: University Press.

Lemarchand, R. (2008). *The Burundi Killings of 1972.* Viewed from http://bit.ly/2Th1vNe [Accessed 29 August 2017].

Louw, D. (2008). *Cura Vitae. Illness and the healing of life in pastoral care and counselling.* A guide for caregivers. Wellington: Lux Verbi.

Lowery, D.K. (2000). *'1 & 2 Corinthians,'* in Walvoord, J.F. and Zuck, R.B. (eds.) *The Bible Knowledge Commentary. An Exposition of the Scriptures by Dallas Seminary Faculty.* [New Testament.] Colorado: Cook Communications Ministries, pp.505-551.

Mbaku, J.M. (2017). *Election spotlights: Kenya and Rwanda.* Nonresident Senior Fellow, Africa Growth Initiative, Global Economy and Development, Brookings Institution. Viewed from https://brook.gs/2HNqEID [Accessed 10 June 2017].

Mbiatem, A. (2015). *Presidential Term Limit Divide in Democratic Republic of Congo: Another Security Threat in the Great Lakes Region? ALC Newsletter African Leadership Centre III,* (No. 1, Sept) pp.8-15. Issue Contributions by ALC Fellows, Alumni, Staff and other stakeholders. Viewed from www.africanleadershipcentre.org. [Accessed 18 June 2017].

Media Support (2015). *Burundi's Media During the 2015 Election Crisis.* Viewed from http://bit.ly/2HSdqdT [Accessed 26 August 2017].

Merdassa, D. (2014). *God's Act of Reconciling Sinful Humanity with Himself. "A Christian View of Reconciliation".* School of Mission and Theology [Online]. Viewed from http://bit.ly/37Tt7Mr [Accessed: 28 August 2017.]

Musser, M. (2015). *Peacebuilding thrives amidst Burundi unrest.* Viewed from http://bit.ly/2vxEM6k [Accessed 24 August 2017].

Ndayizigiye, J.B. (2005). *Humiliation and Violent Conflicts in Burundi.* Paper prepared for Round Table 1 of the 2005 Workshop on Humiliation and Violent Conflict, Columbia University, New York, 15-16 December 2005. Viewed from http://bit.ly/2wXU6cP [Accessed 22 June 2017].

Ndikumana, L. (2005). Distributional Conflict, the State, and Peace Building in Burundi. University of Massachusetts - Amherst ScholarWorks@UMass. Amherst Economics Department Working Paper Series. Viewed from http://bit.ly/3cwMRsX [Accessed 22 August 2017].

Ndlovu, T.J. (1999). The Church as an Agent of Reconciliation in the Thought of Desmond Tutu. Andrews University. Viewed from http://bit.ly/38kHjOO [Accessed 27 August 2017].

Niyonkuru, R.C. (2012). *Building Peace Architecture From Bottom-up: The Experience of Local Peace Committees in Burundi.* Viewed from http://bit.ly/39ZXP7W [Accessed 28 August 2017].

Niyungeko, S. (2015). *Burundi's Catholic Church Withdraws Support for Elections*. Viewed from https://nyti.ms/2PkN6Nt [Accessed 27 August 2017].

Ntahombaye, P. and Nduwayo, G. (2007). *Identity and Cultural Diversity in Conflict Resolution and Democratisation for the African Renaissance*. The Case of Burundi. Viewed from http://bit.ly/2SWUXTX [Accessed 26 May 2017]. https://doi.org/10.4314/ajcr.v7i2.39417

Ntamahungiro, J. (2014). *Ou En Est-On Avec La Reconciliation Au Burundi?* Viewed from http://bit.ly/2PhHy6k [Accessed 20 January 2017].

Omondi, G. (2015). *The New Assault On Presidential Term Limits In Africa: Focus On Burundi*. Viewed from http://bit.ly/2PIk2Wb [Accessed 21 June 2017].

Polling, J.N. (2010). 'Toward a Constructive Practical Theology: A Process-Relational Perspective,' *International Journal of Practical Theology*, 13(2):199–216. https://doi.org/10.1515/ijpt.2009.13

Prunier, G. (1994). *Burundi: A Manageable Crisis?* WRITENET (UK). Viewed from http://bit.ly/2v1AnIT [Accessed 28 August 2017].

Riedl, R.B. (2015). *No Separation: Can The Church Calm The Crisis in Burundi? Pacific standard*. Viewed from http://bit.ly/2wKAXLD [Accessed 25 August 2017].

Robinson, L.E. (2011). *The Influence of Social Context on a Theology of Reconciliation: Case Studies in Nothern Ireland*. Unpublished dissertation, Doctor of Philosophy, The University of Edinburgh.

Schreiter, R. (2013). 'Reconciliation as a Model for Mission: Biblical Foundations,' in Schreiter, R. and Jørgensen, K. (eds.) *Mission as Ministry of Reconciliation*. Vol. 16. Edinburgh: Regnum, pp.9-29.

The Electoral Commission of Uganda. (2016). *2015/2016 General Elections Report*. Submitted to Parliament through the Ministry of Justice and Constitutional Affairs in accordance with the provisions of Section 12 (1) (o) of the Electoral Commission Act, Cap 140 (as amended). Viewed from http://bit.ly/2w36K9S [Accessed 18 June 2017].

Turaki, Y. (2006). 'Ephesians,' in Adeyemo, T. (ed.) *Africa Bible Commentary. A One-Volume Commentary Written by 70 African Scholars*. Nairobi: Word Alive Publishers, pp.1425-1438.

'UN Urges DR Congo Leader to Keep Promise to Step Down', *Gulf Times*, 1 January 2018. Viewed from http://bit.ly/37Vt6aN [Accessed 25 January 2018].

Vandeginste, S. (2014). 'Governing ethnicity after genocide: ethnic amnesia in Rwanda versus ethnic power-sharing in Burundi,' *Journal of Eastern African Studies*, (2):263-277. https://doi.org/10.1080/17531055.2014.891784

Vandeginste, S. (2015). *Burundi's crisis and the Arusha Peace and Reconciliation Agreement: which way forward?* Viewed from http://bit.ly/3aOujPE

Wallis, A. (2015). *Burundi: Crisis and Warning*. Viewed from http://bit.ly/2Igd7JW [Accessed 26 August 2017].

Waters, T. (2008). *Ethnicity and Burundi's Refugees.* Viewed from http://bit.ly/2x6t3MG [Accessed 24 August 2017].

Witmer, J.A. (2000). 'Romans,' in Walvoord, J.F. and Zuck, R.B. (eds.) *The Bible Knowledge Commentary: An Exposition of the Scriptures* by Dallas Seminary Faculty [New Testament]. Colorado: Cook Communications Ministries, pp.435-504.

A Pastoral Care Approach

*Oholiabs D. Tuduks[1]*

## INTRODUCTION

Nigeria as a multi-religious country has three main religious groups – Christians, Muslims, and the adherents of traditional religions. But the most populous of the three are Christians and Muslims, while the former are found more in the south-east and south-west of the country among the Igbo and Yoruba major ethnic groups, the latter are concentrated more in the north among the Hausa/Fulani[2] major ethnic group. Impliedly, in Northern Nigeria Christians constitute the minority who comes from the minority ethnic groups and a meagre number from the Hausa/Fulani major ethnic group. The two religious groups live together in the same communities with some families having mix-religious adherents as a result of inter-marriages and or proselytisation. But despite this togetherness, Christians and Muslims continue to experience inter-religious tension.

Historically, Northern Nigeria is known for its periodic religious crises which has caused a lot of havoc among the Christians and Muslims in the region. Research has shown that Northern Nigeria has been under religious crises from 1980 to the present and this has claimed numerous lives including destruction of properties (Best, 2001; cf. Sodiq, 2009; Sampson, 2012; Adegbulu, 2013; Mulders, 2016). The religious crises can be divided into two different stages: the early stage (1980 to 2008), and the late stage (2009 to present). The major divide of these stages was the advent of a dreaded Islamic group popularly known as *Boko Haram*[3] in 2009. The early stage originated with a religious attack by a group known as the Maitatsine[4] (1980 to 1985) who caused

---

1 Rev Oholiabs D. Tuduks is an ordained minister in the Evangelical Church Winning All (ECWA), as well as a lecturer in the Department of Religious Studies at Gombe State University, Nigeria. He is currently a PhD candidate at Stellenbosch University.

2 Hausa/Fulani were two different ethnic groups before the colonial era, but later became assimilated into one, and known today as Hausa/Fulani ethnic group.

3 This is a radical Islamic sect called "Jama'atu Ahlis Sunna Lidda'awati Wal-Jihad", but widely known as *Boko Haram*. The word *Boko* in Hausa is an equivocal term which means either 'western' or 'foreign'; while *Haram* is an Arabic derivative meaning 'forbidden'. Therefore, the two words put together means 'to forbid anything that is western and western education' (Adegbulu, 2013).

4 The Islamic group was nicknamed after the name of the leader – 'Maitatsine' (Ibighbi, 1987).

serious harm among the two religious groups but more especially the Christians. By 1987 there were inter-religious crises as the results of religious intolerance, religious solidarity, and alleged blasphemy which continued periodically to 2008 while claiming the lives of many of these religious groups. The late stage from 2009 to the present started with the emergence of the *Boko Haram* whose activities are no longer news in Northern Nigeria today. It is worth noting that the crises in the early and late stages include religious attack and inter-religious crises. And in the case of religious attack where Christians[5] are made the target, Muslims[6] are not totally exempted particularly with the current *Boko Haram* attacks. The effect of these religious attack and inter-religious crises trigger the practice of dysfunctional exclusion[7] among the two religious groups as will be discussed in the next section.

Nonetheless, according to Yusufu Turaki, the dysfunctional exclusion and the religious crises experienced today in Northern Nigeria originated in the British colonial era when religious intolerance and prejudice between the Muslims and non-Muslims were encouraged (Turaki, 1993). This assertion was affirmed by the report on the inter-religious crises in Nigeria by the International Joint Delegation of the World Council of Churches (WCC) and the Royal Aal al-Bayt Institute for Islamic Thought (The Royal Islamic Strategic Studies Centre, 2012). The reports explained the dysfunctional exclusion in the geographical polarisation of Muslims and Christians, where Christian residential areas, and in some cases local markets, are segregated from those of Muslims. It is this situation of exclusion that results in the dysfunctional relationship where the practice of exclusion and marginalisation of the minority religious group becomes a common practice in Northern Nigeria. And these practices continue to trigger religious tension leading to violence among the religious groups. As a result of these practices the adherents of the two religions do not trust one another or each other as group, they rather live with concealed anger, yet with fear of one another. Several attempts have been made by different peace brokers to address the challenges through inter-religious dialogue and by means of religious tolerance, yet the two religious groups continue to live in a dysfunctional relationship that triggers religious tension.

In view of the introduction above, this chapter will reconsider the praxis of reconciliation among the two religious groups in addressing the dysfunctional relationship and inter-religious crises in Northern Nigeria. It will first examine the

---

5    Sodiq (2009:669) further states, "Whenever any sect of modern revivalism of Islam attacks Westerners or denounces modern materialism, these movements always assume that Christians are agents of the West; therefore, Christians are directly or indirectly seen as agents of oppression against Islam and Muslims." This might be the reason why some Muslims attacked Christians and their places of worship.

6    Bitrus (2016) argues that the involvement of Muslims in *Boko Haram*'s attack is designed to blindfold the public from perceiving the reality of the *Boko Haram*'s mission against the Christians. And, on the other hand, he explains that Muslims are also attacked because they are perceived as threat to *Boko Haram*'s mission and or perceived as collaborators with government to fight against them.

7    Dysfunctional exclusion refers to the practice in a relationship that keeps off an individual or group for one's personal or group interest thus making relationship vulnerable to crisis. In other words, it is an exclusion that causes an impaired relationship thus creating more emotional turmoil than satisfaction (Urell, 2013).

challenge of Christian/Muslim relationship in Northern Nigeria. Secondly, it will reconsider the praxis of reconciliation and its challenges among the two religious groups. And lastly, it will pragmatically approach reconciliation from a pastoral care perspective with an inter-religious consciousness towards promoting Christian/ Muslim inter-religious co-existence in Northern Nigeria.

## THE CHALLENGE OF CHRISTIAN/MUSLIM RELATIONSHIP IN NORTHERN NIGERIA

Christians and Muslims in Northern Nigeria continued to experience periodic religious crises among themselves. Speaking on the causes of crises, Joseph and Rothfuss (2012) indicates that Christians in Northern Nigeria have been occasionally subjected to mob attacks from followers of the Islamic faith as a result of perceived *provocation*. Gwamna (2010) further argues that the perceived provocations made Christians in Northern Nigeria suffer attacks from their Muslims counterpart. He asserts that some of the crises are so-called *misplaced aggression* for example the Osama Bin Laden riot (2001), the Miss World Pageant crisis (2002) and the Prophet Mohammad Cartoon crisis (2006) which were not perpetrated by Northern Nigerian Christians. In this context, Northern Nigerian Christians were made scapegoats of perceived atrocities of the West who are identified as being Christians (Griswold, 2010). They have thus experienced numerous attacks and killings in response to these alleged blasphemies.[8]

On the other hand, Christians have also complained of blasphemous statements spoken against the person of Jesus Christ by some Muslims. For example, Malam Nasir El-Rufai[9] who blasphemed on two different occasions about Jesus Christ (Eyoboka, 2016; cf. Erunke, 2013). In response to the blasphemies, the Christian Association of Nigeria (CAN) asserts that it is due to the maturity, fortitude, patience, decency, forgiving nature and deep sense of restraint that the majority of Christians have in Nigeria which prevented them from retaliating against El-Rufai for his blasphemous statements (Erunke, 2013). In regard to the killing of Christians in Northern Nigeria, CAN[10] blames the President of the Federal Republic of Nigeria for keeping silent (Obi, 2016). Joseph and Rothfuss (2012) have earlier noted that the government of the Federal Republic of Nigeria has failed in taking action against the perpetrations of evil on the innocent, rather regarded the actions of the mob as being carried out by hoodlums, thereby dismissing the issue. Omotosho (2003) blames the

---

8    For example, more recently in Niger state, Mr. Methodus Chimaije Emmanuel on 29 May 2016 was killed over alleged blasphemous comments about Prophet Mohammed on the social media (Omonobi, 2016). Mrs Bridget Agbahime was brutally killed in Kano state on 2 June 2016 on the ground of alleged blasphemy against Prophet Mohammed (World Watch Monitor, 2016). And on 22 August 2016 on the account of alleged blasphemy against the Prophet Muhammad in Zamfara state, eight were set ablaze in a house to their total annihilation (Nwachukwu, 2016).

9    Malam Nasir El-Rufai is the present Governor of Kaduna state, Nigeria. His administration is believed by many Christians as capable of causing religious crisis in Kaduna state.

10   The Christian Association of Nigeria (CAN) cited the example of Mrs Eunice Elisha who was killed in Abuja on 9 July 2016 noting that she is not sure whether the killings of Christians bother the President or not (Obi, 2016).

two religious leaders for being responsible for the acts of provocation that triggers religious violence. He cites examples of some of the Christian and Muslim polemics who engaged in provocation, thereby causing violence among the two religious groups. For Omotosho, the major factors responsible for the cause of inter-religious violence are, lack of recognition of one another; campaigns of hatred and blackmail; lack of genuine desire to understand each other's belief and culture; and extremism. He therefore argues that to end religious violence in Nigeria, the government must set up a religious committee who would serve as regulatory body for religious activities and at the same time serve as advisory body to the government (Omotosho, 2003). In assessing the inter-religious bridge-building efforts of peace brokers[11] from governmental and non-governmental organisations, Ojo and Lateju (2010) remarks that most of the Nigeria's peace brokers responded to the religious crisis only after its escalation to violence, which made it very difficult to address. They noted that the grassroots where the flame of religious crisis is normally seen are often forgotten in nominating members of the dialogue team. Ojo and Lateju therefore argue for the inclusion of people at grassroots level in the inter-religious dialogue team.

There is also the challenge of confronting the truth among the religious groups when there is an act of perpetration by one group against the other, the perpetrators are hardly ever confronted by their respective religious leaders who would rather choose to remain silent over the perpetration. Consequently, the silence or assuming the position of neutrality, communicates the message of affirmation as alluded in the words of the Archbishop Emeritus Desmond Tutu: "If you are neutral in situations of injustice, you have chosen the side of the oppressor."[12] In this context, Thesnaar (2008) uses the term "offenders" in preference to "perpetrators", as offenders in addition to perpetrators includes direct or indirect supporters. The evilness of injustice implies a commitment to disturb the peaceful coexistence of people in a society and as long as the injustice continue it further implies an act of threat that there will be no peace in the society (Esack, 2002).

## THE PRAXIS OF RECONCILIATION AMONG RELIGIOUS GROUPS IN NORTHERN NIGERIA

In the event of inter-religious conflict in Northern Nigeria, dialogue and tolerance have often been considered by peace brokers as major tools for reconciliation. Reflecting on the history of inter-religious dialogue in Nigeria, Dopamu (1989) asserts that the first major attempt for introducing the inter-religious discussion was in 1975 by a group called Nigerian Association for the Study of Religions (NASR). But according to Sodiq (2009), inter-religious dialogue started in the 1960s with the activities and participation of some Christian and Muslim leaders in inter-religious

11    Such as the Advisory Council on Religious Affairs (ACRA) 1987; Nigeria Inter Religious Council (NIREC) 2000; Programme for Christian–Muslim Relations in Africa (PROCMURA); Centre for Interfaith Relations and Cross-Cultural Outreach; Justice, Peace and Reconciliation Movement (JPRM); Bridge Builders; West Africa Network for Peace Building; Interfaith Mediation Centre; Muslim–Christian Dialogue Forum.

12    See Goodreads, *Desmond Tutu Quotes*, viewed from http://bit.ly/2TI6uWf [Accessed 19 March 2017].

discussion. Inter-religious dialogue therefore continued with an increasing number of proponents. The 1980s reoccurrence of inter-religious crises between Christians and Muslims, which affected the Northern Nigerian region, prompted the military administration of General Ibrahim Badamasi Babangida to consider inter-religious dialogue as a matter of priority in addressing the crisis. In 1988, General Babangida appointed an advisory council of twenty-four members, comprising twelve Muslims and twelve Christians, to find ways that all religions in Nigeria could live together in harmony. In 1999 when the inter-religious crisis still persisted, the Nigeria Inter-Religious Council (NIREC) was formed through the joint efforts of the Nigeria Supreme Council for Islamic Affairs (NSCIA) and Christian Association of Nigeria (CAN) to serve as peace brokers. In the efforts of NIREC, Joseph and Rothfuss (2012) noted the ineffectiveness of the use of dialogue, and therefore argues for reconsideration of their approach. Meanwhile, the International Joint Delegation of the World Council of Churches and the Royal Aal al-Bayt Institute for Islamic Thought in its report on inter-religious crises in Northern Nigeria identified the ineffective cooperation within NIREC as a key factor behind the inter-religious tensions and crises in Northern Nigeria (The Royal Islamic Strategic Studies Centre, 2012). Therefore, the inter-religious dialogue among Christians and Muslims needs to be assessed to find out the challenges that make it unsuccessful.

## The challenge of inter-religious dialogue

Inter-religious dialogue has faced challenges which has made it less effective among the religious groups. It has been observed that the idea of inter-religious dialogue is still a controversial subject in an intra-religious setting. For example, Sodiq (1994), from a Muslim perspective pointed out that the two religious groups are not in congruence on the idea of religious dialogue and its practice. He commended the Christian leaders for their initiative and support for dialogue, but on the other hand, Sodiq (1994) reveals that some Muslims are not in support of dialogue for the following reasons. Firstly, Muslims feel a need for self-sufficiency as they believe that Islam is seen as a system of belief that is completed by Allah, therefore Muslims need nothing outside it to borrow or learn from other religions. Secondly, Muslims resent dialogue thinking that Christians consciously employed various methods of winning them to Christianity and they assume dialogue may be one of these, and therefore were afraid of total engagement. The third reason was the argument that there were fewer Muslim scholars who were knowledgeable enough in Christian thought to engage on an equal level together with Christian scholars in dialogue; by this, they believe, dialogue give Christians an advantage over them, allowing Christian scholars to dominate and control the dialogue table at many conferences.

Arguing against the resentment of some Muslims about dialogue, Omotosho (2003), an Islamic scholar, explains that Muslims believe that Islam has always recognised and practiced genuine dialogue with Christianity right from the inception of Islam, and hold that, on the subject of dialogue they have made giant strides on fundamental issues that are yet to be reciprocated by Christians (Omotosho, 2003). In support of Omotosho, Acar (2005) speaks from the Islamic historical perspective, on the investigatory dialogue between the delegation of the Najran Christians and the

Prophet Muhammad in Medina, which is understood as a successful and peaceful dialogue that concluded with peaceful farewell words "O, Abu al-Qasim, we decided to leave you as you are and you leave us as we are" (Acar, 2005:3). According to Acar, the dialogue ended with a written agreement between the Christians and the Prophet Muhammad about the security of the lives, property and religion of the Christians, and this was signed by witnesses.

It is believed that in the early period in Medina, the inhabitants were largely Christians and Jews, who were known as *people of the Book* and with whom the Muslims had cordial relationship and that they invited them for dialogue (Omotosho, 2003). This interest in dialogue is inscribed in the Qur'an: "Say O people of the Book! Come to common terms as between you and us that we worship none but God; that we associate no partners with Him; that we erect not from among ourselves Lords and patrons other than God ..." (Qur'an 3:64). Such dialogue suggests the interest of the Qur'an in inter-religious peaceful coexistence and reconciliation. Despite the fact that the Qur'an reveals that mankind was one community (Qur'an 2:213), which according to Al-Qurtubi (Fazaluddin, 2016) implies oneness of religion. The Qur'an holds to the unity of faith, talking of a common foundation for success between Muslims, Sabians, Jews and Christians who all believe in God, the Judgement Day and the doing of good deeds (Fazaluddin, 2016). Muslims are admonished not to engage in a senseless argument with the people of the Book,[13] as this would be capable of creating a crisis, for the Christians have the same source of revelation, and the same God whom they all worship (Qur'an 29:46). In another development, Christians are singled out for special respect by Muslims as their affection (Qur'an 5:82). These perspectives serve as motivation to Muslims for peaceful relationship with Christians today.

Other area of challenge to Christian/Muslim inter-religious dialogue is the practice of fundamentalism among some religious leaders. Yakubu Yahya, a Muslim activist noted that if there is any grievance between Muslims and the government, the only place of settlement is not the dialogue table but battlefield. To this view of Yahya, Kwashi asked, if Muslims are prepared to settle grievances with the government only on the battlefield, where else can they settle grievances with Christians? (Kwashi, 2004). Notwithstanding, it is worth noting that this statement of Yakubu Yahya does not necessarily represent the view and opinion of all Muslims in Northern Nigeria. On the other hand, the late Evangelist Paul Gindiri, a renowned Christian preacher of Northern Nigeria has been described as a confrontational preacher who's preaching lacked diplomacy as he often attacked Muslims (Gaiya, 2004). From these two examples, it is clear that fundamentalism is a challenge to Christian/Muslim coexistence in Northern Nigeria.

---

13    In the Qur'an and Hadith, the term People of the Book (Ahl al-Kitāb) is used to refer to followers of certain monotheistic faiths which pre-date the advent of Islam. In particular, it refers to the Christians, Jews, and Sabians. Viewed from http://bit.ly/2Tpff8x [Accessed 20 August 2019].

## Reconsideration of inter-religious dialogue and religious tolerance for effective usage

Religious leaders need to understand the concept of inter-religious dialogue and how it should be practiced inter-religiously. It is more than just coming to sit around a table, what is brought to the table and how it is presented matters. Gwamna (2010:174-177) understands inter-religious dialogue and classifies it into four types. *The dialogue of life*, which he explains as relationships at the level of the ordinary, the everyday life of the religious adherents. Second, the *dialogue of discourse* which involves the coming together of different religious adherents in interaction with basic information and ideas on their respective religious beliefs and practices. The third type is the *dialogue of spirituality* which has to do with the totality of the person's religious experience, in meditation, prayer, faith and its expression, and can also be referred to as the *dialogue of the heart*. The fourth one is the *dialogue of action* which refers to dialogue through cooperative joint efforts towards the promotion of human development.

In concurring with Gwamna, Bakker (2014) summarised the four types into the dialogues of life, heart, and mind. He merged Gwamna's second and fourth categories under the dialogue of mind. The categorisation of dialogue into these three crucial places of human activities suggest dialogue as an existential phenomenon which automatically puts dialogue at the disposal of human life. Bartholomew (2010) understands dialogue as the most fundamental experience of life and the most powerful means of communication. He stressed the fact that dialogue promotes knowledge, abolishes fear and prejudice, and broadens horizons. Bartholomew warns that to engage in dialogue is not to undertake arguments against one's opponents in the framework of conflict. But rather dialogue is to be approached in a spirit of love, sincerity, and honesty. In this respect he believes that dialogue implies equality that speaks humility (Bartholomew, 2010). Therefore, with equality and humility dialogue becomes a simple way of life among religious groups that dispels hostility and arrogance. Song (2012) rightly asserts that inter-religious dialogue is possible if people recognise the web of relationships, the inevitable interconnectedness they already and inevitably participate in. She asserts that when the walls of individuality, or *ego* is broken down something much more powerful takes over—the fount of wisdom and empathy emerge. So, the Golden Rule of *Do not do to others what you would not have them do to you*, naturally comes to the fore with ease and without resistance.

To promote and sanitise inter-religious dialogue at a round table its guideline needs to be respected and adhered to. The *Dialogue Decalogue* formulated in the work of Leonard Swidler (1983) should be upheld: *First Commandment* – The primary purpose of dialogue is to change and grow in the perception and understanding of reality and then to act accordingly. *Second Commandment*: Inter-religious dialogue must be a two-sided project – within each religious community and between religious communities. *Third Commandment*: Each participant must come to the dialogue with complete honesty and sincerity. *Fourth Commandment*: Each participant must assume a similar commitment of complete honesty and sincerity in the other partners. *Fifth*

*Commandment*: Each participant must define himself. *Sixth Commandment*: Each participant must come to the dialogue with no hard-and-fast assumptions as to where the points of disagreement are. *Seventh Commandment*: Dialogue can take place only between equals or *par cum pari* as Vatican II put it. *Eighth Commandment*: Dialogue can take place only on the basis of mutual trust. *Ninth Commandment*: Persons entering into inter-religious dialogue must be at least minimally self-critical of both themselves and their own religious traditions. *Tenth Commandment*: Each participant eventually must attempt to experience the partner's religion from within. If religious leaders or dialogue participants are guided by these *Dialogue Decalogue* it will increase the chances of realising a successful inter-religious dialogue result. Furthermore, the four theses of Paul F. Knitter (2012) serves as a caution as it explains the power of religion in conflict resolution or escalation. His first thesis argues that, unless the religions become part of the solutions, they will certainly continue to be part of the problem. The second thesis is formulated on the grounds that the causes of religious violence can be likened to bad breath, which requires other people to conscientise you. Therefore, the thesis argues for the need of religions to become part of the solution together, and not separately. The third thesis states that, to become part of the solution, religions must confront the reason for being part of the problem. The fourth thesis asserts that one of the reasons why religions are easily exploited for the purposes of violence and hatred is because each religion makes exclusivist claims. Knitter's theses explain the need for inter-religious understanding that helps in the practice of inter-religious dialogue and religious tolerance.

For religious tolerance to be proclaimed among religious adherents, its concept needs to be understood. Thomas Jefferson's understanding of tolerance is *bearing with* or *suffering*. This supports the Oxford English Dictionary that defines tolerance as to endure, or to sustain pain or hardship, without interference or molestation. The tolerant person "suffers" or "endures" or "bears with" precisely by restraining rather than releasing the impulse to punish or muzzle the opponent by violence (Little, 1998). According to Little, a person who is tolerant is open-minded with an interest in diversity, and as found in the dictionary's elegant words, has a *catholicity of spirit*. The *catholicity of spirit* was found in Mother Theresa who in her lifetime committed herself to serving humanity regardless of their religious affiliations (Wuthnow, 2005:3). In living her Christian religious life inter-religiously Mother Theresa proclaimed *I see God in every human being* (Wuthnow, 2005:1). This is the kind of mind-set that gives birth to the practice of tolerance. In describing the feature of tolerance Potgieter et al. (2014) identified one as ethical behaviour, explaining that a person who is tolerant believes that people in a community benefits when different lifestyles are allowed to flourish as they represent the experience of diversity where much can be learned to better the human condition. They believe that the ability to allow, to permit, to comply, and to forbear constitutes a form of tolerance enjoyed in a community as the people have and exercise the right of living their own lives. Tolerance implies that we are made to be different (Potgieter, van der Walt, & Wolhuter, 2014). Difference must be appreciated for its ability to make us develop desire for something we do not have. The Archbishop Emeritus Desmond Tutu says, "Differences are not intended to separate, to alienate. We are different precisely in order to realise our need of one another."[14] For tolerance to find a fertile ground for flourishing among the adherents of the two religious groups there is a need for an accurate knowledge of the beliefs and practices of Christians and Muslims (Azumah, 2008). Tolerance makes more sense when there is an understanding of what one is to tolerate. This calls for inter-religious understanding among the religious groups.

The following examples of centres and individuals who are committed to promoting inter-religious discussion show that inter-religious understanding is feasible. The efforts of Pastor James Wuye and the Imam Muhammad Ashafa, who are popularly known as *the pastor and the Imam*, are acknowledged often in the promotion of inter-religious understanding. In the past, the two religious leaders were enemies, religious fundamentalists, but today they are partners heading an organisation together called Interfaith Mediation Centre in Kaduna, the north-western part of Nigeria. Pastor Wuye and Imam Ashafa are passionately engaged in creating awareness for an inter-religious understanding towards peaceful co-existence and healing of the wounded relationship among the Christians and Muslims in Northern Nigeria (Sennott, 2014). The example of these men is a motivation for inter-religious understanding towards peaceful coexistence, or as the archbishop of Canterbury, Dr. Rowan Williams, calls it *a model for Christian Muslim relations* (Henderson, 2015:1).

The Da'wah[15] Institute of Nigeria (DIN) of the Islamic Education Trust in Minna, the north-central part of Nigeria is committed to both intra and inter-religious awareness on inter-religious understanding. The awareness is crucial for the fact that Christians and Muslims in Northern Nigeria have limited inter-religious understanding. Again, DIN believes that *bad people* who are always involved in the act of perpetrating violence are found in both the religions thus the need for inter-religious understanding (Da'wah Institute of Nigeria, 2009). Archbishop Ignatius Kaigama has also been pictured as another example of an inclusive faith leader who engages in inter-religious discussion aiming at fostering the peaceful coexistence between Christians and Muslims. In his efforts to address the divide between the two religious groups in Jos, where in some communities, the two religious groups live in exclusion, the Archbishop engages in organising training and inter-religious discussions aimed at creating an inclusive functional coexistence (Verwoerd, 2015). For this reason, he established an inter-religious centre in the north-central part of Nigeria known as *Jos Interfaith Centre* where inter-religious training and dialogue are conducted.

Another example of a discussion that promotes inter-religious understanding is the nonviolence approach to reconciliation among Christians and Muslims passionately embarked on by Rev. Abare Yunusa Kallah, the chairman of The Christian Association of Nigeria (CAN) – North-eastern zone. Rev. Kallah engages in organising and conducting trainings and seminars among religious leaders promoting nonviolence, peace and dialogue engagement (Kallah, 2015). He was motivated by his leadership

---

14    See Goodreads, *Desmond Tutu Quotes*. Viewed fromhttp://bit.ly/2Tl6uWf [Accessed 19 March 2017].

15    *Da'wah* is an Arabic word which means to invite or summon someone. This term is often used to describe when Muslims share their faith with others, in order to teach them more about Islam. This definition is provided by Thoughtco. Viewed from http://bit.ly/2TmTKpb [Accessed 16 March 2017].

experience where he discovered the possibility of engaging in inter-religious discussion among Christian and Muslim leaders to develop a nonviolence approach to reconciliation. These examples serve as motivation for a pastoral care approach through inter-religious learning and understanding among the religious groups.

## A PASTORAL CARE APPROACH TO RECONCILIATION AMONG RELIGIOUS GROUPS

Pastoral care is not a biblical concept, it stems from the ancient Greek use of *soul care* (Louw, 1998). Nonetheless, the concept gained acceptance within the Christian tradition but over the course of time it developed new meanings. For example, the orthodox approach to *pastoral care* regards it as a process of learning towards an understanding and insight into ecclesiastical doctrine; the reformed tradition considered the concept towards the purification and sanctification of human life through relationship with Christ (Louw, 1998). Clebsch and Jaekle (1964) defines pastoral care as activities of help done by representative Christian persons directed to heal, to sustain, to guide, and to reconcile the persons in trouble. They emphasised that pastoral care is a ministry to be performed by persons of Christian faith not necessarily a pastor or any church leadership person. Clebsch and Jaekle (1964) believe that pastoral care requires Christian faith resources. History might show that people from different disciplines and religions were involved in soul care but that does not make their activities pastoral care. The definition of pastoral care by Clebsch and Jaekle is crucial, where emphasis is placed on Christian faith. In this context, the role of pastoral care can further be summarised into three dimensions: faith care (*cura animarum*) – theological dimension; life care (*cura vitae*) – therapeutic dimension; and victorious resurrection care (hope care) – spiritual dimension (Louw, 2008). The practice of pastoral care expresses a deep concern for human beings without discrimination (Lartey, 2003). It engages in the affairs of human suffering, creating an environment that makes people live in hope with human dignity in the face of their sufferings (Louw, 2008). The functions of pastoral care include healing, sustaining, guiding, reconciling, nurturing, liberating, and empowering Lartey (2003). Louw (2008) added the act of interpreting to Lartey's list. These functions are aimed at improving both spiritual and physical maturity (Louw, 2008).

In his book *Pastoral Care to Muslims: Building Bridges*, Kirkwood (2002) differentiates between pastoral care and Christian pastoral care. He explains the latter as having a Christian dimension, sustained by Christian faith; while he understands the former as care provided to the needy by anyone and thus not necessarily by a Christian. Kirkwood (2002) specifically mentions the possibility of pastoral care being offered by a Muslim to a Christian, a Buddhist to a Christian, and a Hindu to a Christian or vice versa. He emphasises that pastoral care is a responsibility of anyone who is in position and has the spiritual sensor, is obliged to render pastoral care unconditionally. In describing the responsibilities of pastoral care giver, Lartey (2003) outlined its model as therapy, ministry,[16] social action, empowerment, and personal interaction. According to these outlined models and the functions described

---

16    The ministry includes proclamation, teaching, prophecy, service, and worship.

by Lartey and Louw, pastoral care will hardly be the responsibility of everyone. I therefore reaffirm the definition of pastoral care by Clebsch and Jaekle that makes pastoral care a unique Christian responsibility, in contrast to the view of Kirkwood. And as a Christian responsibility, the service is believed to be non-discriminatory focusing on all human beings and their sufferings. A motivating factor for pastoral care, that makes it a Christian service, is the inclusive ministry of Jesus Christ in which the functions of pastoral care are evident in His earthly ministry.

It is worth noting that for pastoral care to be effective there is a need for a hermeneutical approach that explains the process of practicing the functions of pastoral care. According to Louw (1998), hermeneutics involves the process of interpretation where the pastoral care giver operates between the text of the scripture and the context of people (Louw, 1998). The main focus of hermeneutics is the explanation, translation, communication, and interpretation of a message to people who are prepared to hear and understand (Louw, 1998).

In commenting on the hermeneutical characteristics of pastoral interpretation Preston (1977) mentions three phenomena that are frequent in pastoral care: the self of the pastor as interpreter; the uniqueness of every caring situation; and the mutual development of understanding. He added a fourth phenomenon which he describes as having much in common with the traditional hermeneutic endeavour – concerning a time perspective. This has to do with the relative emphasis upon past, present, and future as it illuminates the meanings within the interpretation. In pastoral care the interest is on *human wholeness* according to Louw, with *cura vitae* is meant life should be healed. He explains that in Christian spirituality healing is not merely of a private human soul detached from the body, the existential realities, and the environment; healing is a comprehensive concept (Louw, 2013). Thesnaar (2011) asserts that the hermeneutical process is a deeply transformative process. He states the goal of pastoral care as the understanding of the encounter between God and humans from the perspective of the confronting effect of the grace of God, presence and identifying with the human need and suffering. It should be made clear that within the hermeneutical paradigm, both the perpetrators and victims are in need of healing and wholeness because both have been affected and therefore needs healing that restores their relationships (Thesnaar, 2011).

Towards effective healing, remembrance constitute a part of the reconciliation processes which is often overlooked, or intentionally rejected, by some peace brokers in fear of triggering a crisis. For the present and future to be protected the past need to be remembered. Søren Kierkegaard rightly says, "Those who cannot remember from the past are condemned to repeat it. Life can only be understood backward but must be lived forward" (quoted in Thesnaar, 2011:6). For healing and reconciliation to be effective, pastoral hermeneutics must critically engage with the past in order to transform it in the present and the future (Thesnaar, 2013). Story-telling is the way to the past, the perpetrators and the victims become part of each other's story; telling it gives a sense of acceptance, respect, and care.

And in telling the stories the following must be confessed, *what we have done; what was done to us; and what we failed to do* (Thesnaar, 2011:30). Stories that are sincerely told prepares the ground for healing and reconciliation.

Thesnaar (2003) provides a helpful process towards a meaningful reconciliation, the first step is for the offender to realise that an offence has been committed. The second has to do with a remorseful confession of the offender to the victim. Thirdly, there must be a willingness for reparation, restoration and restitution by the offender. The last step is an expression of the victim's willingness to forgive. Thesnaar's steps to reconciliation concurs with that of Howard J. Clinebell (1966), an early expert in pastoral care and counselling, whose process includes confrontation, confession, forgiveness, restitution, and reconciliation. Clinebell's main emphasis is on the importance of confrontation, where the core truth is supposed to be unveiled. The idea of confrontation in conflict resolution is likened to the idiom of *calling a spade a spade*. According to Clinebell, sometimes guilt is hidden from both parties, and for it to be resolved, the truth about it needs confrontation. In conflict resolution when the truth is not confronted, peace brokers will only be scratching to the pain of the victim's wound. In the context of healing and reconciliation among religious groups, and confrontation of truth, a pastoral care approach needs an inter-religious consciousness.

## Inter-religious pastoral care approach to reconciliation

In promoting religious plurality, Bowden (2005) suggests the need for openness, mutual understanding and respect for one another's truth among the adherents of religions. According to Barnes (2002), the *context of otherness* discloses the *possibility of God*, as God is already working through his Spirit in the *context of otherness*. He urges Christians not to look at their calling only to speak about God that has been revealed through Jesus Christ, but also to critically listen with generosity to what others are saying about God (Barnes, 2002). Knitter (2011) agrees with Barnes, and affirms the terminology of Tillich, that if in Christian theology Christians want to explore more about *God beyond God* than what they have discovered in Jesus Christ, then there is need to turn and give listening ears to the experience and teachings of other religions. He adds that Christian theology is not complete without making an effort to explore beyond the confines of the Christian boundary, because the God who is beyond God is beyond all boundaries. In other words, this God is the boundary, the circle that holds everyone (Knitter, 2011). Knowing about other religions will help Christians to appreciate their unique religion (Knitter, 2011). In stressing Tillich's theology, who was involved in exploring other religious traditions, Knitter asserts that religious diversity is God's will. He explains that, if religious diversity is what it is supposed to be, then the existence of people religiously should be done with consciousness and in co-existence with the other religious people in different ways from theirs. In a language that is more contemporary theological, Knitter (2011:118) states, "To be religious today is to be religious inter-religiously." Wuthnow (2005) points to the example of Mother Teresa, who lived her Christian religious life inter-religiously. The true testimony of her inter-religious ministry was seen by the attendance of her funeral service, where representatives from the world's major religions, Muslims, Buddhists, Hindus, Sikhs and Christians, were represented.

To promote religious life of adherents inter-religiously, I will argue for inter-religious hospitality among Christians and Muslims. According to Cornille (2011), the notion of hospitality entails the recognition of the other different from one's self who is welcomed in spite of fundamental differences in beliefs and practices. In such an atmosphere, friendship and trust are created among the guest and the host so that tolerance produces constructive engagements in those differences. He discussed inter-religious hospitality in three different categories: hospitality at home; ritual hospitality; and doctrinal hospitality. The type of inter-religious hospitality that I am arguing for is the hospitality at home which involves the act of welcoming the adherents of other religions and receiving them into one's home. Cornille (2011) explains that it is in sharing such a meal and home space that opportunity is created between the guest and the host for a more intimate understanding concerning the faith of each other. Inter-religious hospitality will potentially find acceptance among the religious groups as the concept of hospitality is not strange. From a Christian perspective, Hederman (2011) asserts, with two scriptural examples, the implication for hospitality. He observed that sometimes hospitality explains reasons of enlightened self-interest as depicted in Hebrew 13:2 (do not forget to show hospitality to strangers, for by so doing some people have shown hospitality to angels without knowing it). Again, hospitality could sometimes be a means of entering into everlasting life as explained in Matthew 25:31-46, "… come, you who are blessed by my Father; take your inheritance, the kingdom prepared for you since the creation of the world. For I was hungry, and you gave me something to eat, I was thirsty, and you gave me something to drink, I was a stranger and you invited me in …" These texts are believed to serves as motivations for Christians' participation in the practice of hospitality. On the other hand, practicing hospitality from an Islamic perspective is also a strongly held value, it was believed to have been practiced by the Prophet Mohammad and commanded of every Muslim to practice. Prophet Mohammad explained faith in connection to hospitality in terms of giving someone food and exchanging greetings, concluding that good is not found in one who is not hospitable (Lumbard, 2011). According to Da'wah Institute of Nigeria (2009), the Prophet Mohammad welcomed and hosted about sixty Christian delegates from Najran who ate, slept, and even prayed in the Muslim's Mosque in Madinah. Therefore, to visit and host non-Muslims is not only permitted, but encouraged (Da'wah Institute of Nigeria, 2009).

As part of the promotion of inter-religious understanding and tolerance among Christians and Muslims in Northern Nigeria, I want to stress the need for a continuous *multi-religious prayer* at events. In his argument for *inter-religious prayer* instead, Gavin D'Costa (2000) distinguished it from multi-religious prayer. He describes the former as an occasion where people from various religious groups plan, prepare, and participate in prayers that the attendants can or may claim as their prayers. D'Costa describes *multi-religious prayers* as a meeting where the religious groups represented are given opportunity to pray or make contribution in relation to an agreed subject. D'Costa (2000) acknowledges the fact that *inter-religious prayer* is seen by others as marital infidelity as the prayers involve communities that are not theirs, who do not profess the same faith as they, and who pray to gods different from theirs. Meanwhile in Northern Nigeria, it is *multi-religious prayer* that is practiced, but partially. The practice of *multi-religious prayer* will make the two religious groups feel inclusive and inter-religious, and it will conscientise the adherents of the fact that the community is inter-religious related.

In a religious pluralistic society, the dictum of Hans Kung is true and needs to be strengthened, *the peace among nations depends on the peace among religions*, dialogue and collaboration among the religions strengthens the relationship and promotes peaceful co-existence (Knitter, 2011). If the crises among nations and ethnicities have a religious cause, then the solution should be from religion. Tillich puts it that *religion should be used in fighting religion*, but much more now that it has to be done inter-religiously (Knitter, 2011). The assertion of Knitter is worth affirming that, if religions are not found to be part of the solution to the problem of crises between nations, they definitely will continue to exist as part of the problem. Malte C. Boecker (2007) points out that one of the temptations that make mutual respect very difficult among adherents of the religions is the teaching about other religious traditions as false or delusory and incomplete or distorted. He argues for religious resources for a theology of difference, where he affirms that Christian religious beliefs promote respect for others in the need to welcome and treat strangers with respect and kindness. This is also the case in the teaching of Jesus in the parable of the Good Samaritan, where a neighbour could mean anyone outside one's faith. Already Knitter (2011) has made a point regarding the need for doing theology with the consciousness of others from other religions. He noted that to experience being a Christian inter-religiously requires the reflection of Christian theologians in affirming the following needs of other religions in the task of doing theology: the need for religious others in order to know and understand one's own particularity; to be able to understand God's universality; and building the reign or Kingdom of God. There is a need for a development of theologies[17] that are designed to promote reconciliation and a true sense of community towards inter-religious understanding and peaceful co-existence in Northern Nigeria.

Inter-religious understanding leads to proper religious tolerance and respect for one another's religious reliefs and practices. In one of his famous quotes,[18] Miroslav Volf (2001:1) states: "I don't think we need to agree with anyone in order to love the person. The command for Christians to love the other person, to be benevolent and beneficent toward them, is independent of what the other believes." Inter-religiously, love entails respect for one's or group's conviction, this I will describe as inter-religious love. This love will promote inter-religious functional coexistence among the religious groups. Again, in his reflection on the experience of the post September 11 of the World Trade Centre, Volf (2011) identified what he described as debit and credit in the American moral accounts which could be thought provoking to Christian/Muslim relationship in Northern Nigeria. He described the debit side of American moral account in the context of exceptionalism as thus: "In an inter-connected and inter-dependent world we insist on going our own way. We

---

17   This is noted by Meiring (2003:405), as reflected in the final report of the South African Truth and Reconciliation Commission (TRC) from the contribution of the religious faith communities.

18   See BrainyQuote, *Miroslav Volf Quotes*, Viewed from http://bit.ly/32NBKXK [Accessed 19 March 2017].

don't hold ourselves accountable to the norms we hold others accountable to—the moral principle of reciprocity enshrined in the Golden Rule does not apply to us. As a result, we are less liked abroad than ever, and in some parts of the world we have come to be despised as bullying hypocrites" (Volf, 2011:1). On the credit side, Volf affirms the efforts of some Christian leaders who are involved in the promotion of civility and inter-religious understanding among the religious groups. According to Volf (2011:1), the conviction of such Christian leaders is the belief that, "the better Christian you are, the more truthful, just, and loving toward others, including Muslims, you will be." The lesson in Volf's reflection from the post September 11 American experience can be learned by the Christians and Muslims in Northern Nigeria.

## Conclusion

As inter-religious dialogue is often considered as a reconciliation tool among the religious groups in Northern Nigeria, the challenges often faced are the misuse of dialogue, fundamentalism, and government laxity. In assessing the praxis of the reconciliation among Christians and Muslims in Northern Nigeria, the research indicates a lack of proper processes undertaken by the peace brokers which ultimately result in the failure of reconciliation and thereby the persistence of inter-religious crisis and dysfunctional exclusion. This happened when the offenders and victims are not allowed to pass through the reconciliation processes, as a result, the offenders feel protected and the victims suffer the pains. A pastoral care approach to inter-religious challenges through inter-religious understanding is capable of bringing healing and reconciliation among Christians and Muslims in Northern Nigeria.

Finally, in support of the efforts of Pastor Wuye and Imam Ashafa of the Interfaith Mediation Centre (North-western Nigeria); the Da'wah Institute of Nigeria of the Islamic Education Trust (North-central Nigeria); the Archbishop Ignatius Kaigama of the Jos Interfaith Centre (North-central Nigeria); and Rev. Kallah of his nonviolence approach to peace and dialogue engagement (North-eastern Nigeria), I recommend inter-religious learning among the religious groups in Northern Nigeria. It should be made a subject of learning at the grassroots level at public and private schools (primary and secondary) and be made a general course of study at tertiary institutions. Inter-religious hospitality and multi-religious prayer should be encouraged among the religious groups to aid inter-religious understanding and cooperation in the community. Secondly, in the event of inter-religious conflict requiring healing and reconciliation, proper pastoral care hermeneutical processes should be taken into consideration as explained by Clinebell and Thesnaar. And lastly, the Christian/Muslim inter-religious life in public and private sectors should be supported and encouraged by the authorities through ensuring that people are treated inter-religiously.

# References

Abu-Nimer, M. and Nasser, I. (2013). Forgiveness in the Arab and Islamic contexts: Between Theology and Practice. *Journal of Religious Ethics*, 41(3):474–494. https://doi.org/10.1111/jore.12025

Acar, I. (2005). *Interactions between Prophet Muhammad and Christians* [Online]. Viewed from http://bit.ly/2TbwBo1 [Accessed 23 October 2013].

Adegbulu, F. (2013). Boko Haram: the emergence of a terrorist sect in Nigeria 2009–2013. *African Identities*, 11(3):260–273. Viewed from http://bit.ly/32IyVNz [Accessed 24 March 2017]. https://doi.org/10.1080/14725843.2013.839118

Akinloye, B. (2016). There is a grand plan to wipe out Christians in Nigeria—CAN General Secretary Rev. Musa Asake. GbamTV. Viewed from http://bit.ly/32jDJDa [Accessed 13 March 2017].

Azumah, J. (2008). *My Neighbour's Faith: Islam Explained for Christians*. Nairobi: WordAlive Publishers (Hippo Books).

Bakker, F.L. (2014). Inter-religious dialogue and migrants: the case of the Netherlands. *Mission Studies*, 31(2):227-254. https://doi.org/10.1163/15733831-12341335

Barnes, M. (2002). *Theology and the dialogue of religions*. Cambridge: Cambridge University Press. https://doi.org/10.1017/CBO9780511613425

Bartholomew, I. (2010). The imperative of inter-religious dialogue in the modern world. *The Greek Orthodox Theological Review*, 55(1 – 4):310-315.

Best, S.G. (2001). Religion and religious conflicts in Northern Nigeria. *University of Jos Journal of Political Science*, 2(3):64-81.

Bitrus, I. (2016). The Persecution of the Church in Northern Nigeria: A Theological Response. *Word & World*, 36(4):380-389.

Boecker, M.C. (2007). *Paths and pitfalls of interreligious understanding: Discussion paper for the Trilogue Salzburg 2007*. Bertelsmann Stiftung [Online]. Viewed from http://bit.ly/39YVf21 [Accessed 29 September 2014].

Bowden, J. (2005). 'Religious pluralism and the heritage of the Enlightenment,' in Boase, R. (ed.). *Islam and global dialogue: Religious pluralism and the pursuit of peace*. Farnham: Ashgate Publishing Limited, pp.13-20.

Boys, M.C. (1997). *Jewish-Christian dialogue: One woman's experience*. New York: Paulist Press.

BrainyQuote, *Miroslav Volf Quotes*, Viewed from http://bit.ly/32NBKXK [Accessed 18 March 2017].

Christiano, T. (2006). 'Does Religious Toleration Make Any Sense?' in Thomas, L. (ed.) *Contemporary Debates in Social Philosophy*. Oxford: Blackwell Publishers, pp.1-34.

Clebsch, W.A. and Jaekle, C.R. (1964). *Pastoral care in historical perspective: An Essay with exhibits*. Englewood Cliffs: Prentice-Hall.

Clinebell, H.J. (1966). *Basic Types of Pastoral Counselling. New resources for ministering to the troubled*. Nashville: Abingdon Press.

Cornille, C. (2011). 'Interreligious Hospitality and its limits,' in Kearney, R. and Taylor, J. (eds). *Hosting the stranger between religions*. New York: Continuum International Publishing Group, pp.35-43.

Da'wah Institute of Nigeria. (2009). *Relations with Non-Muslims: An introductory examination of the Islamic textual evidence for peaceful inter-faith relations*. Minna: Islamic Education Trust.

D'Costa, G. (2000). *The Meeting of Religions and the Trinity*. Maryknoll: Orbis Books.

De Gruchy, J.W. (2002). *Reconciliation Restoring Justice*. Minneapolis: Fortress Press.

Dopamu, P.A. (1989). Religious tolerance and peaceful coexistence: The case of African religion in Nigeria. *Dialogue and Alliance*, 2(4):59-69.

Erunke, J. (2013). CAN Blasts El-Rufai over alleged comment on Jesus Christ … urges FG, JNI to call him to order. Nairaland. Viewed from http://bit.ly/2x7DclX [Accessed 13 March 2017].

Esack, F. (2002). 'An Islamic view of conflict and reconciliation in the South African situation,' in Gort, J.D., Jansen, H. and Vroom H.M. (eds.) *Religion, Conflict and Reconciliation: Multifaith Ideals and Realities*. Amsterdam/New York: Rodopi, pp.290-297.

Eyoboka, S. (2016). El-Rufai is stoking Religious Tensions—Okogie. *Vanguard*, 18 June 2016. Viewed from http://bit.ly/2TwqcUI [Accessed 13 March 2017].

Fazaluddin, S. (2016). Conciliation Ethics in the Qur'an. *International Journal for the Semiotics of Law*, 29(2):333–358. https://doi.org/10.1007/s11196-016-9455-z

Gaiya, M.A.B. (2004). Paul Gofo Gunen Gindiri 1935 to 1996 Evangelical Church of West Africa / New Life for All / Gospel Team Nigeria. *Dictionary of African Christian Biography*. Available from http://www.dacb.org/stories/nigeria/gindiri_paul.html [Accessed 30 November 2015].

Goodreads. *Desmond Tutu – Quotes*. Viewed from http://bit.ly/2PJmhTm [Accessed 19 March 2017].

Griswold, E. (2010). Christian-Muslim encounters in Nigeria on the fault line. *Christian Century*, 127(22):22-25.

Gwamna, J.D. (2010). *Religion and politics in Nigeria*. Jos: African Christian Textbooks.

Hederman, M.P. (2011). 'Hospitable by calling, inhospitable by nature,' in R. Kearney and Taylor, J. (eds.). *Hosting the stranger: Between religions*. New York: Continuum International Publishing Group, pp.87-94.

Holy Quran. (1930). English translation by Mohammed Marmaduke Pickthall. Karachi: Fazleesons.

Huda, I. (2018). *The meaning of Da'wah in Islam.* Viewed from http://bit.ly/2TmTKpb [Accessed 1 April 2019].

Ibighbi, E. (1987). The Maitatsine risings in Nigeria 1980-85: A revolt of the disinherited. *Journal of Religion in Africa*, 17(3):194–208. https://doi.org/10.1163/157006687X00136

Joseph, Y. and Rothfuss, R. (2012). Threats to religious freedom in Nigeria: Analysis of a Complex scenario, *International Journal for Religious Freedom*, 5(1):73-85.

Kallah, A. (2015). Centre for Nonviolence & Peace studies. Promoting peace and a global beloved community through nonviolence. University of Rhode Island. Viewed from http://web.uri.edu/nonviolence/abare-kallah/ [Accessed 11 May 2017].

Kirkwood, N.A. (2002). *Pastoral care to Muslims: Building Bridges.* New York: The Haworth Pastoral Press.

Knitter, P.F. (2002). *Introducing theologies of religions.* Maryknoll: Orbis Books.

Knitter, P.F. (2011). Doing theology interreligiously: Union and the legacy of Paul Tillich. *Cross Currents*, 61(1):117-132. https://doi.org/10.1111/j.1939-3881.2010.00165.x

Knitter, P.F. (2012). Challenges of interreligious and intercultural cooperation today. *Political Theology*, 13(3):397-399. https://doi.org/10.1558/poth.v13i4.397

Kwashi, B. (2004). Conflict, suffering and peace in Nigeria. *Transformation*, 21(1):60-69. https://doi.org/10.1177/026537880402100113

Lartey, E.Y. (2003). *In living colour: An intercultural approach to pastoral care and counselling.* London: Jessica Kingsley.

Little, D. (1998). Religious Tolerance and the Challenge of Peace: Tolerance, carefully defined, has an important role in the peaceable kingdom. *Church & Society*, 88(4):59-66.

Louw, D.J. (1998). *A pastoral hermeneutics of care and encounter: A Theological design for a basic theory, anthropology, method and therapy.* Cape Town: Lux Verbi.

Louw, D.J. (2008). *Cura vitae. Illness and the healing of life.* Wellington: Lux Verbi.

Louw, D.J. (2013). *Cura vitae*: the hermeneutics of spiritual healing and the beautification of life. *Scriptura*, 112:1-16. https://doi.org/10.7833/112-0-60

Lumbard, J. (2011). 'Some reflections on hospitality in Islam,' in Kearney, R. and Taylor, J. (eds.). *Hosting the stranger between religions.*
New York: Continuum International Publishing Group, pp.133-138.

Meiring, P. (2003). The Muslim voice in South Africa – in the era of truth and reconciliation. *Deel*, 44(3 & 4):399-406.

Merdjanova, I. (2016). Overhauling interreligious dialogue for peacebuilding. *Religion in Eastern Europe*, 36(1):26-33 [Online]. Viewed from http://bit.ly/2Tai10b [Accessed 20 March 2017].

Mosher, L. (2011). Walking deliberately into difference: A theology of enabling interreligious understanding, *Anglican Theological Review*, 93(4):637-644.

Mulders, A. (2016). Crushed but not defeated: The impact of persistent violence on the Church in Northern Nigeria – Summary report. *Open doors international* [Online]. Viewed from https://www.worldwatchmonitor.org/research/4316020 [Accessed 23 August 2016].

NewsRescue.com. (2012). Jos Arch. Bishop visits Central Mosque; urges Muslim-Christian unity. *Newsrescue.com* [Online]. Viewed from http://bit.ly/37Sul55 [Accessed 17 September 2015].

Nwachukwu, J.O. (2016). Blasphemy: Killers of 8 people in Zamfara will be brought to book – Buhari. *Dailypost.ng* [Online]. Viewed from http://bit.ly/2wAALhE [Accessed 13 March 2017].

Ogbuehi, F.I. (2016). Critical appraisal of dialogue as a strategy for religious conflict resolution in Nigeria. *Journal of Religion and Human Relations*, 8(2):158-174.

Ojo, M.A. and Lateju, F.T. (2010). Christian–Muslim conflicts and interfaith bridge-building efforts in Nigeria, *The Review of Faith & International Affairs*, 8(1):31-38. https://doi.org/10.1080/15570271003707762

Oloyede, I.O. (2011). NIREC and conflict management in Nigeria [Online]. Viewed from http://bit.ly/2TxsKCa [Accessed 22 September 2015].

Omonobi, K. (2016). 4 killed, church, others burnt as religious violence breaks out in Niger. *The Vanguard* (Online). Viewed from http://bit.ly/2VC1AwB [Accessed 13 March 2017].

Omonokhua C. (2012). *The need for inter-religious dialogue*. The Guardian, Monday, July 2, 2012.

Omotosho, A.O. (2003). Religious Violence in Nigeria – the Causes and Solutions: An Islamic Perspective. *Swedish Missiological Themes*, 91(1):15-31.

Potgieter, F.J., van der Walt, J.L. and Wolhuter, C.C. (2014). Towards understanding (religious) (in)tolerance in education. *HTS Teologiese Studies/Theological Studies*, 70(3):1-8. https://doi.org/10.4102/hts.v70i3.1977

Preston, R.A. (1977). Hermeneutic processes and pastoral care. *Lexington Theological Quarterly*, 12(4):128-136.

Sampson, I.T. (2012). Religious violence in Nigeria: Causal diagnoses and strategic recommendations to the state and religious communities. *African Journal on Conflict Resolution*, 12(1):103-134.

Sennott, C.M. (2014). Once enemies, a pastor and an imam wage peace in Nigeria. *PRI*. Viewed from http://bit.ly/2VfJ8cU [Accessed 14 April 2017].

Sodiq, Y. (1994). Muslim-Christian relations in Nigeria: Causes of tensions. *Journal of Ecumenical Studies*, 31(3-4):279-306.

Sodiq, Y. (2009). Can Muslims and Christians live together peacefully in Nigeria? *The Muslim World*, 99(4):646-688. https://doi.org/10.1111/j.1478-1913.2009.01292.x

Song, G. (2012). The nonduality of diversity: dialogue among religious traditions. *Cross Currents*, 62(3):381-388. https://doi.org/10.1111/j.1939-3881.2012.00249.x

Swidler, L. (1983). The dialogue decalogue: Ground rules for interreligious dialogue. *Journal of Ecumenical Studies*, 20(1):1-4.

The Royal Islamic Strategic Studies Centre. (2012). Report on the Inter-Religious Tensions and Crisis in Nigeria of the International Joint Delegation of the World Council of Churches and the Royal Aal al-Bayt Institute for Islamic Thought *Dublin.anglican.org* [Online]. Viewed from http://bit.ly/37OJU3a [Accessed 30 November 2015].

Thesnaar, C.H. (2003). Facilitating healing and reconciliation with young people living in the aftermath of political and cultural conflict: the challenge to the church and its youth ministry. *The Journal of Youth Ministry*, 2(1):29-48. https://doi.org/10.1163/24055093-90000201

Thesnaar, C.H. (2008). Restorative Justice as a Key for Healing Communities. *Religion & Theology*, 15:53-73. https://doi.org/10.1163/157430108X308154

Thesnaar, C.H. (2011). Healing the scars: a theological-hermeneutical analysis of violence from the perspectives of both Perpetrators and victims. *Scriptura*, 106:26-37. https://doi.org/10.7833/106-0-144

Thesnaar, C.H. (2013). Embodying collective memory: towards responsible engagement with the 'other'. *Scriptura*, 112:1-15. https://doi.org/10.7833/112-0-75

Obi, Paul. (2016). Nigeria: CAN Advises Christians to Defend Themselves after Murder of Female Pastor in Abuja. *This Day*, 13 July 2016. Viewed from http://bit.ly/2HQQbRj [Accessed 13 March 2017].

Turaki, Y. (1993). *The British colonial legacy in Northern Nigeria: A social ethical analysis of the colonial and post-colonial society and politics in Nigeria*. Jos: Challenge Press.

Turaki, Y. (2010). *Tainted Legacy: Islam, Colonialism and Slavery in Northern Nigeria*. McLean: Isaac Publishing.

Tyagananda, S. (2011). Doing dialogue interreligiously. *A Journal of Theology*, 50(3):227-230. https://doi.org/10.1111/j.1540-6385.2011.00627.x

Urell, B. (2013). Nine warning signs of a dysfunctional relationship. Selfgrowth.com [Online]. Viewed from http://bit.ly/32kwISu [Accessed 5 September 2013].

Verwoerd, W. (2015). "Seeking Communities of Enlightened Justice" Evaluation Report: A Promising Harvest of Practical Wisdom. *Project 3306*. July 2015.

Volf, M. (1996). *Exclusion and embrace. A theological exploration of identity, otherness, and reconciliation*. Nashville: Abingdon Press.

Volf, M. (2001). *Brainy quote*. Viewed from http://bit.ly/32mLh7Y [18 March 2017].

Volf, M. (2011). Did 9/11 Make Us Morally 'Better'? *Huffpost* [Online]. Viewed from http://bit.ly/38SGdLi [Accessed 9 January 2018).

Wikilslam. (n.d.) Islam and the People of the Book. *Wikilslam.com*. Viewed from https://wikiislam.net/wiki/Islam_and_the_People_of_the_Book [Accessed 20 August 2019].

World Watch Monitor. (2016). Nigeria: Pastor's wife killed after blasphemy accusation. *World Watch Monitor*, 8 June 2016 [Online]. Viewed from http://bit.ly/37VSs8i [Accessed 13 March 2017].

Wuthnow, R. (2005). *America and the challenges of religious diversity.* Princeton: Princeton University Press. https://doi.org/10.1515/9781400837243

Zodhiates, S. (ed.). (1984). *Lexical aids to the New Testament. The Hebrew-Greek key study Bible (NASB)* (Red letter edition). Chattanooga: AMG Publishers.

*Wilhelm Verwoerd[1]*

## From clenched fists to open hands

Ugandan Catholic Archbishop John Odama visited Belfast in March 2012, towards the end of my decade as a peace practitioner on the island of Ireland. During this visit a few colleagues and I spent a precious few hours around a small, round table with him. He told us about going into very dangerous remote areas to meet with leaders of the Lord's Resistance Army (LRA), including the notorious Joseph Kony. For Archbishop Odama it was about being true to his calling as a peacemaker. He also talked about the Acholi Religious Leaders Peace Initiative (ARLPI), which includes the Anglican Archbishop, an Orthodox Christian leader and a Muslim Imam.[2] He then demonstrated his solidarity with humanity by relating to my colleagues how he prayed for them during the "Troubles", the euphemistic term often used for the deeply rooted, bloody conflict in and about Northern Ireland. He fasts every Thursday and prays for every conflict in the world that he is aware of. Then he held up his hands in the familiar gesture of prayer – with the palms and fingers against each other – and slowly explained what these two hands symbolise for him. Each finger represents one of the five continents; one hand stands for men, the other for women; his light brown palms bring to mind all people who are light-skinned, the dark brown on the outside reminds him to pray for all people of color.

I was deeply moved that such a simple gesture could become the symbol of compassion without borders. Spontaneously I began to thank him: "Archbishop Odama, you make me realise again how much I miss South Africa, you remind me so much of Archbishop Tutu…" Searching for words I continued, "But I am also filled with sadness. When I think of the tragedy of apartheid, of the fear amongst the Afrikaners, the community I come from…" Without thinking about it I started to clench my hands into two opposing fists, "This is what I grew up with!"

---

1    Dr Wilhelm Verwoerd is a Researcher at the Beyers Naudé Centre for Public Theology, Stellenbosch University.

2    For more details see Katongole (2017:14): "John Baptist Odama was installed as archbishop of Gulu diocese, in Northern Uganda, in 1999, where from 1986 until recently a group calling itself the Lord's Resistance Army [LRA] waged war against the Ugandan government, terrorised the civilian population…and abducted over 23,000 children as a means of recruitment into their fighting ranks. Odama became a fierce critic of the war, moving back and forth between Kony's fighters and the Museveni government seeking to mediate an end of hostilities, building a coalition of cultural and religious leaders (ARLPI) …"

Pointing to my fists, "These are the contracted, inward-looking, fearful, defensive, confrontational hands that I grew up with, which caused so much destruction to others...and ourselves. What a contrast with your all-embracing hands!"

Again without much premeditation I started to open my clenched hands into that prayer gesture, with the soft, vulnerable palms touching each other. Looking at my colleagues I wondered out loud, "Is this not what our peace work is about? How do we transform closed fists into united hands...that stay open, and connected, despite so many risks?"

## Christian violence

A number of chapters in this book reminded me of this powerful encounter, of the tragic contrast between my white, Afrikaner Nationalist, Dutch Reformed Church fists and the open-hearted hands of so many fellow Christians represented by people like John Odama and Desmond Tutu (see Verwoerd, 2019; Van der Westhuizen, 2016). An underlying theme in these chapters is the stark contrast between the ongoing, multi-dimensional contribution of the Christian religion to those violent fists, versus the life-giving, transformative, radically inclusive potential of a faith imbued by the kenotic Spirit of Christ.[3]

In my experience a major challenge for real, deep reconciliation is making this closed-fists-open-hands contrast fully visible, especially when the fists have become collective, institutionalised, systemic and span across generations. Botha's critique of (white, Western) Christianity's service of "Empire" and Brown's post-colonial, feminist challenge to the "Son of Man" ideology expand my understanding of the long religious fingers that continue to enclose racialised power and privilege. These chapters affirm the need for a nuanced, far-reaching religious dimension to "white work" in the current South African context of growing black disillusionment with shallow rainbow-reconciliation (see also Thesnaar chapter and Forster 2017, 2018).[4]

Sadly the challenge of making the alarming connections between Christianity and violence visible is not restricted to the more systemic level. Other authors in this book highlight the more obvious, physical, intergroup violence that Christians continue to also be involved in, for example, Nigeria, Ethiopia, and Burundi.

However, even these highly visible, physical killings of Christians killing (mostly) other Christians are typically "explained away", as pointed out by Michael Budde (2016:5):

---

3    See K. Armstrong (2014) Fields of Blood: *Religion and the history of violence* regarding religion and violence in general.

4    The cultivation of self-critical intragroup awareness and a creative sense of shared historical responsibility, especially within the Dutch Reformed Church, has indeed become an increasing focus of my facilitation practice since returning to South Africa at the end of 2012. The purpose of this "white work" is preparation for more humble, restitutional involvement in reconciliation across apartheid divides. On "white work" in the South African context see Steyn (2001, 2012) and within the Dutch Reformed Church see Van Wyngaard (2011).

> World War I is described as interstate rivalry run amok, not the industrial butchering of Christians of one another; Rwanda symbolises the ugliness of ethnic conflict rather than Catholics massacring Catholics; the U.S. wars in Central America are charged to the Cold War account instead of Christians in the United States abetting the killing of Nicaraguan, Salvadoran, and Guatamalan Christians by one another. That no one describes these events as a scandal to the gospel, a cruel inversion of the unity of the body of Christ, is among the most embarrassing charges against contemporary Christians.

I was alerted to Budde's work by Ugandan-Rwandese theologian Emmanuel Katongole (2017) in his recent book *The Journey of Reconciliation: Groaning for a New Creation in Africa*. I strongly resonate with much of what he writes about his (theological) journey to discovering "Word made flesh" reconciliation as the heart of his faith. With my own personal-professional journey in mind and two recent visits to Rwanda fresh in my memory, I identified in particular with the profound questions raised for him upon visiting the country of his birth a few years after the 1994 genocide. Standing in "horrified silence" in the church of Nyamata, one of the killing fields during the genocide, he asked himself: "How could this have happened in this beautiful and deeply Christian country? Why was the Catholic Church [70% of population, Protestant 15%] never able to provide a bulwark against the slaughter of Rwandans by their neighbours, but was rather, as some cases indicated, a contributing factor in the killing?" (2017: 66).

His heart was filled with more questions, questions which apply to all the above examples of Christians – directly and indirectly, individually and collectively, physically and structurally – killing other Christians: "Was all the talk of new identity, new life with God nothing but mere spiritual platitudes that actually meant very little in the 'real' world?" With refreshing honesty he probed even further: "What, then, is the relationship between one's biological, national, racial, or ethnic identity and the reality of baptism? Does the blood of tribalism run deeper than the waters of baptism?" (p.67)

I'm hesitant to use the language of "tribalism" given the primordialist, ahistorical overemphasis on "God-given" ethnic identities within the apartheid ideology of "Separate Development" (Verwoerd, 2019). But Katangole's troubling question about the depth of the "blood of tribalism" lies at the heart of my own personal and my professional journeys of reconciliation.

Most of my facilitation work on the island of Ireland was with former combatants and survivors from across the political spectrum. Gradually I came to appreciate the complex interplay between British-Irish-Northern Irish ethno-national identities, Protestant-Catholic sectarian divisions and more working class-based Loyalist-Republican organisational and regional dynamics. In a context where the majority of those involved would describe themselves as Christian the answer to Katangole's question is an overwhelming "yes". I saw first-hand that for most people the "blood" of family type group bonds run deeper than the blood circulating in the veins of the body of Christ, especially when the human boundaries of belonging are sanctified by (sectarian) religion and soaked in the sacrificial, covenantal blood of martyrs.

The same can be said of the Afrikaner "white tribe" that I'm linked to, where "Christian" revealingly functioned as an adjective within the ideology of "Christian Nationalism" that shaped my socialisation and education in pre-1994 South Africa.

## RECONCILIATION AS BETRAYAL?

My emerging understanding is that the scandal of these answers will not (only) be changed by righteous indignation, by moral judgment or prophetic theological condemnation. Transforming this "cruel inversion of the unity of the body of Christ" (Budde, 2016) demands, perhaps firstly, a willingness, to go deeper into Plato's cave, a further descent into the dark illusions that keep "Us" opposed to "Them", before we can start to use the less shadowy, light-filled language of rainbows.[5] Put differently, a key root of deep reconciliation for me is increasingly about facing the murky, often unconscious reality of exclusive group identities. This underground, dark, root work is not about avoiding shared responsibility for my groups' violence. This diagnostic phase is intended to inform the shaping of humanising processes, including language, that will actually encourage people with clenched fists to journey *through* the bloodied boundaries of narrow, exclusive belonging into the dangerous, profoundly unsettling territory of enemy love.

For my personal reconciliation journey and my work with "veteran peacemakers" from South Africa, Ireland-Northern Ireland and Israel-Palestine has taught me how truly radical Jesus' command to love your enemies is – enemies who actually have the blood of "your people" on their hands. For example, during a recent international Beyond Dehumanisation research project, Themba Lonzi summarised the profound challenge of cross-border compassion as follows:

> You feel like you are betraying your community and your people by empathising with someone you see as an enemy. [Your] people get angry with you. They will say 'you're turning soft now, you're soft.'[6]

I am also thinking of Chen Alon, the inspirational co-founder of Combatants for Peace,[7] who participated in the Israel/Palestine leg of the Beyond Dehumanisation project. Despite a strong Zionist socialisation, having lost family members in the Holocaust, he reached a point where he refused to serve as a soldier in the Occupied

5    Alistair Little first formulated this challenge to Plato's famous analogy of the cave (in *The Republic*), during one of our many late night conversations. See footnote 9 for more detail regarding Alistair's remarkable journey from killing to peacemaking.

6    Themba Lonzi was an ANC-aligned anti-apartheid youth activist in the 1980s and through a long "healing of memories" process in the 1990s became a dedicated reconciliation-with-justice practitioner. I co-facilitated this Beyond Dehumanisation project between 2012-2014, which involved a series of reflective workshops and interviews, in South Africa, Ireland-Northern Ireland and Israel-Palestine, with small, diverse groups of (mostly) former combatants/veterans who became peacemakers. Quotes from this project are taken from unpublished transcripts of these interviews and reflective workshops.

7    See www.cfpeace.org and their inspiring sister organisation *The Parents' Circle-Family Forum* (comprising Israeli and Palestinian survivors committed to "breaking the cycles of blood" that cost the lives of their loved ones (www.theparentscircle.com).

Territories. He became convinced that it would be in the interests of everyone peacefully to change the injustice of the Occupation. Thus working with the enemy, however, broke powerful taboos in his own community:

> A few years earlier I couldn't even have imagined doing this. Initially I was terrified. You know I was the son. My parents were proud of their son, a major serving in a combatant unit. All the friends and the family were proud of me. When I told my parents that I am about to form Combatants for Peace the first thing that my mother asked me was, 'Isn't that dangerous for you?'

> This working with the enemy was something exceptionally dangerous for her: to be banned, not to belong to society, not to belong to the mainstream, to the narrative ... not to belong to the 'US'.

> A very close friend of my parents said to my father, 'I saw the name of your son in the newspaper, but let's not get into it because you know what I think. I think they should put them against the wall and shoot all of them, all these traitors.'

My close colleague, mentor and friend, Alistair Little[8] dug a bit deeper to explain the above dynamics:

> [B]etraying all of what you've been conditioned to believe is the right thing to do, feels like breaking 'sacred bonds'. If you speak out against this conditioning you're 'supporting the enemy' or you're 'agreeing with the enemy'. And therefore the blood of your friends, your community is not only on the hands of the enemy, this blood is also on your hands, because you're supporting those who did the killing.

Those of us involved in violent conflict therefore tend to keep our hands closed, because if we shake hands with the enemy, then those hands also become tainted with the blood of "our people", and then "your people" can turn their fists on you, with the extra intensity of excluding "one of us".

The hard-won practical wisdom of these veteran peacemakers help me to understand why the language of reconciliation can so easily morph into domesticated "spiritual platitudes" (Katongole, 2017a) that leave high walls between conflicting groups intact. For real, radical reconciliation – at least at the levels of interpersonal and intergroup relations – cannot avoid, I believe, the uprooting existential dynamics of betrayal. As the hard-line Northern Irish Protestant political leader, Rev. Ian Paisley, put it while stoking the fires of "the Troubles": "Bridges and traitors have one thing in common, they both go over to the other side." Paisley intended this statement to keep his political flock even more tightly together. In the process he provides another tragic, all too common demonstration of the "cruel inversion" (Budde) of the message of the "Saviour" he professed to follow. For Jesus very clearly stated – "If anyone comes to me and does not hate his own father...he cannot be my disciple" (Luke 14:26-27). And following this Jesus undoubtedly includes "love of enemies" (Matt 5:44)

---

8    Alistair became involved with a Loyalist (British) paramilitary organisation, the Ulster Volunteer Force (UVF), at the age of fourteen, committed acts of serious violence and was imprisoned for 13 years at the age of seventeen (Little & Scott, 2009).

I am not used to quoting Scripture in writing about reconciliation/(re)humanisation, neither am I a biblical scholar. The chapters by Nel, Endale and others are sobering reminders of the humility and care with which one should approach the biblical text, to avoid, amongst others, the pitfalls of anachronistic, self-serving interpretations. But those verses in Luke 14 (and Matt 10:34-36) played a critical role in my faith-based decision to join the ANC in the early 1990s, despite my father's agreement with Paisley and despite my mother's tears (Verwoerd, 2019). Having been immersed for those 12 years on the island of Ireland in supporting bridge-building between former enemies, I now see a strong connection between Luke 14:26-27 and Matthew 5:44. In other words, I now find it very helpful to understand Luke 14:26-27 not as the long-term rejection of genealogical family or ethnic "family", but rather as a truthful process-oriented, preparatory prediction of the unavoidable in-group relational realities when a group member dares to journey towards the "Other" side.

This intimate, very uncomfortable connection between (intergroup) reconciliation and the dynamics of (intragroup) betrayal is theoretically supported by Thesnaar's very helpful employment of Boszormenyi-Nagy's framework of (horizontal and vertical) "loyalty networks" (chapter 7), as well as Forster's highlighting of the power of social identities (chapter 4). My growing conviction that there is a biblical linkage between enemy love and family hatred can also be fleshed out philosophically using Margalit's illuminating distinction between "thick" and "thin" human relationships (2002; 2017).

"Thin" refers to the basic respect, dignity, non-humiliation that should characterise our relation to all other human beings. As demonstrated by the two paradigmatic models of thick relations – family and friends – these relations are much more limited. "Thickness" is a metaphor for a number of interwoven strands, like trees making up a thick forest, that characterise these relationships. First among these strands is the emphasis on *belonging* rather than *achievement* – mutual care that is to a large degree unconditional is central to family ties and friendship loyalties in contrast to the (often contractually enforced) good performance required to maintain, say, a typical employment relationship. Family type thick relations furthermore contribute significantly to the *meaning* of one's life, which also has to do with the importance of sharing many *memories*.

Much more can be said about the reach and nature of thick relations beyond biological family ties and beyond relationships with the living. At this stage I just want to agree with Margalit that exclusivity unavoidably flows from this kind of thickness. As well as the accompanying risk that distinctions between "family" and "strangers" can slide into "friends" vs. "enemies". When those outside the boundaries of thick relations become enemies it is unlikely that the "thinness" of relations will fulfill its purpose of serving as a bulwark against the dehumanisation of any human being.

For Margalit betrayal amounts to the "undermining of thick relations" (2017), as illustrated by the existential intensity – the emotional and epistemic shock – of, for example, adultery or, more traditionally, apostasy. Judas has become a lasting symbol of betrayal primarily because he was a *friend* of Jesus, Margalit argues convincingly.

This fleshed-out understanding of the dynamics of betrayal resonate strongly with my personal journey as well as the experiences of many veteran peacemakers such as Themba Lonzi, Chen Alon and Alistair Little. Along this way I've come to understand that real bridge-building also requires a journeying through a dark valley of betrayal-of-Us and a sense of self-betrayal. Deep, radically inclusive humanisation demands the transformation of thick intragroup and intrapersonal relationships.

This understanding has significant implications for the language and processes that would be appropriate in the aftermath of violent political conflict. In my experience the language of "perpetrators" and "victims" and the accompanying stress on the need for apology and forgiveness can actually be counter-productive to draw (literal and metaphoric) "brothers-in-arms" into truly facing the consequences of violent actions and to form meaningful (thickish) relationships with (former) enemies. I am *not* questioning the need to fully acknowledge the devastating impact of violence and prioritising the needs of those directly and indirectly affected. I have experienced though the alienating potential of insisting on the need for apology (and restitution) at the *early* stages of reconciliation journeys. For example, many veterans, especially former political prisoners, would not enter the room with survivors/victims at Glencree[9] if they were expected to apologise at the start of the dialogue. To acknowledge wrongdoing would amount for many of them to a betrayal of their cause, their community, their comrades (especially those who died during the conflict), and the sense of themselves as committed political activists. These participants taught me that not only forgiveness but also apology is a process. And we've found that preparatory "single identity", intragroup workshops and the language of humanising empathy and compassion can open doors to intergroup reconciliatory processes that will hopefully lead to the acceptance of restitutional responsibility (Verwoerd & Little, 2018a).

## Towards an embodied spirituality of reconciliation

A burning question raised by the highly conflictual, deeply disruptive understanding of reconciliation-as-betrayal is this: where does one get the energy, the courage to start and especially to continue this kind of radical relational journeying? What is the taproot of this kind of costly, cross-border compassion?

This question is implicit in Brown's advocacy of pursuing a kenotic genre of Jesus (chapter 6) and in Botha's emphasis that a decolonising approach to mission must be rooted in one's primary relationship with God (chapter 7).

This brings me back to Odama's open hands. In an interview with Katangole (July 2009) he noted that his life has been "one long journey of conversion" and stressed that "we must all learn to see beyond tribe, race and nation – and recognise that we are first and foremost human beings created in the image of God" (quoted in Katangole, 2017:128).

---

9    The Glencree Centre for Peace and Reconciliation, a residential centre located in a restored British military barracks, in the Wicklow hills outside Dublin (www.glencree.ie). I worked as co-co-ordinator of the Glencree Survivors and Former Combatants Programme between 2002 and 2008.

Katangole then asked the crucial question of "what kept him going through the years of war and fuelled his endless advocacy on behalf of the local population". Odama responded "it was the practice of setting aside Thursday and spending the entire day in prayer, fasting and meditation before the Blessed Sacrament" (2017:14). In a later interview (Jan 2011) we get more insight into the motivation behind this spiritual practice: "So that I may not take myself too seriously. The mission of peace is not mine. I do not own it. It is owned by God and I am merely the servant … I take to him what is going on. This time [before the Blessed Sacrament] keeps me focused and I 'listen' … In this way, I can remain hopeful. For I hear God saying, 'Do not lose hope. Do not be afraid. I am with you always." Why a whole day? "Connecting with God takes time. [And] I pray for all humanity …" (quoted in Katangole, 2017a:132), with both hands, in the way he explained to me in Belfast.

Katangole's questions spring from his own understanding of reconciliation, with which I resonate strongly. For him questions such as "'Why go on?' will constantly confront us at critical times when the cost is high, forgiveness too painful, the hurt too deep, and the resistance too strong" (2017:12). Therefore the journey of reconciliation "requires the cultivation of spiritual and other resources necessary to sustain the journey over the long haul" (2017:xv). He is very clear that this journey is about "the endless advocacy for peace, justice, human rights, and an end to war and violence in the world", but he stresses that it is also a "deeply personal journey" (2017:12-13). This personal dimension includes cultivating leadership capacities – "for scriptural imagination, mediation, negotiation, patience, and all forms of skillful advocacy and improvisation" (2017:xv), and it involves "intimacy with God" – which requires "moments of prayer, silence, and devotion" (2017:13).

As far as I'm aware this deeply personal dimension of reconciliation is the heart of Archbishop Tutu's radically inclusive, highly political journey. And this is also my personal experience over the last twenty years. Without a committed discipline of (contemplative) "Centering Prayer" and "Welcoming Prayer"[10] I simply could not sustain my work within the TRC, as a facilitator of cross-border compassion, or complete a book on the transformation of the (individual and systemic) sins of the fathers (Verwoerd, 2019).

As a researcher and as a practitioner I am therefore increasingly convinced that more attention needs to be given to cultivate an embodied spirituality of reconciliation. My own interest is the potential contribution of a contemplative root in this spirituality, drawing on the apophatic tradition represented by *The Cloud of Unknowing* (Verwoerd, 2018b). I am particularly interested in learning how to more fully understand and more effectively finesse the "amygdala factor" (Fitzduff, 2015), which seems to be a significant bodily contribution to conflict and violence. I am fascinated by the encouraging evidence emerging from the burgeoning field of contemplative neuroscience, affirming the potential of dedicated contemplative practices to, literally, rewire the brain towards less reactivity, towards reducing the instinctive power of our fight-flight-freeze (fisting) "old brain", and towards increasing "new

---

10    See Keating (1994), Bourgeault (2016), www.contemplativeoutreach.org.

brain" (prefrontal cortex) capacity for compassion (Goleman & Davidson, 2017; Troskie, 2018). My hunch is that this provides a fruitful connection with our call as Christians to participate in the mystery of the Incarnation. Especially when so many people directly and indirectly affected by violence live with the embodied realities of trauma. The language of "trauma" opens up a huge new theme, but at this stage I just want to point to the promising connection between trauma healing and "re-fleshed" spiritual practices such as yoga (Shoop, 2018, Van der Kolk, 2014).

I hasten to add that an embodied spirituality of reconciliation also needs to have an ecological dimension, as alluded to in the Chapter by Brown. Again, this is not the place to go into much detail. I just want to mention that nature-based activities in the Wicklow mountains outside Dublin, in the Scottish highlands and especially five day wilderness trails in Hluhluwe-Imfolozi Nature Reserve in South Africa grew into a central strand of the "Journey through Conflict" approach that my colleague Alistair Little and I developed over a period of 10 years (Little and Verwoerd, 2013). Underlying this approach is an understanding that sustainable peace requires a "trinity" of healthy relationships between people, between people and God, and between people and the environment. This understanding inspired me to become part of the Lynedoch EcoVillage since my return to South Africa at the end of 2012. This small potential prototype of semi-rural land reform is an attempt practically to combine an ecological vision with concretely addressing the legacy of racial (and class) separation in South Africa.[11] The founders of our village were inspired by the Schumacher College's approach, beautifully captured in these words by Satish Kumar (2000):

> Even an event as historically important as the French Revolution presented only a one-dimensional vision. Its cry – Liberté, Egalité, Fraternité – was a social trinity. The natural world and the spiritual dimension were left out. Americans created a trinity of life, liberty and the pursuit of happiness. This, too, lacks the ecological and the spiritual dimensions. In recent times the New Age movement developed a personal trinity – Mind, Body, Spirit. But this replaces one partial view with another... Over the years Resurgence has explored, examined and expounded a holistic trinity: Soil, Soul, Society. Soil represents the natural world: we come from the earth and return to the earth... While we respect soil, we also take care of the soul, which is the vessel for mind, body and spirit. [Social stands for] social justice, restrained consumption, sustainable economics, a sense of community and the diversity of cultures... This trinity of Soil, Soul, Society is one single reality, for each is always implicit in the other.

With this broad and deep vision of corporeally, socio-politically, ecologically embodied reconciliation in mind I want to conclude by returning once more to Odama's hands, my symbolic fists and Katangole's haunting question about the 'deepest' blood.

---

11    See www.sustainabilityinstitute.net/lynedoch ecovillage

Dorothee Sölle's (1990) *The Window of Vulnerability: A Political Spirituality* helps me to see that the hands I referred to around that table with Archbishop Odama were not only clenched in fists. They were also covered in invisible scales - my socialisation during the heyday of apartheid shared the spirit of Siegfried, the most powerful hero in German mythology. Sölle explains that "[h]e kills a dragon and bathes in the monster's hot blood. This bath gives him a horny skin no sword can penetrate; he becomes invulnerable." The dream behind this myth is "a male fantasy, to be the strongest and at the same time to be invulnerable. Dragon's blood is the sacramental sign of the powerful. They have bathed in it. They want to wall up all the windows. No light is to peak in; nothing must ever touch them" (1990:ix).

Her contextual application of the power of "dragon's blood" to wealth in the West can also be applied to 'whiteness' and white South Africans in particular. She echoes Forster's (chapter 4) warning against language of "post-apartheid": "Wealth functions like a wall, much more impenetrable than the famous Berlin wall. We [members of First World] keep ourselves apart, we make ourselves untouchable; our wall is soundproof, so that we cannot hear the cries of the poor and oppressed. Apartheid is not merely a political system in one country in Africa; apartheid is a particular way of thinking, feeling and living without consciousness of what is going on all around us. There is a way of doing theology without ever letting the poor and the economically exploited become visible and audible – that is apartheid theology" (p.17).

She continues to describe how "dangerous" the transcendence of genuine religion is, because "it makes us vulnerable". It therefore becomes so tempting to worship the "idol of invulnerability in the name of 'security'", a "false transcendence that has reduced itself to the otherworldly and the individual". In language that reminds me of Brown's contribution she leaves no room for superficial reconciliation in the name of Christ: "The masculine myth of the invulnerable hero is opposed to the unarmed carpenter's son from Galilee: there is nothing here to harmonise. [I]n Christianity [vulnerability] is driven to the limit: in Christ, God makes Godself vulnerable."

I am inspired by this kind of political spirituality.[12] And I am reminded of the practical wisdom of fellow South Africans with whom I am privileged to do reconciliation work that feels real. During the South African leg of the Beyond Dehumanisation research project, sitting in a circle on the edge of District Six in Cape Town, Themba Lonzi highlighted the need for hardened combatants to become "tender" again.

"My experience of the past has hardened me. And in order for me to feel tender, I have to really connect with people coming from different backgrounds, at a point when I get to question myself and my actions and my perceptions."

Pumla Gobodo-Madikizela responded warmly: "This notion of restoring the tenderness is so important. It's such a simple statement, but it's really the crux of the

RECONCILIATION, FORGIVENESS AND VIOLENCE IN AFRICA

12    See also Sölle (2001), Katangole (2017b) and Holmes (2017).

matter. People commit these terrible deeds - they lose this sense of tenderness, either towards themselves or towards the other. And that's why it's possible, then, to hurt the other in so many ways, because there is no connection - the natural connection, the human connection of tenderness towards another is gone."[13]

In a later workshop Themba Lonzi made it clear that the tenderness required by (re) humanising reconciliation is not to be confused with "becoming soft":

> I think it's one of the toughest choices when you choose the path of trying to reconcile people. I think the easiest thing is to pick up arms and fight. I think for me that's very easy. But the most difficult is to try to bring people together.

---

13    Prof. Gobodo-Madikizela (Chair, Studies in Historical Trauma and Transformation Studies, Stellenbosch University) was a participant at this workshop and has published widely on trauma and reconciliation-related themes. See, for example, Gobodo-Madikizela (2003, 2016).

## REFERENCES

Armstrong, K. (2014). *Fields of Blood: Religion and the history of violence.* Canada: Knopf.

Bourgeault, C. (2016). *The Heart of Centering Prayer: Nondual Christianity in theory and practice,* Boulder, CO: Shambhala.

Budde, M.L. (ed.). (2016). *Beyond the Borders of Baptism: Catholicity, Allegiances and Lived Identities.* Eugene, OR: Cascade Books.

Fitzduff, M. (2015). *Introduction to Neuroscience for the Peacebuilder.*

Forster, D.A. (2017). *The (im)possibility of forgiveness? An empirical intercultural Bible reading of Matthew 18:15-35.* 1st ed. Vol. XI. (Beyers Naudé Centre Series on Public Theology). Stellenbosch, South Africa: African Sun Media.

Forster, D.A. (2018). 'Translation and a politics of forgiveness in South Africa? What black Christians believe, and white Christians do not seem to understand', *Stellenbosch Theological Journal.* 14(2):77–94. https://doi.org/10.17570/stj.2018.v4n2.a04

Gobodo-Madikizela, P. (2003). *A human being died that night: A South African story of forgiveness.* Cape Town: David Phillip Publishers.

Gobodo-Madikizela, P. (2016). 'What Does It Mean to be Human in the Aftermath of Mass Trauma and Violence? Towards the Horizon of an Ethics of Care', *Journal of the Society of Christian Ethics,* 36(2):64-91. https://doi.org/10.1353/sce.2016.0030

Holmes, B.A. (2017). Joy Unspeakable: Contemplative Practices of the Black Church (2nd edition). Minneapolis: Fortress Press. https://doi.org/10.2307/j.ctt1tm7hhz

Keating, T. (1994). Intimacy with God: An Introduction to Centering Prayer. New York: The Crossroad Publishing Company.

Katongole, E. (2017). *The Journey of Reconciliation: Groaning for a New Creation in Africa.* Maryknoll: Orbis Books.

Katangole, E. (2017b). *Born from Lament: The Theology and Politics of Hope in Africa.* Grand Rapids: W.B. Eerdmans.

Kumar, S. (2000). 'Preface', in J. Lane and Mitchell, M.K. (eds.) *Only Connect: Soil, Soul, Society.* Dartington, Totnes, Devon, UK: Green Books.

Little, A. with Ruth Scott. (2009). *Give a Boy a Gun: From Killing to Peace-making.* London: Darton, Longman and Todd.

Little, A. and Verwoerd, W.J. (2013). *Journey through Conflict Trail Guide: Introduction,* Trafford Publishing.

Margalit, A. (2002). *The Ethics of Memory.* Cambridge, Mass.: Harvard University Press.

Margalit, A. (2017). *On Betrayal.* Cambridge, Mass.: Harvard University Press. https://doi.org/10.4159/9780674973930

Shoop, M.M. (2018). 'Body-wise: Re-fleshing Christian spiritual practice in trauma's wake', in Boynton, E. and Capretto, P. (eds.) *Trauma and Transcendence: Suffering and the limits of theory*. New York: Fordham University Press, pp.240-255. https://doi.org/10.2307/j.ctv19x52c.14

Sölle, D. (1990). *The Window of Vulnerability: A Political Spirituality*. Minneapolis: Fortress Press.

Sölle, D. (2001). *The Silent Cry: Mysticism and Resistance*. Minneapolis: Fortress Press.

Steyn, M. (2001). *Whiteness Just Isn't What It Used To Be*. New York: SUNY Press.

Steyn, M. (2012). "The ignorance contract: recollections of apartheid childhoods and the construction of epistemologies of ignorance", *Identities*, 19(1):8-25. https://doi.org/10.1080/1070289X.2012.672840

*The Cloud of Unknowing*. (2009). New Translation by Carmen Acevedo Butcher. Boston: Shambhala.

Troskie, S. (2018) 'Self, religie en homeostase: 'n Neuroteoretiese verkenning van die vroeë Boeddhisme', *LitNet Akademies*, 15(1).

Van der Kolk, B. (2014). *The body keeps the score: Mind and body in the healing of trauma*, Penguin Books, New York.

Van der Westhuizen, C. (2016). 'Afrikaners in post-apartheid South Africa: Inward migration and enclave nationalism', *HTS Teologiese Studies / Theological Studies*, 72(4):1-9. https://doi.org/10.4102/hts.v72i4.3351

Van Wyngaard, C. (2011). Post-Apartheid Whiteness and the Challenge of Youth Ministry in the Dutch Reformed Church, *Journal for Youth and Theology*, 21(2):23–34. https://doi.org/10.1163/24055093-90000037

Verwoerd, W.J. and Little, A. (2018a). 'Beyond a Dilemma of Apology: Transforming (Veteran) Resistance to Reconciliation in Northern Ireland and South Africa', in B. Kröndorfer (ed.) *Reconciliation in Global Context: Why It Is Needed and How It Works*. SUNY Press: New York.

Verwoerd, W.J. (2018b). 'Towards hospitality between enemies', in Veldsman, D.P. and Steenkamp, Y. (eds.) *Debating Otherness with Richard Kearney: Perspectives from South Africa*. Cape Town: AOSIS, pp.287-306. https://doi.org/10.4102/aosis.2018.BK94.14

Verwoerd, W.J. (2019). *Verwoerd: My Journey through Family Betrayals*, Cape Town: Tafelberg.